Cracking Morse Code

Semiotics and Television Drama

D0522526

Cracking Morse Code

Semiotics and Television Drama

UNIVERSITY
OF LUTON

press

British Library Cataloguing in Publication Data
A catalogue record for this book is available from the British Library

ISBN: 1 86020 570 4

Published by
University of Luton Press
University of Luton
75 Castle Street
Luton
Bedfordshire LU1 3AJ
United Kingdom

Tel: +44 (0)1582 743297; Fax: +44 (0)1582 743298
e-mail: ulp@luton.ac.uk
www.ulp.org.uk

Cover Design by Gary Gravatt
Typeset in Van Dijck MT and Helvetica
Printed in Great Britain by Thanet Press, Margate, Kent

Contents

Acknowledgements

This book represents the culmination of a considerable period of work with a range of colleagues. I am deeply grateful to the team of editors of *The Year's Work in Critical and Cultural Theory* for supplying me with review copies of many of the books I have cited. In addition, my students have contributed far more than they perhaps know to the realisation of this project. My colleagues, Geoffrey Nowell-Smith and Sarah Shrive displayed patience, tact and kindness in dealing with my shortcomings and they have made an enormous difference. Manuel Alvarado has been a wonderful editor whose cheerfulness and professional acumen has sustained me throughout.

Above all I must thank Gilly, Josh and Eloise for tolerating my endless hours on the computer when I should have been more sociable. I promise to let you play Quake 4 now.

Adrian Page
December 2000

Introduction

Any writer who chooses the topic of television drama risks the charge that they are begging the questions they raise. The definition of television drama is often contested, so it would be possible to define 'drama' in the way which suits the writer and then to draw conclusions based purely on the dramas which have been selected. The phrase, 'television drama' may be used to distinguish between 'serious' drama and popular forms such as soap opera, by comparing television drama with theatre and cinema drama where quality is already acknowledged (see Caughie, 2000, for example). Other writers such as Sean Day-Lewis, by contrast, prefer a 'purist' definition: 'small screen drama that is not adapted novel, imitation theatre or would-be cinema, but television' (Day-Lewis, 1998, vii). Alternatively the phrase may be used more broadly to refer to the entire output of fictionalised narratives which are acted out on the small screen by characters in order to avoid divisive value-distinctions. Raymond Williams argued, however, that the:

> ...attempt to hold a hard line between absolutely separated categories (of television) seems to depend on a fiction about reality itself. It depends also on the convention that 'factual' television simply shows, neutrally, what is happening. (Williams, 1974:73)

Thus even the news can be seen as a dramatised media offering which is presented as deliberately heightened episodes of crisis in human affairs. Drama can be found in many types of television. As Barthes said in another context, 'The filmic is not the same as the film' (Barthes, 1977: 65). The term 'television drama', may come to be regarded not as a definable genre, but as a style which many genres can adopt.

Whichever approach is adopted, it seems that the ability to 'read' television drama and to express its cultural significance and value must precede evaluative distinctions. The irony is that, as John Caughie comments, 'the development of television studies is not anchored in the way that film studies is, by the analytical reading of texts, or more exactly, it is hard to find textual analyses of television as a signifying practice which move with explanatory power from the specifics of the text to the generation of signification and the signifying system' (Caughie, 2000a). The following study sets out to remedy this lack, and therefore examines 'serious drama' such as Samuel Beckett's television plays, literary adaptations and more popular forms such as *ER*, and does not distinguish rigidly between drama on tape and film. This is in order to demonstrate how semiotic approaches might begin to offer a more systematic base for both readings and evaluation of drama on television. Rather than implying a canon, the choices are designed to cover a significant range of genres within this umbrella term in order to test the applicability of the methodology developed. A more varied choice of texts will hopefully demonstrate the usefulness of the theoretical strategy outlined in the first section which follows.

In contemporary academic studies of television, however, drama has not yet begun to be studied as seriously as might be expected now that its texts are available on video and some drama which has not been broadcast since the 1960s can now be viewed at leisure. Contemporary academic theory has examined its dominant naturalistic form and largely condemned it. Although television dramatists such as Trevor Griffiths have hailed television as the medium which can make an impact on the political consciousness of the majority, naturalism is not usually seen as a form which is capable of providing politically relevant commentary. Thus Patrice Pavis, Professor of Theatre Studies at the University of Paris, and a leading semiotician, writes that 'Television drama is consumed in the same way as television news, weather or commercials' (Pavis, 1992: 109). The close resemblance which television drama bears to other genres of broadcasting which are largely informative means that it can be assimilated into this ceaseless media flow. Tony Garnett's recent series *The Cops* takes naturalism to such a degree that some viewers thought they were watching a documentary rather than drama.

Garnett's now famous sixties drama *Cathy Come Home*, however, is a landmark in naturalistic television drama. *Cathy Come Home* is almost a paradigm of 'drama for pleasure and drama for instruction' to coin a Brechtian phrase. This is one outstanding example of how a drama could stand out from the 'ceaseless flow' and arouse anger against social injustice. The narrative about the tragedy of a family being made homeless by a heartless Local Authority led to the formation of the pressure group Shelter to lobby for the homeless. John Fiske has argued that television upholds the interests of the socially dominant ideology when it presents 'uniaccentuality', or a dramatic narrative which appears to have one clear meaning, yet in this case, an oppositional ideology was made abundantly clear to a large proportion of the population.

In contemporary writing about television, however, drama is seen as fundamentally conservative. David Morley, in his celebrated 1980 study, *The 'Nationwide' Audience*, discovered that television can suppress its conventions and naturalise its own ideological practices. Drama perhaps suffers from being seen as an extension of this process. Within naturalism, ideology is not foregrounded and consequently can make the dominant culture seem to be inevitable and necessary. As Horace Newcomb writes, 'Television drama is seen as mainstream, maintaining the status quo despite potentially more progressive values among producers' (Klaus Bruhn Jensen and Nicholas W. Jankowski eds, 1991:96).

Postmodern theories place drama on television within the television practice that simply recycles images to entertain without informing. Writers such as Dennis Potter have attacked the medium within which they work: 'By far the dominant mode in television is Naturalism and so it is that television ends up offering its viewers a means of orientating themselves towards generally received notions of 'reality' – that is the way things are, which is more or less the way things *have* to be. There is not much space left for what it is that 'Art can do...' (Potter, 1984 : 30).

The example of *Cathy Come Home* is one striking case where naturalism was not supporting the *status quo*, the art of the drama makers was evident, and the ideological practices of the makers were obvious to the audience. There was no doubting the skill which changed attitudes on a national scale. The reasons for the ideological impact of television drama are often institutional, and can often be accounted for by examining the various pressures which combine to shape a final broadcast. Rodney Buxton, in an article entitled, 'After it happened...: the Battle to Present Aids in Television Drama', describes how the producers of an American drama series responded to public pressure not to misrepresent the disease and changed the output after battling with their own institution. One fruitful area of investigation is what Horace Newcomb calls 'production research' in which the institutional and ideological factors which shaped the final version are explored. The fact that television companies demand ratings and audiences demand accurate representation might help to explain why producers may feel that they are not entirely free to create the drama they would like to see. Television drama is one genre which is often reminded of its social responsibility when its representations impinge on social reality, and this highlights the ideological transparency which some television drama achieves. Alan Bleasdale's *The Monocled Mutineer*, for example, which dealt with a historical mutiny in the British army brought about by harsh conditions, and caused questions to be raised in the House of Commons about the accuracy of the events portrayed. The subversive influence of the drama was a sensitive issue.

Production research offers an extremely valuable insight into the process of making drama, and may reveal the expectations which limit the horizons of drama writers and producers, but the following research does not attempt to study drama on television from this perspective. Production research may help to discriminate between the intentions of the collaborative team who make television drama: the producer, or the camera operator or the writer, to name but a few. Although it is unfashionable to speak of the makers' intentions, as if the signs of drama on screen signified only ideas in the minds of the creators, it is undoubtedly true that some intended effects and meanings are achieved. The theoretical objection about references to intention stems from the belief that any discussion of this kind suggests that meanings are pre-determined. In fact, as Colin MacCabe wrote in 1989 in an article entitled, 'The Revenge of the Author', the dialectic 'does not place the author outside the text but within its process of its production' (MacCabe, 1989 : 9). MacCabe's approach stresses that the author does not rigidly determine meaning nor yield such a role to the audience, but instead contributes to the process of making. Like the architect who designs a building as a church, the original intentions may govern some of the uses to which it is later put, but not dictate them absolutely. The television text according to the semiotic theory proposed here has meaning which neither the author nor the audience have fixed for themselves.

At the opposite end of the spectrum to the view that authors determine the meaning of signs, is the belief that audiences can read television texts such as drama in their own ways, and that the text only really exists in the readings which audiences make of it. John Fiske has written about the practice of ethnosemiotics:

> What excites me are the signs that we may be developing a semiotic ethnography... In these moments there are no texts, no audiences. There is only an instance of the making and circulating of meanings and pleasures. (Fiske, 1988:250)

The view that *only* the effects of drama on audience members should be taken into account as the real, and that the practice of making texts and creating meaning is irrelevant is a kind of pragmatism. Fiske does not say so explicitly, but it is worth noting that such an extreme view rules out the influence of drama-makers. The landmark dramas have shown that this is untenable. In a subject area which encompasses sociology and literary criticism, it is not surprising that textual analysis and audience ethnography should sit uneasily alongside each other, since their object of study is said to be the same whereas their purposes are different. It is not surprising, therefore, that they might criticise each other's conclusions. Media Theory has progressed by what Bakhtin calls 'the apophatic method'. Speaking of literary history, he says that 'Each phenomenon is studied primarily or even exclusively as the negation of what preceded it, in a sort of pseudo-dialectic' (Bakhtin and Medvedev,1978 : 92).

Thus the study of the auteur gave way to the study of the text and the study of the text has now been succeeded by the study of audiences. Perhaps the phenomenon of television drama is large enough to be studied from a number of complementary angles, incorporating pre-production, the production itself and post production, plus reception. It may not be necessary to advance a theory of which element has precedence. The theory advanced here presupposes that the context of broadcasting is foremost and this can mean that any element can dominate depending on the circumstances.

The following study of television drama, however, reverts to a close examination of how media artists create texts which produce meaning through the use of signs. This might seem to be a backward step towards studying the domination of a television auteur, but semiotics has changed considerably since the heyday of auteur theory and this is no longer the case. Semiotics derived from a need to theorise how meaning was independent of individuals and could be detailed by reference to socially-understood procedures. Barthes' essay 'The Death of the Author', is a classic statement of this position. The consequences of accepting this theoretical orientation, however, were that textual analysis seemed to become much like Leavisite literary criticism. The theory of signs which was found in the journal *Screen* has been described as 'producing readings independently of grounding that reading within specific determinants' (MacCabe, 1989: 8). Detailed textual analysis can seem to lead on occasions to a situation where the viewer apparently cannot but interpret the signs in the author's or critic's own, sophisticated manner. This is partly due to the popularity of the theory that semiotics works by exploiting 'codes' of meaning and that to read a media text is to decode it. Codes give little room for manoeuvre, and although they can be part of a polysemic text which uses many, they nonetheless seem to dictate the manner in which they are understood. In the following studies, I have referred to clearly encoded meanings as 'Morse code' to draw attention to the way in which some television drama such as *Inspector Morse* does use a set of naturalistic sign conventions to make its meaning clear. Signs taken from the world we know seem to be regarded as having one clear meaning which can be authenticated by referring to conventions. In general, however, I would argue that the conventional signs are those which are less interesting and do not always reflect the increasing skill which is being incorporated into drama. Dramas such as *Inspector Morse* have a dominant social meaning in their codes which has to be 'cracked', or broken and exposed to reveal its polysemic potential. Lyn Thomas' article for *Feminist Review*, 'In Love with *Inspector Morse*: Feminist Subcultures and Quality Television' (1995) details the struggle to overcome the appeal of *Inspector Morse* as a feminist, for example, and illustrates how the dominant code sometimes has to be opposed.

The theory of *semiosis* or sign-production can be much more flexible than code analysis, and in the approach which is developed in the succeeding pages, signs are regarded as ways of indicating phenomena which can be ambiguous or multi-faceted. I have used the term 'semiotics' quite freely so far to signify the study of signs without necessarily subscribing to its Peircean origins. The dramas studied here are meant to exemplify signification: the practice of drawing attention to things we recognise through signs, but which we may not yet be able to name. Where the meaning of a sign is not encoded, viewers can read the sign in the manner of their choosing. Creativity on the part of drama-makers does not imply subservience on the part of their audience, or a lofty position from which they can hand down ideas that are beyond dispute. F.R. Leavis wrote of conventional drama that 'The dramatic imagination at work is an intensely moral imagination, the vividness of which is inalienably a judging and a valuing' (Leavis, 1962:42). In Leavis' theory, the understanding of a stage drama would simultaneously involve grasping the judgement passed on the scenes witnessed. This would ensure that culture transmitted not just knowledge but also values. Signs in such a scenario, are determined by a writer, who has worthy values to transmit. In naturalistic television drama particularly, many writers disclaim any responsibility to offer solutions to moral problems, only to reveal them more clearly. The study of dramatic signs which have no clear signified and may only be described, therefore contributes to those studies which have tried to show how audiences can be much freer in their understanding of media texts.

Taking the text as the primary point of study does not necessarily mean that the text is 'privileged' as has sometimes been argued. The analysis of drama found here attempts to avoid empty formalism which examines only the internal characteristics of the text as if it were entirely separate from the world in which it is found. Television drama, as we have mentioned, often recognises an obligation to society to represent social groups and history in a manner which is historically verifiable and progressive. In an essay on the poetics of culture, Stephen Greenblatt recounts the story of Gary Gilmore, the American man who insisted on being executed for murder. As Norman Mailer compiled the story of his life, another, prisoner, Jack Abbott, wrote to Mailer and volunteered information on the reality of prison life. Mailer accepted and eventually published a book, *The Executioner's Song* about the life and times of Gilmore. A film and television mini-series followed. Abbott's work was also published as a book, *In the Belly of the Beast* and described the violence of prison life and the savage struggles for survival. On his release, however, Abbott mistook a waiter's gesture of following him outside a restaurant as an aggressive act and stabbed him to death. He was convicted of murder again. The incident was then represented in a play also called *In the Belly of the Beast*. Greenblatt's conclusion is that the social sphere and the aesthetic realm are not separate but that there is a circulation of material between them. The problem is that there are no adequate terms to describe this process. The term 'shuttling' might help to describe the process of exchange which Greenblatt refers to, since it implies movement back and forth. 'We need to develop terms to describe the ways in which material − here official documents, private papers, newspaper clippings, and so forth, is transferred from one sphere to another and becomes aesthetic property' (Greenblatt, 1990:157). Considering the text, therefore, does not involve appreciating an independent aesthetic object, but rather in coming to an understanding of how it mediates recognised events in a form which is still recognisable but additionally meaningful. Texts cannot be isolated from their cultural contexts within which they acquire meaning.

The closest which semiotics comes to a term to capture the interrelatedness of culture and text is through 'social semiotics'. An example of this is found, for example, in Yuri Lotman's work, *Universe of the Mind* (1990) where the notion of the 'semiosphere' or the society of signs is developed. In developing a form of social semiotics which sees the sign as a both a formal and a socially-derived phenomenon, the work of Bakhtin is immeasurably valuable. Bakhtin famously asserts that a text has no meaning until it is used in a context. By defining the meaning of a text and its constituent signs as the relationship between signs and culture, the rejoinder to prior events in the media or society, Bakhtin ensures that the interpretation of signs is inevitably culturally aware. Bakhtin's notion of dialogism adds more terminology to solve the problem described by Greenblatt. Jimmie L. Reeves, in a chapter entitled, 'Rewriting Culture: a Dialogic View of Television Authorship', shows how contemporary television rewrites previous texts in a novel manner. The echoing of dramatists such as Strindberg on contemporary television, for example, is rarely commented on, but can be shown to occur. Dialogism proposes that all uses of sign-systems such as language are in reality uses of other's words. Signs are not produced by individuals, since that would lead to private languages. Hence it would seem quite understandable that a complex sign such as a television drama can be analysed as a set of fragments collected from social life. Despite the fact that dramas may consist of fragments of the lives of others, and the author is absent from the dramatic text as Bakhtin puts it, the author remains a significant figure. The authorial position can be inferred from the choices of others' words they have made, but they do not hold the key to the textual meaning. The signs have meaning by virtue of their social relevance and not by virtue of authors' intentions.

Artistic productions such as drama are, therefore, not simply a set of texts with meaning but part of a social signifying practice. Drama is an activity as well as a collection of texts: it is often made to influence and intervene in a situation it also borrows from in order to represent anything at all. As such television drama in particular is creative. Media arts students are taught to create innovatory practices in production work whilst elsewhere on the same course they may be lectured about the fact that originality is really a concept that belongs with Romanticism. As new social situations, new contexts, come into being, so too new signs are needed to designate them. If signs have meaning only in contexts and contexts continually change, then so do signs. The idea that signs are continually generated in a practice rather than pre-existing, appears at first to be a repetition of the aesthetic autonomy of the traditional auteur, but this is not so. Volosinov stresses the originality of linguistic production, but only within existing social practices. Practices have to change before signs can change with them.

The studies which follow are, therefore, aimed at revealing the ways that signs offer possibilities for audience interpretation. John Fiske, for example, has recognised the usefulness of Bakhtin's theory of 'multiaccentuality' as a way of explaining the many interpretations of television, but it is not enough to state that these many ways of reading are simply available. Bakhtin's theories are especially useful here because they reconcile textual groundedness in the social with openness and plurivocality. The authors of *New Vocabularies in Film Semiotics* (Robert Stam, Robert Burgoyne and Sandy Flitterman-Lewis 1992), state that 'Bakhtin's formulation avoids a naïvely 'realistic' view of artistic representation, then, without acceding to a "hermeneutic nihilism" whereby all texts are seen as nothing more than an infinite play of signification' (217). Whilst infinite readings may be *possible*, Bakhtinian theory also stresses the conditions which make such readings *feasible* in society. So far we have had research which focuses on the results of aberrant decoding by audiences, but far less work has been completed on the actual processes by which viewers might reach these results. Subversive and diverse readings of signs, however, need a different set of signifying practices to overcome hegemonic influences. Semiotics as a form of communication is often highly conservative. To signify a gay man on mainstream television with a brief set of images, for example, it might be necessary to play to all the existing cultural stereotypes if we used codes.

In Barthes' essay, 'The Third Meaning', he voices his concerns that the Saussurean theory of codes linking all signifiers and signifieds does not always appear to be borne out in practice. Dick Hebdige, in *Subculture: The Meaning of Style*, pointed out that Barthes' essay reveals that the notions of 'significance' and 'the obtuse meaning' 'suggest the presence in the text of an intrinsically subversive component' (Hebdige, 1978:125). These uncoded signs are the elements which audiences can seize on as open to radical interpretation even against the grain of the conventional forms of communication. In developing a neo-Bakhtinian theory of signs, therefore, it is necessary to include this vital element which helps to explain how audiences can find a new context for a sign which re-accentuates it and gives it a new significance. Greenblatt calls for 'a negotiation between a creator or class of creators equipped with a complex, communally shared repertoire of conventions and the institutions and practices of society'. But, 'In order to achieve the negotiation, artists need to create a currency that is valid for a meaningful, mutually profitable exchange' (Greenblatt, 1990:158). Readers may notice the confusion here between 'communally shared' conventions and newly-created ones.

It seems to be inevitable that signs will have to be generated to meet the needs of new situations. They cannot always, therefore, be communally shared at the moment of creation. In retrospect we can imagine the difficulty of signifying a phenomenon such as transexuality in the 1960s before it was a commonly-recognised gender. Sometimes new phenomena call for new ways of signifying things to enlarge our understanding of the world. Saussurean linguistics has been criticised for failing to theorise a diachronic dimension to language, but in semiotics, this criticism has not been so prominent. Any theory of sign-making must show how signs change with history.

The first section which follows is a theoretical defence of an interpretive semiotics where signs are used to detect and identify phenomena which can reinvigorate our understanding of dramatic texts and challenge conventional coded readings. The aim of the first section is to outline a theoretical strategy for reading television drama which will focus on the inventiveness of drama-makers where signs are concerned, and the opportunities for interpretation which this leaves for audiences. Rather than considering either the makers or the audience as the arbiters of meaning, here the argument is that they can be complementary to differing degrees in each drama. Naturalism tends to conceal the role of signs as it adapts authentic behaviour and locations, and this may mean that audiences do need to be aware of the signifying strategies which they have observed, but not articulated. Existing semiotic theory tends to deny radical functions of signs by confining them to codes. Media education may be necessary in this respect for both makers and viewers of drama. The Bakhtinian influence is considerable, but this is not entirely a homage to Bakhtin. He did not create a theory of semiotics as such, and his remarks serve only to form a framework. The first, theoretical section is necessary because no account of semiotics based on Bakhtin's scattered writings exists which can readily be used in textual analysis. To show the potential of television drama for creating meaning, it is essential to create such a theory, and to add to it and criticise where necessary. The theory is not intended to be an absolutely faithful account of Bakhtin's own pronouncements on the subject. The theory is developed in order to pave the way for a range of studies of dramatic television texts which illustrate how it might work. If there are flaws in the approach, they are mine, not Bakhtin's.

The one vital Bakhtinian point, however, to perhaps stress is that in the case of television drama we can find what he calls 'Understanding as dialogue'. Whereas Leavis assimilated understanding and moral judgements, television drama is not usually so didactic. A neo-Bakhtinian theory of signs assimilates understanding whilst entering into the social debate within which the drama both describes and intervenes. To grasp the sign's function is simultaneously to be empowered either to respond to the social controversy which the drama has presented, or to act. We may not automatically leap to a moral judgement, but we are 'played in' to the game of debating the issue. This is what Bakhtin calls 'responsive understanding'. Television drama above all is popular culture in the Brechtian sense that it does not present any insuperable obstacle to understanding, such as works of literature might. In principle, it is part of the 'semiotic democracy', although drama-makers and audiences may need to be encouraged to seize the initiative by demonstrating how signs work. The playwright John McGrath once referred disparagingly to 'the high priests of semiotics', as if the readings which were produced by theorists bore no relation to the reactions of popular audiences. In the following examples the hope is that the readings offered will seem to meet viewers on their own ground and connect the popular knowledge of the media they have, with the strategies of dramatists to enlarge it.

Charlotte Brunsdon, in a chapter entitled 'What is the "Television" of Television Studies?', points out the implications of the texts which are selected for study in books such as Brandt's, *British Television Drama* (1981). The texts selected here are not intended to represent the 'canon' of good television drama, or just the ideologically progressive texts which would be approved by students of Cultural Studies. The drama chosen, in fact, is deliberately not tendentious political polemic, but examples of ideologically ambiguous characters who require us to consider our responses carefully. The aim is to illustrate the semiotic theory in action in the range of television drama to which it can be usefully applied. Hence not all the drama selected is attributable to an 'auteur' such as Dennis Potter, who has already been covered in a considerable body of work. In some shows, the writer is subservient to the series and fulfills a brief which is already established and successful. Also the implication throughout these studies is that the drama-makers, as I call them in the plural, includes producers, camera people, designers and all the other necessary functions in addition to writing. The sample here is also not meant to be fully representative of the current spectrum of television. I have chosen, for example, to avoid a specific study of Potter since it is important to resist the temptation to cover the 'greats' of television drama and to appear to have a definition of value before establishing an effective method of study. There is no attempt here to summarise the current state of television or its major achievements, which is a vast undertaking beyond the scope of this book. The dramas chosen illustrate how the theory developed in the first section can be applied to textual analysis, and the reasons for the choices are summarised below.

Troy Kennedy Martin once offered a vision of what a radical television drama that avoided the pitfalls of naturalism would be like. The view that television is a medium which by its very nature had to be confined to naturalism, needed to be challenged. Kennedy Martin offered a vision of the antithesis of naturalism:

> The new drama will be based on story rather than plot; it will relate directly Man's relation to God, to other men and to himself. Its action will be distilled and presented in a condensed form. It will be much more personal in style. It will compress information and emphasis fluidity, free the camera from photographing faces and free the structure from the naturalist tyranny of time. Through stream of consciousness and diary form it will lead to interior thought, interior characterisation.

It is, however, very difficult to find a television drama which has fulfilled this mission. Naturalism has remained the dominant form. Beckett's television drama, written as an explicit rejoinder to the television institutions, corresponds to many of the elements which Troy Kennedy Martin identifies. It is not popular culture, but its principal dialogue is with the makers of television and those who are sufficiently informed to recognise when current television practice is reversed and critiqued. As such it shows us how, by disobeying the 'rules' of television drama which institutions seem to have allowed to develop into almost unwritten laws, the signifying potential of television can be greatly increased. Signs in Beckett are radically different and encourage the viewer to acknowledge and challenge the standard practices of television. This, I would argue, is where semiotic subversion should begin. Beckett is also a challenge to the theory I have proposed in that his drama is known for lacking a clear context. The reading of these signs, therefore, shows how a radical approach to the use of the television medium can generate unusual new signs which nonetheless have their origins in social practices.

The Politician's Wife offers one of the clearest examples of how a drama cannot be fully understood unless the signs are taken to allude to a social reality and comprise a rejoinder to that situation. The many examples of 'sleaze' in the Tory party during its period in office comprise a media dialogue which is easily available through press and television to the viewers. The naturalism, therefore, builds on this basis to offer a radical reaction to the treatment of the wives of Tory politicians who have been the victims of these events. This is not tendentious drama which simply attacks the political right, since there is a mixture of criticism and sympathy for the wife. This drama may create divided loyalties in the viewers and raises the interesting question of whether such a retaliatory action as the wife's is, in fact progressive, however justified. Naturalism is here shown to be critical, in other words, and the signs which it uses are interpreted as opportunities to enter into this debate, not to close it. It is interesting, of course to note that drama is as Greenblatt noted, never separate from real life and that American politicians' wronged wives such as Hilary Clinton have acted similarly.

Big Women, from the novel by Fay Weldon, also deals with media events in a manner which interrogates the ideology we have come to recognise easily. Feminism as represented here in a historical perspective, is seen to affect women involved in publishing differently. The criticism of naturalism that it shows the *status quo* as inevitable because it is determined, is shown not to be true. This drama illustrates how by revealing many responses to a historical situation, determinism is overcome and the ongoing dialogue is stimulated. Choice is represented. Here also, we can distinguish between the semiotic inventiveness of the makers and the intellectual content of the novel. The drama reinforces some points through signs in a manner which is different to the novel. It is not simply a faithful 'translation' of literature: television drama is an artistic product in its own right.

Both *ER* and *NYPD Blue* are well known for their use of techniques such as the steadicam which allows the production itself to be much more stimulating and to contribute to the themes. The dominance of technique is what obscures the underlying content here and a theory of the unconscious of television is proposed to explain how the drama might condense more semiotic meaning than viewers are aware. Viewers can often discuss signs in these dramas in a fluent manner which reveals a much greater understanding of the issues which appear to lie dormant. The actual dialogues which these drama participate in, however, such as sociobiology and ethics, are only revealed by a more intensive analysis of the themes. Viewers can, therefore, find themselves empowered to discuss issues of social justice and fairness, although the ideological values of these dramas can be argued to be more conservative. A monologic position seems to lie behind much of American television drama which offers a vision of the pragmatic professional who solves moral problems. Even so, the demand for a continuing story line in a series means that certain subversive signifiers can be found.

The comparison between *Inspector Morse* and *Cracker* shows how sometimes a new sign is needed to represent a changing society. *Inspector Morse* clearly deals in naturalistic signs to offer us a conventional message in keeping with the *status quo*. It is one of the most popular current dramas on British television. If we attend only to the coded signs, our reading of this drama will be equally conventional. It is necessary to find the subversive uncoded signs in dialogue with the themes which propose what Barthes calls a 'counter-narrative' in order to understand just how restrictive 'Morse code' actually is. Morse code invites us to accept simple dichotomies such as good and bad and men and women. Cracker himself is a sign which is new: he combines the intellectual acuity of many detectives with an irrepressible humanity that makes him less of an agent of the state and more of a policeman of the unconscious. *Cracker* is a series which takes many conventional signs such as the detective and constructs them in a way which is novel, compelling us to ask questions about the moral status of the people who discover wrongdoings. *Cracker* is a rejoinder to series such as *Inspector Morse* in that it lays bare the kinds of personal failings hinted at in *Morse* and suggests new consequences. It does this by reaccentuating the sign of the detective. The argument is that *Cracker* is responsible, through its implicit dialogue with preceding police series, for bringing about a radical reappraisal of the semiotics of *Inspector Morse*.

The American version of *Cracker*, is different again, and in the land of individualism sees the drama's emphasis on individual responsibility as a highly relevant theme. A fairly conservative emphasis is again evident. In this case also, by casting Robbie Coltrane, the English *Cracker*, as the villain, the drama exemplifies the fact that all drama works on two levels: in terms of its content and its relation to reality, and in terms of the act of broadcasting as a social gesture in international media debates about performances.

The X-Files is read in a manner which coincides with this view of semiotics as a practice and not just a set of codes. This illustrates how we should focus on the process of sign-making, or semiosis, rather than semiotics, or what signs mean at the moment. As a social activity the drama fulfills an anthropological function for many viewers which enables them to negotiate their values in a world which has lost its moral stability. The interpretation suggests that viewers are not necessarily naïvely accepting the fantasy elements of the series, but that they can adapt its signs to reflect their own struggles with faith and politics. This process involves a certain distance from the sci-fi elements and a critical dialogue with the contemporary world.

If the preceding studies have demonstrated the potential of television, it may still be worth asking why it has not been exploited more fully. The answer may lie to an extent in the capacity of the technology to generate signs. *Wilderness* is an example of a drama which uses the ability to morph images digitally to create a sign which has no precedent and originates in the drama. This approach to signifying the trials of the main female character poses questions about women's social roles in a new way. The increasing availability of new technology to drama-makers also makes a new style of drama possible which is expressionist and creates signs which point to the inner reality of consciousness as well as the social context. These may conflict with, or complement, naturalism. The conclusion raises the possibility that television drama might exploit new technology to represent dialogism and to multiply the perspectives available to the viewer.

Part One

Theory

Why do we need a new semiotics theory to understand television drama?

In Jimmy McGovern's episode of the television drama *Cracker* entitled, 'The Madwoman in the Attic', a young woman who is one of Fitz's students of psychology, has been brutally murdered on a train. Fitz is deeply disturbed by this and is keen to fulfil his role as a forensic psychologist by finding the murderer. The police have the task of informing the student's parents. Shortly before the police visit the parents, we see a woman singing 'Summertime' behind a microphone in a restaurant where Fitz is eating. The song has an unpleasant ironic aspect: the lullaby expresses parental love and is intercut with scenes of the parents visiting the morgue to identify their dead daughter. The lyrics purport to comfort a crying child, but the harsh irony is that this daughter has suffered a terrible death. The rhythm of the piece is dictated by the music, which is echoed in the gently-moving camera, and smooth pace.

Whilst these two parallel events are shown, Fitz's personal life is also featured. He is seen in the restaurant with his wife and another couple ordering wine. The song is being sung in the restaurant adding a further layer of irony. Fitz is able to socialise while this terrible grief is enacted elsewhere. The camera tracks Fitz from a number of angles to find his face as he is hectoring the wife of the other couple about her moral scruples. Fitz is berating her for the fact that she pays other women to look after her children and clean her house while she goes to work. Fitz appears to be trying to convince her that she cannot remain ideologically aloof and not become embroiled in contradictions. He is asked to refrain from his belligerent behaviour and the tracking camera reveals a number of anxious faces around the table. Fitz is particularly scathing about the fact that the woman employs a black woman to clean her house and then goes out to earn a much greater sum 'teaching Women's Studies'. At this point the camera cuts to a black waitress who is coming to serve Fitz. Eventually, in frustration as Fitz becomes most vociferous, the woman throws a glass of wine over him. She too 'cracks' under Fitz's onslaught. Fitz exclaims, ' I think that what we have here is a failure to communicate'.

This line which echoes several famous films suggests that the woman has failed to comprehend Fitz's message. He has been arguing that ideological contradictions are inescapable: that we are all enmeshed in ideology and cannot stand outside it observing the struggles of others complacently from a superior vantage point. One reading of the scene is that Fitz was not attempting to attack the woman personally but merely to point out the inescapable nature of ideology. Althusser has written about the way that we are all in ideology and cannot position ourselves outside it to pass dispassionate judgement: 'As is well known, the accusation of being in ideology only applies to others, never to oneself' (Althusser, 1971 : 49). The drama series *Cracker* takes this particular theme and develops it throughout. Fitz is, after all, shown to be socialising while others suffer intense grief. This reveals the kind of contradiction in his own behaviour which he is pointing out to others.

The woman in the scene described above, however, has taken the point personally, or so it would seem. Throughout the scene, the music underscores the contradiction that involves Fitz himself: he is able to go out and drink copiously while the parents of the student he so admired, suffer. His conscience appears not to trouble him although he browbeats others about their morality. The camera then cuts briefly to the waitress who is coming to Fitz's table. With further irony, it is a black waitress who has the job of asking Fitz to pay and refusing his credit card because his account has been closed. She calls him 'sir', somewhat coldly. The other man at the table has to settle the bill. Fitz has been humbled by the woman whom he too was treating as a servant. Having argued that we cannot escape ideological contradictions, Fitz then finds himself involved in yet another. He is now being waited on by a black woman, and yet he is humbled by her.

The brief scene mentioned here is one which has multiple related meanings which can only be understood if we treat the aspects referred to above as signs: elements of our material world which communicate a generally understood meaning over and above that which they simply represent or mean. Thus the waitress is not merely a minor functional role in the drama but also a sign of ideological contradictions. The classic theories of semiotics derived from Saussure and Peirce and famously implemented by Barthes, suggest that signs are understood because they are constituted by codes. A code is a social convention or rule for relating a signifier, or sign-vehicle to a signified or concept. In the case described above, however, we cannot name a signified for this scene, we can only describe it in detail and interpret what happens, giving it unique significance as a new way of pointing out distinctions in our everyday lives.

Barthes' notion of mythologies is an orthodox concept in the study of the media and explains how social values become involved in signs. Mythologies are examples of how coded meaning serves the hegemonic interests of a society bent on spreading false comfort in order to maximise its profits. In a wrestling match, if one participant exhibits the signs of evil and is defeated by a wrestler who exhibits the signs of decency and fair play, this creates the myth that wrestling is a matter of good conquering evil, or Justice as Barthes describes it. There is a 'second order of signification' operating which makes the victory doubly meaningful. Social conventions associate codes to create beliefs in underlying relations which do not really exist.

The concept of mythologies, however, is rarely invoked to explain the making of new associations, and it is generally used to refer to associated codes with which we have become familiar. Barthes' exhortation to his readers to consider the making of 'artificial myth' (Barthes, 1977 : 135) is considered far less often. When two codes are juxtaposed in an original way for the first time, they need to be interpreted imaginatively. 'All that is needed' remarks Barthes, 'is to use it (existing myth) as the departure point for a third semiological chain, to take its signification as the first term of a second myth'. Thus the sign of the detective, who is usually able to speak with authority about the criminal mind, is used here to show that such statements are made from *within* ideology and do not convey a superior vision detached from personal bias. The code of the insightful detective is retained, but it is also undermined by showing that it can also be challenged. The code which creates comfortable mythologies can be 'broken' by adding to it in a creative practice such as drama. The concept of code-breaking here refers both to understanding mythologies and also seeing how they are unravelled by new signs. While mythologies explain many aspects of semiotics, the theory cannot be applied to new signs which do not signify in conventional terms; a mythology depends on the bringing together of two existing signs. Understanding and destroying codes simultaneously invites the viewer to participate in judging the content of the drama and enter into the dialogue.

The classic theories of signs imply that they exist ready and are waiting to be employed for all purposes. Codes are thought of as pre-existing like a vocabulary waiting to be deployed in a syntagm or sequence of signs. Even mythologies are normally thought of as common beliefs. Hence the analogy between semiotics and language took hold particularly in structuralist circles as the similarities between signs and language were noted. The difficulty which these accepted theories pose for an understanding of the scene outlined above are, however, complex. The scene does not seem simply to draw on a social mythology which already exists but to make a meaningful new distinction for us. What code exists to signify ideological contradiction? As Kaja Silverman notes, 'Saussure's scheme provides no way of distinguishing between linguistic signifiers, photographic signifiers, or signifiers generated by the codes of editing, camera movement, lighting and sound' (Silverman, 1983, p. 22). Saussure's semiology was never intended to do so, of course, but remains one of the most popular methods of semiotic analysis in the study of screen drama. Editing such as that cited above, however, might signify something which language cannot directly approach in a very different manner. Some signs may be constructed by designers, and producers of drama as well as the writers.

Cracker promises to establish new aspects of ideology in the late twentieth-century in a novel form. The scene may draw on certain social codes to create its meaning (black women as examples of exploited people, for example), but their use in this context seems original. When in the television drama, 'The Wench is Dead', Inspector Morse is in hospital, he comments on the 'very nice' West Indian nurse who looks after him and we see him shaking her hand on leaving. This encodes his behaviour as that of a 'gentleman': it is difficult not to feel that he is generously bestowing his compliments on someone who should be grateful to receive them. The scene has connotations of colonialism and class bias. The drama is an utterance about a police officer selflessly pursuing the truth behind a murder committed by lowly workingmen long ago. The utterance is largely concerned with an act of kindness to those who might not expect it. There is a patronising attitude in this moment which is not present in *Cracker*. Morse's relationship is encoded in familiar conventions, but Fitz's behaviour is not so instantly recognisable. In order to read television drama as more challenging, there is a need to 'crack' the code of dramas such as *Morse* and examine how new signs are generated to deal with new social phenomena.

As John O Thompson observed of Raymond Williams, however, it has always been possible to take a different approach to the textual analysis of television drama: 'Wiliams works at what might be termed a macro-semiotic level: he discusses the meaning of whole plays or groups of plays' (Thompson, 1980: 46). Kracauer long ago suggested that a holistic approach to textual signification was needed, and the theory which supports this strategy derives additional support from Bakhtin. Bakhtin acknowledges that codes can exist, but his approach to their use is rather different. He writes that:

> ...secondary (complex) speech genres-novels, dramas...and so forth... arise in more complex and comparatively more highly developed cultural communication. During the process of their formation, they absorb and digest various primary (simple) genres that have taken form in unmediated speech communion. For example, rejoinders of everyday dialogue or letters found in a novel retain their form and their everyday significance only on the plane of the novel's content. These primary genres...enter into actual reality *only via the novel as a whole* [my italics]. The novel as a whole is an utterance, just as rejoinders in every day dialogue are. (Bakhtin, 1986 : 62)

Understanding the two brief scenes from *Cracker* and *Morse* referred to above involves first suggesting the significance of each drama as an utterance in itself. Only then does the precise function of coded elements within the dramas become apparent.

Whereas many semiotic studies have attempted to create readings of audio-visual texts as the *sum* of the codes they contain, Bakhtin argues that the drama itself is an utterance and that all its constituent codes have to be understood as part of this whole. The publication or broadcasting of an utterance in Bakhtin's terms, is a case of performing a meaningful social action. We would not try to understand a sentence simply by defining each of its words in a dictionary, but would also relate it to the context in which it was uttered. Thus for Bakhtin, the sign in use does not have a coded meaning but changes according to the context in which it is deployed – the context of its public use, or utterance. Writers of television drama such as David Bradbury have made their intentions to create a rejoinder to historical circumstances explicit. His play, *The After Dinner Game* was written to express the way in which the humanism of the universities was threatened from without by 'sado-monetarism', or 'economic functionalism' (Bradbury, 1982 : 14).

The examples above illustrate that whatever the codes which are used in a complex sign such as a television drama, the dramatic use of these codes can create a vibrant and original concept which has not been derived from elsewhere. The precise signified, the particular meaning, only exists by virtue of the creation of a particular scene within a particular drama. In an artistic practice such as television drama, the writers and producers of drama can create new signs. Barthes describes this kind of meaningful sign in a phrase derived from Lessing, as a 'pregnant moment', the 'presence of all the absences (memories, lessons, promises) to whose rhythm History becomes both intelligible and desirable' (Barthes, 1977:73). As an example of a pregnant moment, Barthes cites the case of Mother Courage accepting coins as a bribe and thereby causing the events which lead to losing her children. Her financial dealings have led her to this point and will determine her ultimate fate. Such is the relationship between family ties and the need for survival. Such a moment signifies a set of relationships which are uniquely enshrined in this drama, although they are not isolated from issues outside it. This moment unifies three separate aspects of the text's significance: its internal, formal relations, its relations to its contemporary reception at the time of the text's production, and its relation to history in general. Such signs crystallise the text's overall meaning as an utterance and in doing so highlight its various layers of significance. As John Fiske reminds us in his chapter in Robert Allen's collection, *Channels of Discourse* (1992), culture is not a single practice, it is a set of practices which extend throughout a society.

Bakhtin uses the term 'dialogic' to express the relationship between utterances such as new dramas and what has preceded them. The dialogue establishes the meaning of the new sign as a 'rejoinder' to preceding culture. Any utterance has objective relations with relevant utterances which have preceded it in the public sphere. The signifieds attached to signs are, therefore, generated by the specific relationships into which the signifier enters. Rejoinders are forms of reply, such as denouncing, supporting, echoing, rejecting and so forth. The meaning of the sign is the relationship between the new sign and those which have gone before. Hence Fitz's outburst, for example, is a rejoinder in part to the gentility of detectives such as Morse. It is an utterance which signifies that such a complacent picture of detective work is outmoded. In Bakhtin's theory, we would have to decide first of all what the screening of a television drama was intended to signify as an utterance and then derive the meaning of each sign from that. The precise historical context would yield a particular statement which could then be further analysed. For Saussure, the meaning of each individual sign in the drama is already established and cannot change dramatically with a new context.

Saussurean semiotics has been responsible for establishing and perpetuating an unnecessarily formalist approach to audio-visual texts. Since the Saussurean sign gathers meaning by virtue of its differences from other signs in the same system, it can be used to spend an inordinate amount of time on the demonstrable features of the textual signifiers. This is often to the exclusion of the way in which the text interweaves references to real issues. On the other hand, it is equally wrong to treat dramatic texts on television as if they clearly yielded an unadulterated vision of the real world. Between the excessive formalism of Saussure, and the simple realism which views the text as transparent, lie theories such as Bakhtin's.

Bakhtin paves the way for a theoretical approach which is neither exclusively formalist nor simply realist but which merges the two. A television drama such as *Cracker* is a complex cultural form which contains a number of formal codes, yet their actual meaning in this context depends on the value of the drama conceived as an utterance in history. In Althusser's words, the sign therefore 'alludes' to reality rather than duplicating it, and the organisation of its formal structures constitutes the response to the real situation. Audiences may have the opportunity to develop interpretations of new formal signifiers, however, as they decide how to interpret the rejoinder.

To lay emphasis on textual analysis can nowadays seem to be returning to the notion of a television 'auteur' who is able to communicate meanings with complete cultural authority to an audience who have no choice but to consume them. The Bakhtinian approach therefore does not suggest that texts are either determined by authors or by the audience. Some aspects of texts are pre-established by the drama-makers (and not merely the writers) such as the orientation towards certain historical and social events. This is how the text itself can be an author's polemical gesture in a social campaign – something which frequently happens in television drama. The actual evaluative slant which the text is taking towards the identifiable realities alluded to, however, remains open to debate. We may understand that the scene from *Cracker* is a rejoinder to ideological contradiction, but whether it should be seen as sympathetic or condemnatory, or perhaps neutral, is not easily settled. This may depend on, for example, whether the viewer is a man or a woman.

The linguistic approach which such an approach to signification adopts, therefore, is that of pragmatics, the interpretation of meaning afresh in each new context. Pragmatism, on the other hand is a philosophical theory which lays great stress on the audience's interpretation of works of art. C.S. Peirce, the other great figure in the history of semiotic theory besides Saussure, seems to support the view that the meaning of a sign is the 'interpretant', or the conception which people have that links a signifier with a referent. Hence our concept of ideology may determine how we judge Fitz's outburst. The adoption of Peirce's view seems to liberate the text from the authoritarian domination of the author and free the audience to make of drama what they will. This, however, represents an extreme reaction against the notion of textual authority embedded in formalist semiotics. It is important to distinguish between pragmatics as an approach to meaning and *pragmatism*. Pragmatics emphasises the merging of a formal sign system with its context, whereas *pragmatism* suggests that audiences alone determine the meaning of texts.

The Bakhtinian sign is born again each time it is broadcast in a new context and its use in a new context as a rejoinder to new circumstances, creates a new signified and may modify the dialogue it responds to. *Cracker*, for example is a drama which has permanently extended the repertoire of detective fiction on screen. The effect of watching *Cracker* may be to recognise immediately that *Inspector Morse* has been relegated to a sub-genre of genteel 'murder mystery' rather than claiming a place as an archetypal detective drama.

Inspector Morse is an example of the kind of television drama which it is easy to assimilate into traditional semiotics. It uses many conventional codes, such as that of the detective with one or two vices who sees the detection of crime as a hobby. In this respect he is clearly in the Sherlock Holmes paradigm. *Cracker* can be seen as a historical rejoinder to this. The mythology of Sherlock Holmes solving a crime is a matter of deduction but an excess of logic is associated with eccentricity. Detectives are therefore unusual people. Morse solves crimes by virtue of his knowledge of human nature. He is also superior to others, and at least highly individual if not eccentric, but not because of his *academic* intellect. In 'The Wench is Dead' Morse proves to an academic historian that her historical account of a murder is wrong. In this case he solves the nineteenth-century murder when he is off work through illness, hence it is a hobby. The fact that Morse has 'good' taste in music and cars also helps to establish his social status as a 'gentleman' rather like Holmes. The mythology which is constructed around Morse therefore characterises him as a detective who is essentially disinterested. His selfless motivation to unravel the truth appears not merely to be the cause of his desire to detect, but the very reason why he is able to do so. His vision is not clouded by unprofessional motives.

Mythologies operate somewhat like syllogisms: More is disinterested, Morse solves crimes, hence disinterestedness is the key to solving crimes. Morse signifies the belief that love of the truth is what solves crimes, hence it is given only to a certain class of person to act in this manner. The codes which identify Morse as a 'gentleman' of the old school, make it clear that he therefore does not necessarily act out of a desire to make a living. In 'The Wench is Dead', he refuses to retire early, despite a serious illness. The temporary amateur status he enjoys in hospital helps to define him as a lover of truth for its own sake.

This is a recognisable code which derives from the detective drama genre. Whereas Holmes solves crimes by virtue of logic, Morse approaches them from the point of view of rationality. The contradiction is that he must use his personal qualities and he must be able to think in terms of a universal human nature. In 'The Wench is Dead', he states that the process of detection involves continually asking why the suspects acted as they did. The solution only emerges, however, when there is a rational person who is wickedly attempting to further their own self-interest. When Fitz asks why, the cases he considers have a more contemporary feel and often have no rational motive. In contemporary crime, some attacks are prompted by abnormal psychology, rather than the greedy mentality of an otherwise conventional citizen. Spectacularly gruesome murders such as that of Fitz's student involve a warped mind which is perverted by religious symbolism. In the historical development of the detective genre, these three examples show a progression towards a more intimate involvement with the mentality of the criminal. Fitz must understand why in terms of psychological causation rather than motives. His struggles are not with people who think the same way as himself or the rest of us, but he must know something of their temptations and repressed desires. In the interrogation scene in this drama when the murderer is finally caught, Fitz builds up a verbal picture of the attractiveness of the young woman on the train and the appeal of her thighs to the man sitting opposite. Morse would always be morally superior to his quarry, but Fitz reveals that he can envisage the same feelings as the murderer. This would be repugnant to Morse.

In this one scene it is possible to see the kind of mentality Fitz has always had and will continue to suffer from. The blindness of others is something which Fitz can see but not escape. His own myopia explains the problems he has, his failing marriage, for example, his gambling and looks both backwards and forwards. Throughout the series, this television drama shows characters 'cracking' as Fitz identifies the unbearably sensitive aspects of their psyche. The incident at the restaurant table is an example of the kind of interrogation which Fitz conducts throughout the series. His arrogance and domineering manner are due to his insights, but also help to damage his personal life. Barthes also compares some signs to Brecht's social gests which are actions that are more than a merely personal action provoked by emotion but can also be read as signifying a social phenomenon. Throwing the drink at Fitz is a gestic action in Brecht's terms since it signifies a social attitude: those who believe in a worthy ideology cannot see how they might offend against it. An attempt to attack an individual's ideology is seen as an attack on them. In the late twentieth-century, ideologies obscured attempts at mutual understanding. Barthes' words underline what happens in this scene:

> It thus appears that it is extremely difficult to vanquish myth from the inside; for the very effort one makes in order to escape the stranglehold becomes in its turn the prey of myth: myth can always, as a last resort, signify the resistance which is brought to bear against it. (Barthes, 1977 : 135)

The brief scene from *Cracker* is a sign because it signifies a number of things which are not explicit in the text itself – they are absences. It helps to make the text itself cohere by explaining how various internal signs inter-relate. It addresses the knowledge of the contemporary audience in that it asks us to recognise the situation where ideological contradictions are exposed and bitterness ensues, and it also foregrounds the historical rejoinder that forensic psychology is no longer just the pursuit of the rational motive. The woman who takes offence at Fitz's remarks is a sign which can be read in various ways. The pregnant moment is one where the sign's threefold function is momentarily prominent. Furthermore the Bakhtinian concept of dialogue embraces these three functions. Dialogues can be internal in that two signs seem to 'speak' to each other; or external in that they address the audience or historical events. The term 'dialogic' is also used by Bakhtin to characterise all signs such as language, since all signs must be original uses of signifiers but refer back to existing practices to which they respond. In this sense, all communication is both original but derivative. In any one person's voice and actions the words and signs of others are always presupposed. The term 'cracker' for example derives from many codes: someone who 'cracks up', a safebreaker, or a highly attractive person (a 'real cracker'), for example, yet the combination of these as personified by Robbie Coltrane, is unique.

The aspects of television drama which the example above has revealed, therefore are as follows. The signs of television drama are not linear in syntagmatic chains, but instead several signs may exist in any one frame and different signifying systems such as music and images may create a meaningful dialogue between each other. The social meaning of the drama at the time that it is broadcast, its place in a scheme of cultural change, is also highly significant in establishing meaning. Signs also change their signification according to where and when they are used. The use of a code in a particular television drama has to be seen as mediated through that drama and its impact on social dialogues.

The approach to semiotics which is not derived from Saussure or Peirce is referred to as 'interpretive' or 'interrogative' semiotics. This approach regards the sign as configuring the world for us in a new way rather than representing our existing knowledge. In representation we can distinguish between what is represented and the manner of its portrayal. Hence we can talk about the representation of women, or the general conclusions about women which can be drawn from their mode of representation.

In the television drama, *The Lifes and Loves of a She-Devil* as Liz Bird and Jo Eliot point out, the final scenes contain the somewhat surprising transformation of the she-devil who has personified a woman's anger against the husband and the romantic novelist he has betrayed her with, into the romantic novelist herself. This is an ambiguous sign: it could signify that the she-devil wishes to be like her rival, or that she has successfully taken over her role. Liz Bird and Jo Eliot remark, 'it is impossible to say this is "a feminist text"' (Brandt, 1993 : 225). Despite their analysis of 'woman as sign' this sign is original: it has no precedent in codes. We cannot distinguish here between the subject of the representation and the representation itself. If we want to decide which of the possible interpretations is valid, we have to interrogate the actual transformation further and look more closely at its characteristics. In other words, the form of representation and the subject are indistinguishable. Elisabeth Bronfen's reading of this transformation as a sign in her study of women and death, *Over Her Dead Body*, is that, ' In the monstrous act of totally refashioning her body, she both is and isn't the first Mary Fisher; she confirms and critiques the textual models of Pygmalion's and Frankenstein's creations' (Bronfen, 1992 : 414). This reading indicates that the sign is a new way of viewing old codes. It is a rejoinder to previous dramatic transformations and gains meaning from this dialogue with the past at this point in History. We might need to return to the overall purpose of the drama as an utterance and consider its social repercussions. Does this sign have a function rather than a meaning? Is a question rather than a statement communicated by this sign?

In the education of young media arts students, they are encouraged to practice creativity and to surpass current conventions rather than imitate them. A semiotic theory which acknowledges the leading role of innovatory practitioners is needed to appreciate and evaluate their creativity within the limits of ideology.

The example above indicates some of the features of television drama which we might expect any thorough semiotic analysis to reveal. The available writing on the textual analysis of television drama, however, is very limited and says little about semiotics. The most directly relevant contribution is perhaps Ellen Seiter's chapter on a semiotic approach to television in Robert C. Allen's *Channels of Discourse* (1992). Seiter relies heavily on Hodge and Tripp's book, *Children and Television, a Semiotic Approach* (1986). Their later work, *Social Semiotics* is not applied to the study of television drama in the revised edition of Seiter's work. The small number of books dedicated to television drama, Brandt (1992), Tulloch (1990) and more recently, Nelson (1997), do not discuss semiotic approaches in detail. An introductory textbook on the study of television such as that of Selby and Cowdery (1995) , takes it as axiomatic that semiotics means a Saussurean study of how signifiers such as a zoom in, have a specific signified associated with them. The most familiar approach to television drama semiotics is typified by Fiske and Hartley in their brief analysis of *Cathy Come Home* which uses the Saussurean concepts of paradigm and syntagm (Fiske and Hartley, 1978). In Hodge and Tripp's early work, semiotics is seen as a process of encoding by the television makers and decoding by the audience. This familiar model which echoes Stuart Hall's famous article on this subject (see Hall, 1973) relies on the analysis of what Hodge and Tripp call 'rule systems' which govern what signs can mean. In contemporary media theory, the term 'code' is used to describe rule systems.

The aim of existing semiotic approaches is largely to reveal a matrix of choices which determine clearly what each individual sign can mean. Existing social conventions delimit the range of signification and can be described explicitly to establish the principles on which all signs are attributed with meaning. It is assumed that the structures and conventions are common to both the sender and the receiver of the message. Structuralists soon adapted the fundamental principles of the approach to accommodate the existence of ambiguities and multiple meanings. Barthes' concept of polysemy allowed for the simultaneous existence of a number of codes which determine meaning. Thus the existence of many meanings can be acknowledged whilst the principle of socially-determined codes is retained.

Semiotics itself, however, has developed apace in recent years and is now responding to the influence of poststructuralist theories. The editors of *New Vocabularies in Film Semiotics* (Robert Stam, Robert Burgoyne and Sandy Flitterman-Lewis, 1992) argue that Derrida has been mainly responsible for challenging the notion of the stable relationship between signifier and signified which is fundamental to the notion of codes of meaning, since the mid 1960s. The authors of this summary of development in media semiotics point out how poststructuralism can enable an analysis of the conflicting ideological currents in a work and allow for their simultaneous existence. This approach, by de-stabilising the signifying relationship, can help to represent the actual condition of contemporary society. The post-structuralist denial of stability, however, may also fail to capture the social consequences of certain signifying practices. As Robin Nelson writes, for example, the television drama *Baywatch* is irredeemably sexist. The Russian Formalists coined the term 'the dominant' for the interpretation of a sign which was prevalent in any society, and it would appear to be difficult, if not impossible to account for this through poststructuralism which insists that texts cannot be so stable.

The explanation for this lack in poststructuralism may lie in the fact that it can be accused of an excessively formal approach to textual analysis. It tends to focus on the inter-relationship between signs within the text rather than examining the referents of signs. The referent, in poststructuralism, is always at one step from discovery, eluding any attempt at capture. Pierre Macherey also criticised structuralism in the mid 1960s, although from an alternative angle. In his writing on literary criticism, Macherey argued that structuralism subsumed the study of literary narratives into 'an aspect of the theory of communication' (Macherey, 1978 : 144). This may account for the continued popularity of structuralist assumptions amongst media academics. For Macherey, a true analysis ' confronts the silences, the denials and the resistance in the object – not that compliant implied discourse which offers itself to discovery but the condition which makes the work possible. which precedes the work so absolutely that it cannot be found in the work' (Macherey, 1978:130). The conditions of literary production were, according to Macherey, in the context of production and not necessarily in the work. Thus what was important was the 'silent signification', or what the text was signifying but not saying. This means that the non-formalist analysis of texts should focus on the presence of absences as Macherey put it, the notable omissions in the work which enable it to be related to a historical context and thereby to its conditions of production. The only published work which deals with Macherey's theory in relation to the media is Manuel Alvarado's pamphlet *Authorship, Origination and Production* (University of London Institute of Education, 1982).

The television drama *Tumbledown* written by Charles Wood, is the story of the disillusionment of a British Officer who was wounded on Mount Tumbledown during the Falklands conflict. It is a drama which reveals the brutality of war and exposes the emptiness of the chauvinistic rhetoric which sends people willingly into battle. In his introduction to the published text of *Tumbledown* (1987), Wood argues that defiant patriotism is often associated with a certain social group: the notions of honour and duty mean most to the privileged. The drama therefore opens with signs which clearly connote this particular social group from which the young officers have come. The first scene shows a green Panther sports car winding its way through a beautiful part of the Cotswolds. Although it is not stated explicitly, the significant absence here of any other social group tends to reinforce the belief, which Wood himself expresses, about the popularity of patriotism. What is not said – that these kinds of people are the breeding ground for patriotic ideology – is nonetheless clearly understood. The absent history of social class which readers can be relied upon to have experienced, ensures that the meaning lies in the relationship between the text and society and not in some structure held mysteriously within the text. Ray Jenkins (1995). analyses the opening scene and points out how the drama relies on signs which provoke audience reactions.

The developments in theory then, made the task for textual analysis harder still: the text had to be susceptible of many readings, rather than understood as harbouring one structure, yet it also should be related to its historical moment which governs the way in which it produces meaning. Semiotics faced a particularly difficult challenge: the discipline had originated within structuralism and yet now had to qualify its acceptance of 'structures', and concede that signification could be unstable. On the other hand, it had to offer an explanation of how signs could have referents and could not fail to relate to society in some way. Semiotics began as a means of situating art within material cultural practices, but post-structuralism tended to undermine this enterprise.

Whereas structuralist-inspired readings of film appeared in the journal *Screen*, suggesting that signs operated to 'position' the viewer in a particular ideology, postmodernism liberated the viewer and maintained that viewers had virtually unlimited freedom to interpret signs how they chose, since all signs were unstable. Both extremes in these camps, however, concentrated on the relationships between signs and the audience. Hodge and Tripp eventually joined those who called for a ' social semiotics' which would treat all analysable texts as existing in what they call the 'mimetic plane' (standing in some relation to reality) and the 'semiosic plane' (reflecting a formal relationship amongst signs and sign-systems) (Hodge and Tripp, 1988 : 262).

For many theorists concerned with semiotics, Charles Sanders Peirce seemed to present a way out of this dilemma. Julia Kristeva, for example, adopts many of

Peirce's ideas. Peirce's system is more complex than Saussure's and relies on a fundamental trichotomy of sign, referent and interpretant. The interpretant is the idea in the mind of the sign-user by which he or she relates the sign to its referent. In addition, any item in this three-way relationship can also become a sign in its turn. The Peircean view that signs were everywhere in social life and existed both in consciousness and in society, enabled semiotics to break down the dualism of the mind and the world. It also fulfils Hodge and Tripp's requirement that the mimetic and semiosic planes would be reconciled. Signs could be used in, for example, psychoanalysis. Kristeva was anxious, however, to break free from *semiology* as practised by Saussure and those who came after him. She emphasised that semiotics was not a sign-system, but a signifying *process*. It was something which people did, not an immutable set of rules which they were obliged to follow. This recognition led her to develop what she called 'semanalysis'. If signs were used by people for their purposes then the study of meaning did not exclude the users, in fact it was obliged to incorporate them and their motives. The vast system which Peirce proposed, led to what he called the 'pan-semiotic universe' where all social life was a matter of signs. The difficulty with Peirce's theories, however, is that whereas Saussure believed that it was social psychology which would explain how signs were used, Peirce ultimately related all sign use to logic. Hence Peircean semiotics can also be applied to the physical sciences.

It was Bakhtin/Volosinov who proposed a theory which could explain how signs might be created by individuals, and yet still constructed only in social life. Kristeva is an enthusiastic disciple of Bakhtin. Prior to Volosinov, it appeared that creativity was suspect because it seemed to rely on a spurious concept of autonomous psychic agency. In *Marxism and the Philosophy of Language* (1973), there is a spirited defence of language as a creative activity analogous to the Marxist conception of history as 'the story of men in pursuit of their ends'. Signs, like history, are shaped in the pursuit of human goals and not by a monolithic system which is somehow outside history. Language too, has to be understood as the attempt to express the ideas of individual subjects but only by reference to the real world.

For Peirce, the meaning of a sign was explained by the philosophy of pragmatism as its 'generalisable effects'. Much of contemporary reception theory could be argued to fall into this tradition. Where audiences are credited with revealing the meanings of a text, this is a kind of pragmatism. As Julia Hallam and Margaret Marshment argue, however, we are 'in danger of fetishizing the "ordinary reader/viewer" in a way that will exclude most actual readers and viewers' (Hallam and Marshment, 1995:13). Audience ethnographies of television drama have discovered ever increasing complexity and differences between viewers. This trend threatens to challenge the notion of a homogeneous audience about which generalisations can be made. The pragmatic emphasis suggests that there is no such thing as the text and that the only meanings exist in the minds of viewers where effects occur. Bakhtin enabled Kristeva to return to a study of the productivity of individuals within a materialist tradition. It is also arguable that the possibility of media education depends on the possibility of being able to reveal further meanings in texts.

The other major step forward which Bakhtinian theory makes is that it links signs to society without narrowing down their meaning to one signified. Bakhtin's notion of dialogue is a relationship which can exist within a dramatic work and between the work and society. Since dialogue continues to reverberate, and is never absolutely clear-cut, it does not confine meaning, but it also represents a relationship between the drama and its social contexts. Bakhtinian semiotics situates the process of using signs within a historical moment and specific social practices where the participants generate meanings. The sign has a specific meaning in a specific context of use, but it is open to multiaccentuality, and can be used in other contexts. It therefore can have specific effects in certain instances, but this does not delimit the meaning of any sign, since it can be re-used. All signs also have accents or ways of being produced, whether it be by voice or on screen. The accentuation of a sign can also change in new contexts. What makes Bakhtinian semiotics so much more amenable to the study of media arts is that what lies behind the signifying practices of the media is not a system but the actual interests and activities of people. Media texts are not simply self-contained stories, but also agit-prop, polemic and other forms of attempted social intervention. Bakhtinian theory continues to espouse some notion of individual agency, but also attempts to situate this within material practices and acknowledge the existence of social institutions which may dominate certain forms of meaning. Peirce's theories tend to suggest that the interpretants in people's minds are the origins of meaning and that to study signs in society is to study individuals and their conceptions of the world. This semiotic theory is also increasingly used to defend a conservative politics with its emphasis on a society of free individuals determining their own future.

Bakhtinian theory has been recognised as a useful addition to the armoury of theories applied to film as the authors of *New Vocabularies in Film Semiotics* have pointed out, but the only major writer on Bakhtinian theory as applied to the media is Robert Stam in works such as *Subversive Pleasures: Bakhtin, Cultural Criticism and Film* (1989). The elaboration of a semiotic approach derived from Bakhtinian principles which can help to detect the subtleties of television drama is the aim of the following studies in textual analysis. Bakhtin, of course, did not write about television drama and there is only an occasional reference to semiotics in his writings. It should be noted, therefore, that in developing a semiotic approach which is greatly indebted to some of Bakhtin's fundamental concepts, there seems to be a need to be eclectic and at times critical of Bakhtin. The approach developed here is not intended to be an extension of Bakhtin's views alone. The primary purpose of using Bakhtin is to assist the understanding of television drama. There are undoubtedly many further subtleties in Bakhtin's huge body of work which can throw more light on this issue, but the intention here is not merely to expound Bakhtin's views.

Naturalism as the dominant aesthetic of television can conceal the function of signs. When a drama is situated in the Oxfordshire countryside, for example, the colour of a passer-by's shirt will be assumed to be incidental. Whereas on stage all the elements are assumed to be significant as Elam (1980) noted, on screen in a naturalistic drama, it is possible to discount certain elements which have simply been transferred wholesale from the location. We assume that they were simply there at the time by chance. Hence television drama usually foregrounds dialogue and reduces the function of setting and location. Signs in television drama are not always the writer's work, however. A text is a collaborative creation and it is possible for the production to incorporate signs which reinforce the dialogue, or exist in some other kind of relationship with it. On occasions, as the *Cracker* example cited earlier shows, there are many factors in an apparently naturalistic scene which can have thematic significance. The emphasis on textual study should not be thought of as privileging the role of the writer, although it does stress the creativity of all those who make such work. Developments in semiotic theory are needed to enable audiences to recognise how to derive further meaning and pleasure from televisual texts.

David Harris has written that the interest in representation of minority groups in television and film is 'no longer sufficient either to explain the production values or to account for the complex pleasures of the audience watching them' (Harris, D. 1996:37). Ideology is, of course vitally important in signifying practices but it is not static and cultural practices are at the forefront of change. Lyn Thomas (1995) , for example, writes about the varied reactions of women watching typical representations of masculinity in the television drama *Inspector Morse*. In this article Thomas deals with the audience's ability to discern signs of quality whilst simultaneously distancing themselves from a conservative representation of men. Thomas therefore acknowledges the actual reactions of women viewers and does not attempt to homogenise them.

The ethnographic study explores the reactions of viewers who were conscious of a contradiction in watching a drama which was regarded by many as 'politically unsound'. This demonstrates, perhaps, that media education has broken the hold of naturalism and has awoken its supposedly passive audience. As Jensen and Jankowski write, 'while Barthes and some later authors have suggested how text and image may be interrelated when they communicate in concert, a detailed typology of the various discourses and genres remains to be constructed' (Jensen and Jankowski, 1991, p. 39). Another aspect of television drama's naturalistic aesthetic is that its elements are usually regarded as unified. This has meant that the interrelationship of elements such as music and dialogue has not been extensively explored. As Brecht put it, we need to regard the 'separation of the elements' of drama as an essential stage in understanding its significance. The following work aims to make a contribution to that area of research.

The Third Meaning: Semantics, and syntax in semiotic theory

In his essay entitled 'The Third Meaning', Barthes discovers some aspects of stills from Eisenstein's films which cannot be accommodated in the Saussurean semiotic system. A close examination of this essay reveals that Barthes was beginning to recognise that a semiotic theory which originates with Bakhtin was needed to explain all the signs he could detect in Eisenstein's work. Lengthy descriptions of particular shots are needed for Barthes to identify elements which have meaning yet cannot be seen as signs with a conventionally-attached concept. The term Barthes uses for this more diffuse meaning is *signifiance*, the generation of 'signifiers without signifieds'. For Saussurean theory, this is completely inexplicable, since the sign is said to consist of a signifier and its socially-related concept or signified. Barthes acknowledges that this discovery leads him 'via the path opened up by Julia Kristeva, to a semiotics of the text' (Barthes, 1977:54). Kristeva's semiotics, is, of course openly indebted to Bakhtin, and Barthes' use of the terms 'carnival' and 'dialogue' in this essay suggest that Bakhtin is a distant influence. In this section, Bakhtin's emphasis on the pragmatics of semiosis is differentiated from previous semiotic theories, using Barthes' essay as a springboard. The essay is used to differentiate between the three main branches of linguistics as models for the analysis of filmic and televisual signs.

'The filmic', according to Barthes, is 'that in the film which cannot be described, the representation which cannot be represented. The filmic begins only where language and metalanguage end' (Barthes, 1977:64). This statement clearly suggests that structuralism, which Barthes defined as the application of theory derived from linguistics to cultural issues, cannot account for some of the meaningful moments which occur in media texts such as television drama. If some non-conventional elements of a text can be regarded as significant, the reason why this cannot be adequately represented in language is that the signified cannot be identified. As Barthes remarked in his essay 'Rhetoric of the Image', 'there is no vocabulary to describe signifieds' (Barthes, 1977 : 47).

The meaning associated by Barthes with certain signifiers can only be approached by further description of the signifier. The signified cannot be named.

The third meaning is discovered by Barthes when he examines a set of stills from Eisenstein's films. After considering the information conveyed and the symbolic dimension he finds that obstinately, there are still aspects of the image which seem to signify but which cannot be assigned to a clear signified. One image is of two courtiers pouring gold coins over the head of the king. The informational and symbolic aspects are clear: the divine one is showered in a suitably lavish cascade of coins to signify his regal stature and declare it officially. This much can be clearly attributed to the film-maker's intentions. The faces of the courtiers, however, display both boredom and diligence. They are aspects of the obtuse meaning which refuses to be reconciled with the previous two meanings. Here there is a lack of the magnificence which is the purpose of the ceremony, a kind of counter-narrative. The third meaning 'structures the film differently without destroying the narrative'. The faces of the courtiers signify the artificiality of the ceremony to the common man and subvert the idea of the consecration of monarchy. Barthes attributes it to the carnival aspect of the film (recalling Bakhtin's theory of the carnivalesque) where distinctions of rank are not observed as the common elements of humanity are celebrated. Nonetheless his kind of signifier cannot be described adequately. You would have to see the expressions to know the precise quality of the attitudes they embody. They constitute part of the 'filmic' – that which cannot be rendered in other terms. As Barthes says, the obtuse meaning disturbs metalanguage: it does not allow a metacommentary to capture its essence.

These perceptions all suggest that the fundamental structuralist approach, to model all signifying systems on language, is mistaken. Visual signifiers can have a symbolic status which endows them with an uncategorisable meaning. The filmic or televisual can signify in ways which language is not equipped to specify as Deleuze has maintained, for example in *Cinema-2: The Time-Image* (1989). Saussure himself postulated a 'General science of signs' of which language was only a part, hence to use linguistic theory alone as he proposed, seems inevitably narrow.

Barthes identifies two more conventional layers of meaning in addition to *signifiance* in this essay: the informational and the symbolic. If these are applied to the *Cracker* example, they are easy to find. At the informational level, we learn that the parents of the dead girl are told of her death and that Fitz goes out to dinner without any money. In symbolic terms, aspects of the scene such as the music clearly connote maternal love and peace which has been brutally broken for the victim's family. If the third or obtuse meaning was eliminated, there would still be communication and signification of aspects such as these. The signs which Barthes is so puzzled by are those which have no existing codified meaning, yet can nonetheless function as signs. As Barthes says, 'the obtuse {or third} meaning is not situated structurally, a semantologist would not agree as to its objective existence (but then what is an 'objective reading'?) (Barthes, 1977 : 60).

There is an obvious analogy between early structuralist approaches to semiotics and semantics. The attempt to give a sign a consistent value by attributing it to a signified recognised by convention, is analogous to the attempt to restrict the meaning of a word. Although linguistics for Saussure is properly part of the general science of semiology, signs are subjected to linguistic analysis in Saussurean thought. As Clive Thomson expresses it, 'a word in a dictionary, for example, that is to say without context, is merely a conventional sign' (Thompson, 1983:18). Thompson goes on to quote Bakhtin's words, 'The connection between meaning and sign in the word taken concretely and independent of the concrete utterance, as in a dictionary, is completely random.' To specify in advance of its use what a word means is only to offer the most vague generalisation. Just as semantics can only partly account for the meanings of words in use, so too codes can only partially tell us what signs signify.

Some signs in our society can, of course, be recognised by convention as Saussure argued. Roses are a code for romance. Just as dictionary definitions are often useful, so too codes often tell us a great deal about a sign's function in a media text. As Volosinov states, however, 'the theme of an utterance is indivisible' (Volosinov, 1973:100). Despite the fact that the *meaning* of the utterance can be broken down into a separate component for each word, meaning alone will not give us the value of a sentence in use. Meaning is an abstract notion, unrelated to actual cases of the use of language. If we know the meaning of each word in a sentence, it does not follow that we know the use of the sentence and its actual meaning when uttered in a specific context. The significance of the words, 'I am a Berliner', extends far beyond their linguistic meaning and has to acknowledge the context of their utterance by President Kennedy during the Cold War in a divided city. An utterance needs to be understood in its entirety first: its meaning cannot be built up by examining the meaning of each sign.

Allocating signs to paradigms is like ascribing a semantic value to them. In Saussurean analyses like this, it is assumed that once the particular choices of paradigms are made, the meaning of the sentence is absolutely clear. In the case of such simple sentences as the above example, this appears to be true. As Ellen Seiter remarks, however, semiotics tends to 'neaten up' the texts it studies (Allen, ed. 1992 : 61). In this case it does so by reducing the possibilities of meaning to a small number of combinations. The dictionary definitions of these words do not give us the full picture of their meaning when used. For example, there is a considerable difference between the sentence, 'The man opened the door' as an answer to the question 'who opened the door?' and as an answer to the question, 'did the man open the door?'. This linguistic example, which is used to illustrate semiotics, is claimed by Hodge and Tripp to illustrate the fundamental nature of signs. It demonstrates how syntagms function at a simplified level. As Saussure reminds us, though, syntagms should not be identified with syntax (which is only one version of a syntagmatic chain), syntagms are defined as 'combinations supported by linearity' (Saussure, 1974 : 123). Hodge and Tripp acknowledge that 'a spoken word followed by a visual gesture constitutes another synchronic syntagm' (Hodge and Tripp, 1986 : 21) for example.

This demonstrates a certain flexibility in Saussurean semiotics, but it restricts analysis to linear sequences. In Barthes' terms, this method does not acknowledge the possibility of what Barthes calls 'vertical' semiotic arrangements, or simultaneous presentation of visual signs in a shot. A further difficulty for the approach via Saussure's syntagms and paradigms is that the approach tends to beg the question. Attributing a character to a paradigm tends to presuppose his or her role within the drama. Fitz, for example, is a father, husband, lover, gambler and a psychologist. There is no Saussurean method to select which of these available paradigms takes precedence here. Once the assumption is made, the approach seems to have rigour, but its foundations are not entirely secure. Semiotics began as an attempt to establish a solid foundation on publicly-observable criteria for communication via art and fiction, but the Saussurean approach has done little to establish an empirical approach which is unchallengeable.

Another example in the scene from *Cracker* illustrates the difficulty of attributing specific, invariable meanings to signs. As Fitz's tirade against his embarrassed friends gathers pace, the camera shows us the expressions on the faces around the table in close up, and in quick succession. The faces register consternation, and this word is possibly the most accurate which can be used, although it does not exhaust the scene's meaning. The semantic analogy, therefore, wears thin, since no meaning can be given with absolute precision. The notion of *signifiance* describes the status of the unstated emotion which rapidly affects the people seated around the table with Fitz. The anxiety which the three people feel can be shown but this term does not fully describe the precise emotion. There is no conventional signified, yet these glances are meaningful. Another example of an obtuse or third meaning might be the black waitress's shaven head. This has no essential place in the narrative, in keeping with the third meaning, but it somehow adds to the visual impact. As Barthes says of the elements of *signifiance* which he discovers, they are 'in subtle dialogue' with the obvious levels of meaning. They do not deny the existence of codified systems of meaning but they play on and between them, qualifying and undermining the codes. In the case of the waitress' shaven head, this makes her both a young, strong and stylish woman, but also recalls earlier images of servitude. The hairstyle can be argued to match the needs of the scene perfectly in its cultural ambiguity. The waitress is both a servant and yet also the person who demands payment from Fitz, thereby embarrassing him. To describe the connotations of her appearance in full, however, takes a great deal of subtlety and skill: it is a blend of ideas which creates a new differentiation for us. It is this subtle relationship between the image which constitute the third meaning and the obvious meaning which Barthes considers to be dialogical. The elements have meaning partly by virtue of their relationship to each other. As Barthes writes, 'the contemporary problem is not to destroy the narrative but to subvert it'. The third meaning does not simply supplement the syntactical structure, but adds another dimension to it.

The third meaning is one which Barthes can only trace within a shot and not in the narrative sequence. Barthes argues that Eisenstein's writings call for a vertical reading: one which examines the shot independently of its function in a sequence. Eisenstein himself came to a similar conclusion later in life. The individual elements of *signifiance* also have meaning in relation to the other elements in the same shot. Their co-existence calls for an understanding of the image as a combination of elements in various relationships to each other, the text's other signs, and the social life of society. Just as semantics can only give the standard or usual meaning of a word, so too, the Saussurean insistence on codes can only give the unexceptional signified attached to any signifier, independent of any specific context.

As Bakhtin remarked, 'a code is a deliberately established, killed context' (Bakhtin, 1986:147). Any attempt to circumscribe the meaning of a sign, whether linguistic or otherwise, in advance of its use must inevitably deny the influence of the context in which it is used. Despite this, there is a frequent assumption in media analysis that to trace a code is to understand a sign. John Corner, for example, in a chapter in Richard Collins *et al* eds. *Media, Culture and Society* (1986) entitled 'Codes and Cultural Analysis', maintains that 'cultural conventions and their variants operate with a degree of internal coherence and regularity comparable to that found in natural language' (Collins, 1986:59). As Bakhtin says, however, 'Semiotics deals primarily with the transmission of ready-made communication using a ready-made code. But in live speech, strictly speaking, communication is first created in the process of transmission and there is, in essence, no code' (Bakhtin, 1986:147). Semantics, the linguistic science of conventional meaning, is only the beginning of a semiotic analysis. Umberto Eco writes that,

> The sign is a *gesture* produced with the *intention of communicating*, that is, in order to transmit one's representation of inner state to another being. The existence of a certain rule (a code) enabling both the sender and the addressee to understand the manifestation in a certain way must, of course, be *presupposed* (my italics) if the transmission is to be successful (Eco, 1986 : 16).

Ellen Seiter's description of 'weak codes' in Eco's theory is that 'they are flexible, changeable and can produce an *unforeseeable* [my italics] number of individual signs' (Allen ed 1992 : 46). If this is the case, then there cannot be a code which is formally in existence 'prior to the act of communication'.

Bakhtin's reason for denying the importance of previously-established codes is that each act of communication is oriented towards a particular context which has not formerly existed: 'In the majority of cases, we presuppose a certain typical and stabilised *social purview* toward which the ideological creativity of our own social group and time is oriented' (Volosinov, 1973 : 87). Like Saussure, Bakhtin believed that there were genres which governed such free acts as ordinary conversation or gestures but these were only realised in actual contexts. What Bakhtin calls ' expressive intonation', for example, ' belongs to the utterance, and not to the word' (Bakhtin, 1986:86). Barthes echoes this idea in his essay when he attributes to the third meaning, 'an emotion-value, an evaluation' (Barthes 1977 :59).

The crucial question, however, is whether codes have to be *presupposed* as Eco claims. This would imply that we cannot understand any signs which we are not already familiar with. Stuart Hall's essay 'Encoding/Decoding' (Hall, *et al*, 1980) is a classic statement of the approach generally taken to the analysis of media texts which ultimately derives from Saussure. Stuart Hall's seminal article also confronts the fundamental theoretical issues which impinge on the study of television drama. To summarise Hall's argument briefly, television does not have unmediated access to reality. Any representation of 'the real' will be edited and composed in such a manner that it is, in fact, a construction by the institutions of television, rather than an unadulterated glimpse of reality. In understanding the television message, we have to decode or, perhaps it would be more appropriate to say, unencode, the way in which the television institution has achieved this construction. Only when we have seen even iconic signs as part of a code-system (images of dreaming spires and gothic architecture signify a traditional university environment in *Inspector Morse* through the code of the establishing shot), can we be said to have understood the real nature of the television message. The semiotic strategy of the television drama makers is compared with our knowledge of traditional university environments and a rapid conclusion is reached in the viewer's mind. Thus, as Hall writes at the end of a polemical section, 'There is no intelligible discourse without the operation of a code'.

This article has set the tone for a great deal of work on media theory and has established the orthodoxy that all mediation is an encoding, because there can be no direct, unadulterated revelation of reality. Saussure's semiotic theory therefore has always provided a valuable source of theory to support this view. The social conventions are the 'rules' which viewers of television have to acknowledge if they are to understand what they see as a code and not simple reality.

We need, however, to understand the polemical debate which this proposes an answer to before we can properly understand the weight attached to these words. The article was written in the course of a dialogue about the 'objectivity' of the media. The article forms a part of Stuart Hall's pioneering work on Marxist approaches to the media, in which he is above all concerned to demonstrate how the media can act to reinforce the hegemony which the State exercises. It is therefore important to stress the way in which the construction of social reality in the media can serve the interests of the powerful by creating a particular impression based on snatches of 'reality'. What is at stake here is the media's inevitable tendency to present a biased view.

Stuart Hall is himself sceptical about the possibility of communication actually taking place. As he says, the meaning structures of the encoder and the decoder may not be the same. There is a permanent possibility that the televisual message is an unrecognised distortion. Hall's theory here is analogous to that of John Locke, (1690) a pioneer in the attempts to theorise semiotics, in describing the Human Understanding in philosophical terms. John Locke argued that when we contemplate a natural object, the object itself is not present to our mind and therefore there must be something which is actually before us. This thing he called an 'idea'. Words stood for ideas in Locke's theory to enable communication. As philosophers such a Gilbert Ryle have pointed out, however, if words are related to an individual's mental activities, then we could not know for certain that the activities I associate with a word are the same as the mental objects which you associate with it. According to Hall's theory a television viewer needs to understand both the code a programme maker uses to give an image meaning and also what that meaning signifies to the maker themselves. This latter stage, however, is a private mental connection forged by the maker and not available to the viewer to see or consider. We could never be certain that we knew exactly what was meant unless we perhaps shared precisely the same human experience as the programme makers. Semiotics deals with public meanings which are independent of the sign-users themselves.

It is possible to accept Hall's position on this without accepting that all signs are pre-established via codes. If reality is fundamentally undifferentiated and any differences are only apparent when we use signs to indicate them, then it follows that new differences can be discovered. If new ways of differentiating the events in the world are found, then they can be repeated until we recognise the same features and come to know the distinction which is being drawn to our attention. This can happen within the time-span of a television drama, which is a cultural practice that exists to enliven our perception in these ways. Any such distinction which is signified within one drama is not yet a code; it is not yet accepted throughout our culture and verifiable through other sources, but it is still a way of mediating the world rather than gaining direct access to it.

William Husson writes in 'A Wittgensteinian critique of the encoding-decoding model of communication', that the central characteristic of the encoding/decoding model in the philosophy of language is its fundamental presupposition of *incommunicability*. The need for us to have a repertoire of inner knowledge that can be related to signs implies that the sign will mean nothing to us by itself (Husson, 1994). Hall's theory demands a decoding and a translation in any one act of television viewing. The decoding finds the signified of the televisual convention ('this is an establishing shot'). The audience must also have their own codes or they would have unmediated access to reality themselves. The content of the establishing shot (dreaming spires) is therefore related to the way in which we would decode this sight in our own experience. The conclusion is that the shot signifies a traditional university environment.

As we have seen, however, in the example from *Cracker*, some signs such as the black waitress coming upon Fitz at a crucial moment in the action, do not have to be understood by reference solely to our own codification of reality. Here the interesting feature is the way in which it might encourage us to adopt a new interpretation of our own lives. This is not a familiar, everyday televisual code, and it can be adapted by the audience to reconfigure their own experience. We might become increasingly conscious of occasions where our utterance has been contradicted by our behaviour. Where a new, original sign is devised, the audience can use this to unite their knowledge of their own experience, society and the televisual text in one act of understanding. If the signs which we use to comprehend reality are arbitrary, they can be constantly re-invented and substituted. In the *Cracker* example, we see how the televisual code can be adapted directly to our own use in everyday life. We do not have unmediated access to reality but an original televisual sign can mediate for us in a new manner. It is still a construction imposed by the medium of television and open to challenge and debate.

Stuart Hall's two acts of decoding are here collapsed into one: to grasp the televisual sign's function is to comprehend a relationship between sign and society in one moment. Thus it is still true that mediated messages are not wholly objective 'slices of life' in the media, and that they are presented in a televisual form, but not that they all draw on a pre-established set of conventions which is shared between television producers and audiences. If there were not the possibility of creating new signs without established meanings, there could be no subversive or deviant activity.

On the question of codes, therefore, we can re-phrase the debate. The issue is not perhaps whether there are codes, since there most certainly are. What is at stake is whether the codes used to signify on television are only those which are pre-established and understood only through prior social conventions. Codes may also be re-accented or given a new meaning which departs from the original codified form. It is the contention of this work that codes do not have to *precede* the television text, since they can also be constructed as they are screened. A social practice needs rules, but those rules do not always precede the practice itself. Social practices develop in action and are not created whole. We can agree that some form of encoding is necessary in any mediated text, by definition, since to mediate means to place an intermediary interpretation between the viewer and reality. Codes, however, are a vocabulary and in interpretation we need to read them in both a syntactical and pragmatic context. I do not want to stress the analogy between semiotics and language, but here it is useful as a means of distinguishing between codes and meaningfulness, To know the full range of codes alone is not sufficient to know how they are used in each context.

A penetrating question to ask of the code theorists is when and how the first discourse began if codes must always precede meaningful articulation. We are entering the age when the media are not the sole property of the rich and powerful and it is increasingly possible to own at least some of the means of technological production. New media artists will increasingly break conventions and establish new practices as they engage in original work. In these new practices, within recognised forms such as television drama, media artists may actually compose codes as they create new forms of social practice. The two activities may be simultaneous. Social practices are systems of conventions. To initiate a new social practice means to create new codes of meaning. Martin Esslin puts the point well in the following passage:

> While certain techniques of this kind – like the slow dissolve that precedes a flashback – have become conventionalised into instantly recognisable 'symbolic' devices immediately understood by the public, it is even here, somewhat problematic to talk about a 'language' with a fixed 'grammar': new and unconventional ways of handling these techniques by innovative directors may well use them in entirely new ways and produce different meanings. Indeed that is the very essence of creativeness in this as in any other medium, so that too rigid a codification of the 'meanings' of specific techniques might become as stultifying as the strict application of the three unities in French classical drama. (Esslin, 1987 : 99)

There has been a confusion in media theory between the call for a semiotics which acknowledges the need for publicly-understood conventions, external to the individual, and social codes which are universally agreed by an entire population. It may be necessary to establish conventions *publicly*, but communication can take place before a code is generally recognised *socially*. As Susan Melrose writes of the theatrical process of staging a text, the ensemble activity of a group of performers may establish connotations of their own and thus the dramatic text is 'not *wholly* socially encoded at the moment of its singular production' (Melrose, 1994 :52). In such a case, however, the ensemble work will nonetheless constitute a public convention amongst a small social group. The same might be said of a television production. This confusion also exists to some extent in Bakhtin/Volosinov's rigid distinction between signals and codes. Bakhtin/Volosiniv does not appear to recognise that what starts as a signal can go on to become a code with time.

Where a media artist creates a new sign, the audience may then use that same sign to recognise and order their own experience. A famous example of this occurred in the television drama *Boys from the Blackstuff* where the cry 'Gissa job!' acted as a sign of a widespread social feeling amongst the unemployed and the disenchanted (Millington and Nelson, 1986). This famous cry acted as an expressive vehicle for many people on football terraces: there was no need to translate it into another, more personal code. Conventions can be established between television drama makers and the audience within the duration of a programme or a series, they do not have to be society-wide to be effective. Patrice Pavis summarises the situation for contemporary semiotics very accurately when he attacks the 'universalising malady' which insists on finding theories which apply across disciplines, genres and even cultures. Pavis opposes 'both a positivism of signs isolated without reference to the audience's ideological situation and a sociologism preoccupied with statistics or socio-professional categorisation of the audience, or an experimental psychology that describes the spectators' reactions without linking them to an aesthetic reflection on the production of meaning' (Pavis, 1992:83).

Another way of phrasing this comment is that any semiotics which does not acknowledge the simultaneous importance of the text, the audience and its particular context, is bound to give only a partial account which privileges one of these aspects. The Saussurean approach is a kind of positivism, in that it tends to see every sign as having a definite fixed signified which derives from social reality (See Aston and Savona, 1992). The aim of semiotics for Pavis must be to preserve the dramatic work's individuality such as its cultural roots and yet to avoid 'scattered, partial and isolated discourses' and to acknowledge history in understanding texts. Robert Stam points out that 'the system of the text, then is the instance that displaces the codes so that they become inflections and substitutions for one another' (Stam, 1989:49). Eco's vast system of 'sinsigns' (a term borrowed from Peirce) which qualify and complicate existing signs is an attempt to predict the unpredictable creation of codes rather than to describe an existing system.

The notion of codes is, then, only the starting-point for a semiotic analysis and not the final stage. As is stated in *New Vocabularies in Film Semiotics*, Will Wright argued that 'the semantic approach is insufficient for comprehending the meaning of narrative' (Stam *et al*, 1992:77). Levi-Strauss and other structuralists had argued that the semantic potential of a text lay in the possibility of interaction between its system of binary opposites, the fundamental semantic building blocks of meaning in structuralism. Wright argued that to ignore plot was to ignore a very obvious element of meaning creation through signs.

In order to maintain the study of culture by using linguistics, structuralists turned to syntax as the language theory which would explain the meaning of signs. The function of a sign depended on its position in a narrative sequence and the other signs with which it was juxtaposed. This allows for a less rigid definition of meaning, since the particular sequence will determine the meaning of a word. As Barthes writes, 'a narrative is never made up of anything other than functions; in differing degrees, everything in it signifies' (Barthes, 1977: 89). The analogy with syntax enabled structuralists to take a somewhat more flexible view of the role of signs, but instead of aiming for a vast 'dictionary', they sought the grammar or rules of syntagmatic combination as if narrative sequences were sentences. The notion of *langue* was simply extended. Structuralists such as Barthes, in their earlier phase, attempted to arrive at the overarching rules of combination which dictated the legitimate meaningful narrative sequences. As Peter Bondanella charts the history of Eco's transition from structuralism to narrative theory, he writes that Eco seized on Peirce's theory of 'unlimited semiosis', as a means of characterising the 'open work' (Bondanella, 1997:76). Barthes, for example, had espoused the kind of narrative theory which Vladimir Propp proposed in his famous *Morphology of the Folk Tale* (1968). In the case of mythology, the syntactical structure was dictated by an uderlying set of narrative functions which transcended time, place and history to form the components of stories world-wide. This is another structural analysis which can indeed be applied to television texts with good results (see Nelson, 1997:33), but it is also ultimately reductive.

We should remember that in a collection of essays such as *Image-Music-Text* (1977), we are not confronted with a consistent theoretical position. The essay on the structural analysis of narratives was written in 1966, whilst the essay on 'The Third Meaning' was written in 1970 and challenges some of the assumptions made earlier. What Barthes really means by a narrative is a sequence of distinguishable actions or events linked by causal principles. When he muses on the possibility of a 'poetical grasp' of a narrative, he is considering the likelihood that an alternative narrative can be made up of perceptions and insights: moments of illumination which do not follow each other in a causal sequence. The discovery that some meaningful elements exist as signs outside the structure of actions and within the shot, encourages Barthes to propose that the contemporary priority is not to 'destroy the narrative but to subvert it' (Barthes, 1977, p. 64). The three types of meaning which Barthes distinguishes in his essay on the 'third meaning' are analogous to semantic, syntactic and pragmatic theory in a Bakhtinian style. As Barthes says of his discoveries, they are 'the epitome of a counter-narrative'.

Barthes speaks of the text as a number of nuclei or pivotal moments where the main character has to choose between mutually-exclusive alternatives which determine the course of events. The example which Barthes gives is of James Bond hearing the telephone ring (Barthes, 1977 : 92). Bond must either answer or not. Inbetween nuclei, catalysers act to precipitate the action required by the nuclei. For example, if there is a knock at the door, Bond's decision becomes all the more urgent. Indices are acts which signify character, such as Bond coolly putting down his cigarette. These actions tell us more about his character and partly determine Bond's response to the imminent decision.

Whilst these terms do characterise some of the functions of signifiers within an audio-visual narrative, they by no means exhaust the possibilities. The tendency in structuralist accounts of narrative is to treat the identifiable elements of plot as if they were irreducible. Semiotic theorists such as Elam (1980) attempted to divide drama into fundamental, irreducible units as in semantics, but eventually conceded failure. The process of making a film or television drama may well consist of uniting indivisible elements such as the shot in editing, but the audience's attention to signs does not necessarily correspond to this. The moment when Fitz is doused with wine is a decisive one, but it does not demand an either/or response. There are many possible reactions: humour, anger, resignation, for example, each of which may take the narrative in a different direction.

A Pragmatics of Signs: Interpretive semiotics

Barthes remarks that the signifiers which do not fit into a conventional narrative can have a subversive function, establishing contradictions or registering defiance of conventions. The term which Barthes uses to describe the impact of the unattached signifiers he finds is that it carries an *emotion value*; it is an *evaluation* (Barthes, 1977:59). This term reveals Barthes' indebtedness to Bakhtin, via Julia Kristeva whom he explicitly acknowledges. Bakhtin writes of 'the speaker's subjective emotional evaluation of the referentially semantic content of the utterance' (Bakhtin, 1986:84). It is Kristeva who is credited with paving the way towards 'a semiotics of the text', although Bakhtin's ideas lie behind her theories. As Kristeva wrote, 'I re-interpreted a writer just re-published in the USSR whom we often read in Eastern Europe, seeing in his work a synthesis of formalism and history: Mikhail Bakhtin' (Oliver, 1997:9). In her prolegomenon to *Revolution in Poetic Language* (1974), Kristeva speaks of *signifiance* as, 'this unlimited and unbounded generating process'. *Signifiance* is not merely a matter of calling on existing sign-systems, but a process of generating new ways of understanding the world with potentially unlimited consequences.

This and the term 'dialogue' as used by Barthes, reveal the fact that Bakhtin's influence was seeping into Barthes views albeit without direct acknowledgement. The assumption that signs represent the world we know lies behind what might now be called 'classical semiotics' and Barthes finds that some signs do not represent the world at all, but re-focus our perception of it. If every utterance contains an 'evaluation of the referentially semantic content', there is no neutral utterance. It must be noted here that the implications for television naturalism are immense. Any act of producing the sign in public such as a television drama cannot simply offer an uncritical, detached 'slice of life' with no implicit evaluation of what is seen. All naturalism has its own accents, or evaluative slants. The impression that naturalism is ideologically passive must be an illusion.

To argue that linguistics cannot provide theoretical frameworks for the analysis of all signs is not to denounce the analogy between language and signs altogether, but to make a claim about the state of the discipline of linguistics. Bakhtin's references to semiotics are often made in the context of discussion of language, hence, he was attempting to develop a broader concept of signifying practices in general which would encompass language. This discipline is called *translinguistics* since it goes beyond traditional linguistics. This fulfils Saussure's original call for a science of signs which would be able to incorporate all signifying practices, even those which clearly operated outside words. Saussure argues that when it is developed as a science, semiology will 'properly include all the modes of expression based on completely natural signs such as pantomime' (Saussure, 1974:68). Bakhtin's translinguistics enables us to see all manner of human behaviour such as this as rejoinders to prior discourses.

A well-known statement from Bakhtin is that 'Context determines text'. Thus, as Gary Saul Morson writes, 'For Bakhtin, everything is pragmatics, and semantic and syntactic codes are really "context in *rigor mortis*"' (Morson, 1982:7). This amounts to saying that no rules of semantics or syntax can, in fact regulate the meaning of signs so that their actual use can be predicted. When signs are used, they must be studied, not in a purely formalist way, by examining the signs and the text alone, but also by examining the relationship between the signs in the text and their context. As Kristeva puts it, this is examining the relation between formalism and history.

The rhetorical emphasis of these statements about Bakhtin's method must be carefully weighed, however. To consider an analogy with political economy is instructive. The methodology known as political economy might be said to claim that 'everything is economics', but this means that all causal relationships can be subsumed by and overshadowed by economics, not that no other relationships exist at all. Economics is the one discipline which can unite these causal explanations into a coherent narrative. Thus recent research has shown that there are very strong parallels between Volosinov's theory of the sign as ideologically neutral (until used) and Saussure's concept of arbitrariness. Paul J. Thibault draws some convincing parallels between the two thinkers (see Thibault, 1997) and maintains that Volosinov cannot ignore the 'lexicogrammatical resource systems ' which make pragmatic relations possible. Semantics and syntax, in other words, are not irrelevant because pragmatics is dominant. This relationship, however, is not clear from Bakhtin's writings and needs further research.

The above argument is important because it distinguishes Bakhtinian semiotics from the pragmatics of Peirce. Peirce is often cited in defence of philosophical pragmatism, since he defines the meaning of a sign, the interpretant, as 'something created in the mind of the interpreter' (quoted in Nöth, 1995:43). It is difficult to imagine this easily reconciled with the view that logic underlies all human discourse. Peirce, however, has been used by contemporary theorists such as Jensen (1995) as the concept of textual meaning has gradually shifted from the author to the text and thence to the audience. Bakhtinian semiotics avoids the conclusion that the meaning of a sign is whatever people generally take it to mean. This places an unrealistic amount of power in the hands of ordinary people and by-passes the social institutions which as Foucault would claim, govern meaning. Even if signs can be created in artistic practices, they can only be developed in the conceptual spaces left free by existing institutions.

Peirce is famous for inventing the semiotic trichotomy of icon, index and symbol. This sequence varies according to the degree of motivation: the icon is the most motivated by virtue of its resemblance to the thing it designates and the symbol is only liked with its referent by agreement or habit. In her early work, Julia Kristeva adopts many of Peirce's concepts. Kristeva charts the development of Western culture as a movement from the symbol which appears to have some resemblance to its signified, to the entirely arbitrary sign (Moi, 1986:62-73). Peirce's other well-known trichotomy of sign, object and interpretant, is a valuable part of Kristeva's argument. Whereas the symbol's supposed resemblance might isolate the sign and make it self-sufficient, the Peircean sign is part of a vast, interdependent system. Each interpretant can in turn act as a sign for another purpose. Thus, Fitz's dousing with wine, can be interpreted as a sign which represents his inability to communicate. This interpretant (Fitz's inability to get his point across) could in turn stand as a sign of his sexist attitude towards women, which could then act as a sign of his general failure to form good relationships, and so on. Peirce's system where each triad of sign, object and interpretant links to another, has been likened to Derrida's view of deconstruction (Merrell, 1997:19) with its infinite deferral of meaning. Peirce's theory is a significant advance for the concept of the sign, since it emphasises that the sign is meaningful because of its function rather than some permanent signified attached to it. In this sense it is analogous to a theory of syntax.

If we take the two great forefathers of semiotics, however, they jointly represent a dilemma for the subject. On the one hand, Saussure is generally thought of as establishing a relationship between the signifier and reality/history via a convention, and on the other Peirce emphasises, like Derrida, that the sign can be made to mean all manner of things in an infinite regress. The meaning of a sign is either fixed or permanently unstable. Bakhtin achieves a compromise between these two extremes via pragmatics.

Bakhtin therefore asserts that we must first understand a work of fiction as the author intended it. This is not because the author has any absolute claim to meaning, but because the author's plan reveals the primary context of reception in which the text is encountered. This process may have some objectivity or even scientific status, but it is not the end of the matter. As Bakhtin also says, 'The interpretation of symbolic structures is forced into an infinity of symbolic contextual meanings and therefore cannot be scientific in the way the precise sciences are scientific' (Bakhtin, 1986:160). This has established the theoretical orientation of Bakhtinian semiotics in relation to 'classical' semiotics. Now it is necessary to derive a methodology from this position and defend it.

The following set of principles sets out the essential aspects of an interpretive semiotics based on Bakhtinian approaches:

- Semiosis is the diachronic process of producing signs to fulfill human purposes.

- Semiotics is the synchronic study of what signs mean.

- The sign, therefore, is used both to represent and to do something.

- What the sign *represents* can be derived from the existing social system of codes in a specific society. No sign is therefore composed entirely new, since all are composed of others' signs which have existed formerly. The sign, however, acquires new meaning when it is used in new contexts and this cannot be inferred from codes alone.

- What the sign *does* depends on the social practice within which it is used, such as story-telling on television. The act of uttering or broadcasting a particular sign at a certain time is a new social action.

- The utterance therefore needs to be examined in its social and historical context in the first instance, in order to see what it signifies to a particular audience.

- Signs can be used to discriminate elements of the material world which have not hitherto been isolated. Signification is the use of a sign to point to an aspect of the social world and identify it for us.

- The sign is not just a signifier with a concept associated with it, but a signifier used within a context where it makes a contribution to an existing social dialogue concerning a particular issue.

- The sign is, therefore, a 'rejoinder', a response to a current dialogue in social life which expresses an evaluation of the issues discussed. It has no meaning in itself from formal features alone, only when it is used in the context of human interaction.

- The evaluation has ideological implications and this is inescapable.

- The signified is, therefore, a relational concept: it is the relation between the use of a sign and the dialogue it responds to that gives it its signification.

- Whereas the *orientation* of a rejoinder towards a particular historical dialogue may be clear in its context of utterance, the precise nature of the rejoinder (rebutting, retaliating, undermining, for example) is open to interpretation by audiences. Each new utterance calls for a new interpretation.

- The same text can, however, signify differently when uttered in another dialogue and another context. The sign can be re-accentuated, or given an entirely different social meaning without changing its material form.

- The fact that all utterances are necessarily accented with an evaluative slant, means that the sign must have an ideological impact.

- The understanding of sign use by audiences should be *responsive*, ie to comprehend the meaning which emerges from dialogue and response , the third party who overhears or witnesses this, has to interpret the evaluative accent of the sign and this means that to understand is to enter into the social dialogue and judge for oneself.

Julia Kristeva argues for the conception of meaning, 'not as a sign-system but as a *signifying process*' (Moi, 1986:28). Teresa de Lauretis also questions the concept of semiotics which derives from Eco's work by harnessing Kristeva's ideas in a chapter entitled, 'Semiotics, Theory and Social Practice', (Burnett, 1991 : 201-221). This is to say that semiotics is rather like Marx's conception of history, 'the story of men in pursuit of their aims' and signs are developed for the purpose of realising aims, not derived from a prior system which determines them. Language for Marx is 'practical consciousness that also exists for other men, and for that reason alone it really exists for me personally as well; language, like consciousness, only arises from the need, the necessity, of intercourse with other men' (Marx, 1977 : 51). Other signs besides language also exist only for the purposes of communication. Roy Harris distinguishes between segregationist theories which presuppose a common set of signs between addresser and addressee, and integrationist theories which maintain that signs are 'created in and by the act of communication' (Harris, 1996:7). The segregationist distinguishes between the sign-system and its users whereas the integrationist believes that signs are only ever meaningful in a context where they are used for human purposes. As Harris notes, virtually all theories of linguistics from Saussure onwards are segregationist. This distinguishes, say, Peircean semiotics from Bakhtinian approaches. In Peirce, there is the sense that meaning as Kristeva puts it, is an act of the *'transcendental ego* cut off from its body, its unconscious and also its history'. Kristeva welcomed Bakhtin's approaches and developed a theory which would relate signs to the fundamental drives which inspired human action and ultimately, history itself. Her concept of 'semanalysis' united psychoanalysis and Marxist theory with semiosis.

Like all human practices, semiotics can be systematised and catalogued, but it can also defy the boundaries of its own definition and expand in unpredictable ways. The proper study of signs is *semiosis*, or sign-making, not the contemporary system of meaning. The systematic collection of regularities in sign use does not amount to the abstraction of immutable 'rules' as structuralism supposed. Texts such as television dramas therefore always have a dual aspect: they both reflect a certain reality and participate in another. Whilst representing the world of the poor, for example, they may participate in the practice of political lobbying on their behalf. A formalist textual analysis may not reveal the actual social function of a set of signs. The Bakhtinian methodology finds the signified in the *relation* between the sign-vehicle and the dialogues it answers. The practice of sign-making constantly extends and reinvents those relations.

The sign is therefore a material aspect of human action and is ultimately understandable only in the context of people's aims and actions. The full implications of regarding semiotics as a social practice and not a system of classifying meanings, are beginning to be made clear. Alec McHoul, in *Semiotic Investigations: Towards an Effective Semiotics* (1996) marries Wittgenstein's theory of meaning as actual use and Nietzsche's theory of the undecidability of history to create a form of semiotic enquiry which will constantly reexamine itself. 'Any sign will have meaning only insofar as it *is* a practice' (McHoul, 1996:9). Social practices change with history, and people's needs change too. Signs may have historical bases, but history itself is prone to deconstruction and can be infinitely complex. The meaning of a photograph from one era may be entirely different in another. McHoul is opposed to a general theory of semiotics which would legislate for all occurrences of a particular sign. Instead all signs must be investigated independently for their own peculiar features with their social world.

Bakhtin/Volosinov distinguishes between two antithetical approaches to language which he describes as 'abstract objectivism' and 'individualistic subjectivism'. The latter is characterised metaphorically as a stream: language is created by the individual's *fiat* and is generated as a continuous, unhindered flow of creativity. This approach to textuality is one which was fiercely resisted in media theory. It was most prominent in literary studies when texts were treated as the direct manifestations of literary genius and the study of the text was regarded as a simultaneous study of the author's mind. The *auteur* theory in film criticism was its nearest equivalent and has become similarly unfashionable. Volosinov's account of language stresses the view that language cannot reflect only one person's mentality, and signs only arise in social contexts. Abstract objectivism, on the other hand is described metaphorically as the rainbow: it is the conception of a vast over-arching system which generates signs and is completely independent of the individual. The abstract concept of language is rather like basic mathematics and individuality and creativity disappear completely as individuals merely refract the immutable laws of the equally immutable system. The Bakhtinian notion of objectivity lies not in a system which permits only certain combinations of signs with a determined value, but in a set of practices which depend on social recognition to enable individual expressiveness. We might label the approach, 'individual objectivism' . There is no limitation to the signs which an individual can create, but only within practices which are situated in a social context.

The Bakhtinian theory of language is of a semiotic system which is both creative, yet external to the individual and public. As Bakhtin says, 'Semiotics deals primarily with the transmission of ready-made communication using a ready-made code. But in live speech, strictly speaking, communication is first created in the process of transmission and there is, in essence, no code'. The codes have to be invented for certain purposes such as art. Robert Stam points out in his survey of Bakhtinian semiotics that 'the system of the text, then is the instance that displaces the codes so that they become inflections and substitutions for one another' (Stam, 1989:49). As Amy Mandelker (1995) adds in her study of Bakhtinian semiotics, Bakhtin adopts an organic metaphor taken from the natural sciences to describe the life of signs, since they can proliferate according to laws of growth, rather than meaning.

Graham Pechey writes, 'The utterance functions in translinguistics as the sign does in linguistics: as the minimal signifying unit of discourse' (Pechey 1989:48). An utterance is the fundamental act which signifies for Bakhtin's 'translinguistics'. The actual broadcast of a drama is in itself the protest despite the fact that there may be specific details within the drama which express it. In ordinary language as Bakhtin points out, language and speech may coincide. The utterance of the sentence 'I promise to pay you £5' means what it *does*. Its illocutionary force, to use the philosopher J.L. Austin's expression, the action which is carried out by uttering the sentence, is that of a promise which coincides exactly with the linguistic, textual meaning. The intonation which we may use in speech to give a sentence an actual meaning (eg we raise our voices when making a statement such as this to indicate disbelief) however, is a part of the utterance, the act of speaking and not the sentence. An utterance may constitute a rejoinder and be structurally simple yet semantically complex. The single word 'Go', for example, as an utterance can be pronounced with various meanings which do not inhere in the semantic meaning of the word.

Television drama can constitute a special kind of utterance in that it addresses social issues which have recently occurred and voices a general reaction to events which it has alluded to. As in the case of the utterance of a single word, the content of the drama may have a relevance which is independent of the explicit text. As Robin Nelson writes about the television drama, *Our Friends in The North*, it 'achieved something of the status of "an event" distantly echoing the days when *The Wednesday Play* provoked discussion in pubs up and down Britain' (Nelson, 1997:246). The act of broadcasting became an utterance. One reason for this is that the allegorical structure of the drama which shadowed the development of Socialism in this country through the lives of various characters, made its unstated referent absolutely clear. The advent of digital television, of course must suggest some change is also likely in this respect.

'The whole utterance', according to Bakhtin, 'is no longer a unit of language (and not a unit of 'speech flow' or the speech chain'), but a unit of speech communication that has not mere formal definition but *contextual meaning* (that is integrated meaning that relates to value – to truth, beauty and so forth – and require a *responsive understanding*, one that includes evaluation)' (Bakhtin, 1986:125). Todorov also highlights the fact that each utterance is unique, since each context is unique and therefore pragmatics is the only discipline which can approach the relationship. *A priori* systems cannot account for this. This is not to say that the initial context of reception is the only one in which the text becomes meaningful. As Bakhtin says, 'Everything that belongs only to the present dies along with the present' (Bakhtin, 1986:4). The rise of cross-cultural media especially places emphasis on the need to consider how the context will affect reception. For Pavis it is now so clear that the performance takes on meaning in relation to the social context of that production that the theoretical notion of reception is now a necessary and prominent aspect of production itself. Pavis argues that the *reterritorialization* of minority theory, its attempts at rediscovering the relations between signs and cultural contexts, is a reaction to the 'crisis' in semiotics. This crisis is the situation where there appear to be no alternatives but to treat the sign as either exclusively textual, or exclusively in the mind of the audience (Pavis, 1992 : 83).

Pavis prefers what he calls, 'sociosemiotics', which explains the process of semiosis in individual cultures, or how meaning is derived from texts. This is the same ambition as Kristeva's: to link formalism and history and to release both text and audience from a theoretical vacuum.

Like Saussure, Bakhtin believed that there were genres which governed such free acts as ordinary conversation or gestures but these were only realised in actual contexts. What Bakhtin calls 'expressive intonation', for example, 'belongs to the utterance, and not to the word' (Bakhtin, 1986, p. 86). If such a vitally-important aspect of meaning could only come into existence when a word was spoken, then it would be impossible to codify all such aspects without knowing in advance all the contexts which could occur. This would be impossible. For Bakhtin, the system of language could not be divorced from speech, its realisation in a material form. Codes could not anticipate the variety of material forms and contexts. Thus Bakhtin can assert that we use words which are 'peopled with the intentions of others', yet not thereby find ourselves repeating their meanings exactly. The words we use are also determined by expressive intonation, the way that they are spoken or used, and this is a feature of a specific human context.

Bakhtin also insists on the necessity for signs which are external to the individual in communication. The comments on formal codes do not mean that he espouses individual subjectivism. As previously stated, the materialist approach to language as taken by Volosinov, demands that signs are used to enable communication and that these are external to the individual. Not all external signs are sufficiently widely-used at the moment of their creation to be conventions. Some conventions are established amongst relatively small social groups such as academics or sub-cultures and take some time to infiltrate the mainstream culture. We should not suppose that all signs have the same provenance: some may be meaningful only to few people at one time. There are parallels between discourse theory and semiotics here. The study of signs, therefore, must regard semiotics as a social practice and focus on *how* signs are made meaningful, not on what they mean. Like some other social practices, such as anti-language, semiotic practices may have to be observed at first hand. There may be no grand scheme from which all such uses can be deduced.

Like Wittgenstein's language games, semiotics may produce a number of theories of how signs come to mean rather than one monolithic theory. A 'code', according to Bakhtin, 'is a deliberately established, killed context' (Bakhtin, 1986:147). In other words, the existence of a code determines the meaning of the sign and neutralises any effect which a new context may have on the sign. If all codes could be pre-determined, then there would be no need for a pragmatics of the sign. This view is in opposition to the prevailing semiotic approaches.

Bakhtin's reason for denying the importance of previously-established codes is that each act of communication is oriented towards a particular context which has not formerly existed: 'In the majority of cases, we presuppose a certain typical and stabilized *social purview* toward which the ideological creativity of our own social group and time is oriented' (Volosinov, 1973:87). Bakhtin and Medvedev write that the work has 'intrinsic thematic determinateness' but that it only realises such a role when it is oriented in the direction of real space and real time: the work is loud or soft, it is associated with the church, or the stage or screen. It is part of a celebration or simply leisure' (Bakhtin and Medvedev, 1978:131).

The concept of dialogism in Bakhtin is vigorously contested, hence it may be best to specify exactly what it means for the purpose of reading television drama. Bakhtin remarks that 'Anything that does not respond to something seems meaningless to us; it is removed from dialogue' (Bakhtin, 1986:145). There can be no contextual meaning for Bakhtin, except 'for another contextual meaning'. This means that there are no isolated uses of signs divorced from all others. Each freely created sign has some formal meaning defined by code-systems and a contextual meaning, but that contextual meaning is governed by the contextual relations it has with other situations. The principle of dialogism is stated most clearly when Bakhtin writes that even a monologic discourse such as a scientific treatise, 'cannot but be in some measure a response to what has already been said about the given topic, on the given issue, even though this responsiveness may not have assumed a clear-cut expression' (Bakhtin, 1986:92). Dialogism also refers to a meaning which only becomes apparent when the relations between a statement and its answer or rejoinder are considered jointly. The relation between statement and rejoinder is only dialogical if a third person (the superaddressee in Bakhtinian terminology) can be supposed who would grasp its meaning.

As with many statements of fundamental principle, the underlying point may be beyond dispute, but the implications can ramify unexpectedly. The use of the term 'dialogue' is metaphorical. We do not literally speak to the past, and the communication can only realistically go one way: the past does not literally speak back to us. Dialogism is a statement about the often unconscious yet demonstrable relations between utterances. It does not follow that all dialogically related utterances are indicative of actual exchanges between social agents. Bakhtin is well-known for the elusive use of terminology, and at times dialogism sounds as if it means actual verbal relations. The concept of dialogical relations used here is akin to that which Fredric Jameson uses in his account of the 'political unconscious' in narrative fiction: 'real social contradictions, insurmountable in themselves, find a purely formal resolution in the aesthetic realm' (Jameson, 1981:79). The resolution to a woman's incompatible feelings in the television drama, *The Life and Loves of a She-Devil* is an aesthetic transformation which implicitly responds to the situation of women.

It is debatable whether all such contradictions do find a resolution or whether they are exposed by some artistic practices, but the fundamental point remains that a narrative produced for television will have some novel relation to existing social situations. The first task in understanding is to construe the whole broadcast as an utterance which is a rejoinder to some social issue. This may be conscious or unconscious.

The fundamental point which Bakhtinian theory is making is that the social meaning of any sign is the relationship between the utterance of that sign and all the signs which precede it which it impinges on. A sign may therefore feature in many discourses, or Wittgensteinian language-games, but there is no one, absolutely definitive use. There can be a theory of sign production in general, but not of all signs.

This must be distinguished from Lyotard's conception of language games, however. For Lyotard, the 'pragmatics of popular narrative' is very simple: it consists merely in recognising the roles of the participants such as addresser and addressee. There is no need for the social group to remember its past: all that we need to do to understand the language game of popular narrative is to acknowledge the respective roles of all concerned (Lyotard, 1979:22). For Lyotard all language games are discrete practices which have their own rules. This helps substantiate Lyotard's postmodern theory where discourses are performances rather than acts of engaging with real issues and events. To perform appropriately is to confer on the discourse the status of knowledge according to Lyotard. The concept of dialogic relations, however, implies that discourses can be created freely, but they are not independent of each other. Signs can be manufactured in a creative activity such as television drama, but not with absolutely any meaning. It would be individual subjectivism and a total denial of semiotics if signs could be constructed without any constraints. The rejoinder to a prior dialogue will be original, but the form and meaning of the rejoinder is partly determined by the foregoing dialogue which it must relate to. Lyotard is attempting to argue for a running-together of legitimation and verification which are not the same things at all. The Bakhtinian sign is freely created but only within the spaces left by existing sign-systems where responses can be made. Each social practice is independent but not isolated from all others.

The Bakhtinian theory of semiotics, therefore is not as it could possibly appear, a theory of creative autonomy, since the individual sign-maker is partly governed by dialogic relation in their selection of a rejoinder. The other main factor which governs the rejoinder is the social practice within which it is created. This may seem as if a supposedly 'free' activity is being hedged about with numerous constraints, but it does not mean that the making of signs is any the less creative. A mathematical formula such as prime numbers restricts creativity, but the range of numbers which can fulfil this formula is still infinite.

The Bakhtinian sign is created within existing social practices as individuals participate and not codified in advance. Roy Harris asks: ' If human beings communicate by means of signs, how does it- or did it-begin?' (Harris, 1996 : 22). This question is aimed at the code-theorists. If we needed a code which had been agreed in advance to understand all signs, signs could never have been invented. Communication must have begun before codes had been devised. The integrationist thesis is that some codes are created within social practices and not in advance of them. Wittgenstein gave a famous example of two builders inventing a language game in which the master-builder uttered the word 'slab' and his assistant brought the slab to him (Wittgenstein, 1951:7). Wittgenstein's argument is that what makes the word 'slab' mean 'bring a slab to me' is whether the assistant catches on and does this. As Wittgenstein puts it, it is agreement in 'forms of life' or social behaviour which confers meaning on this command. The sign has to be *public* in that it has to be external to the individual to avoid pure subjectivity, Wittgenstein's 'private language', but this does not mean that it has to be society-wide to have meaning. Many social practices devise signs without going society-wide to do so. Television is one of them where signs can be created in the course of the practice itself and not before. Volosinov's insistence that signals are not signs seems to derive from his view that individuals cannot make local arrangements which grow into full-scale signs, but this is to make language one vast system, a *langue*, rather than a set of inter-related discourses, such as Wittgenstein describes.

In the television drama, *Rich Deceiver*, a Liverpudlian woman wins the pools but does not tell her husband. Instead she deceives him in the attempt to prove to him that he can succeed in a job by his own talent and not solely by virtue of the money. At the beginning of the drama, the husband is seen tucking into a traditional British breakfast which is full of fat. He says, 'if you ever give me Flora, I'm leaving home'. An essential element of the breakfast is brown sauce in a familiar bottle. The wife's deception creates difficulties and they separate. When the couple are reunited at the end of the drama, we see the man again eating a meal with the wife watching. The camera momentarily focuses on the familiar bottle of sauce in order to present it as a signifier. The return to familiar eating habits signifies a return to domesticity and familiarity at the informational level, but this is an example of symbolic closure, where the image functions like a poetic symbol. Barthes uses the term 'poetical' to describe the grasp of the signifier which has no conventional signified. The 'theoretical individuality' of the signifier means that it can only be re-examined and re-described, just as we seek to find the meaning of a poem by re-examining the words which compose it. The symbol needs to be understood not merely as a cultural icon, which the well-known brown sauce bottle constitutes, but also as a multi-accented sign which can signify many possible meanings. Does this signify a happy resolution or a capitulation, for example? What would a feminist reading reveal? The poetic function of signs is not necessarily related to the narrative sequence, and casts its aura over the entire text, illuminating various aspects in different ways. Like many metaphors, the poetic symbol in television drama is based on a fragment of familiar reality, but uses a known relationship to extend a comparison and create new ways of responding in a 'poetical grasp' of the third meaning.

The precise meaning of the sauce-bottle in this drama is not codified in advance, but is the product of a dialogue between its two appearances within the same dramatic text. No code could predict what the sign means here, despite the fact that the meaning in this context depends on inherited cultural connotations. Television drama is a social practice in which one of the conventions is that signs will be re-accented for the purposes of each dramatic text. The drama is a creative forum for the making of meaning.

Bakhtin's approach to signs, therefore, is rather close to discourse theory. The sign does not acquire a unique value, rather it participates in relatively autonomous signifying practices which have their own rules. What does cause a theoretical problem in Bakhtin, however, is the absolute insistence on context as the sole determinant of meaning. This is true only in a very special sense. Upbringing is the sole determinant of a person's development in the sense that if we are, for example, beaten to death at an early age, we will not fulfil our potential. On the other hand, this is not to say that we were not born with a certain genetic predisposition to acquire certain traits and talents. Upbringing determines the *realisation* of our talents. Similarly, in Marxist theory such as political economy, economics is the final determinant, and a decisive one, but not the only factor to govern human behaviour or artistic form. The fact that financial pressure may dictate whether we see a television drama at all, makes it a decisive determinant, but not a comprehensive one. A decisive determinant is one which is essential for the event to take place as intended. The actual form of the drama in question may be governed by a number of non-economic reasons. The political economy school would undoubtedly point out that even the non-economic factors can be traced to an economic origin, but we could not deduce these characteristics from the basic economic data alone.

The other variety of determinant, I shall call formal determinants, in that they act to shape artistic practice and the nature of art objects such as television drama. Formal determinants are substitutable: they use signs which are not essential to the function of the message in context. Language and existing sign systems do not compel the media artist to use certain signs, but they do delimit the cultural space where invention can take place. Thus in the *Cracker* example, the editing makes a creative point about Fitz's ideology, but does so using a black woman as a sign with cultural and historical associations which the drama-maker has not created. A Filipino woman might not play the same role here, for example. The decisive determinant, however, cannot be exchanged without changing the significance of the message. Such a semiotic point can be proven by using the commutation test as John O. Thompson demonstrates in his article, 'Screen Acting and the Commutation Test' (John O. Thompson, 1978). The text has to acknowledge the existence of prior conventions and decide whether to use them or to create outside of their parameters, but they cannot be ignored for fear of confusing the addressee with a message that has an existing, unintended meaning. As Barthes says, the tableau has 'a meaning not a subject' (Barthes, 1977:75). It does not need to refer to be meaningful in other words. Semio-pragmatics, which considers the context as the final arbiter of meaning therefore, can treat the context as a decisive determinant, but this is not a reason to ignore the textual characteristics and their historical antecedents which act as formal determinants. Disharmonies in music produced at random nonetheless need the traditional harmonies in order to provide them with space to exist.

There have been many attempts to model the semiotic theory of Saussure and Peirce, but Bakhtinian semiotics cannot be so easily captured. The Bakhtinian theory of signs is really a theory of semiosis or sign-making, rather than individual signs. It therefore has to be represented as a *process* rather than a state. The sign's meaning is triangulated between codes, or formal systems, context, or history, and the individual intentions of the user. The sign-user mediates between existing codes and contexts to express an individual meaning. These three factors will take precedence according to the nature of the sign, there is no consistent hierarchy. The following model is an abstraction of the process.

---

(1) Bare Text
A text or sign is employed which has only a codified meaning outside any context. In the case of language, this would be the dictionary definition. This may bring with it a connotation or signified.

(2) Context
The text is uttered within a specific context which gives it meaning. The following factors govern the effect of the context.
social practice
moment of utterance
'social purview'
dialogues

(3) Re-accentuation
In a new context, the text acquires a new evaluative meaning which is peculiar to that context. This process if governed by the following factors.
choice of genre
theme
internal dialogues
       speech-plan of author
       evaluation
       ideology
desired response

(4) Rejoinder
The new use of the sign constitutes an ideological riposte to previous dialogues which also seeks to encourage a suitable action in response.

To take an example from television, in some comedy shows, a text which was formerly spoken by a famous figure might be uttered again but this time by an actor. The same text is now being used in the social practice of satire. As Bakhtin says, 'The author's choice of genre or genres is the first indicator of the intention behind a drama. The speaker's individual speech is manifested only in its choice of a particular genre and perhaps in its expressive intonation' (Bakhtin, 1986:79). Satire in particular is often aimed at a current event and also focused on the politically astute audience, the 'social purview' of the genre. Within the practice of satire, the evaluation of the subject is always derogatory, and often represents the ideology of the majority of the people who are deriding the powerful. A theme such as government ministers and corruption might, therefore, be developed. The desired response is recognition and laughter, but the genre of rejoinders may take many forms.

Internal dialogues can increase the range of signification considerably. Barthes refers to the tenuous dialogism within a shot from a film. The publicity image of Robbie Coltrane as Fitz shows a black and white picture of Fitz's face gazing directly at the camera with a penetrating glare. Cigarette smoke circles about his head to intensify the rather satanic fixity of his gaze. The cigarette which Fitz is holding, however, has about an inch and a half of ash clinging to the end and this is prominently displayed at an upward angle. The ash is about to fall, and this is a feature which, when noticed, detracts from the ferocity of Fitz's gaze. To allow ash to drop is not the action of someone who is in complete control of the situation and is a terrifying interrogator; it will tarnish the image of implacable harshness. The lack of attention paid to the cigarette is, of course, in character, but there is no signified which we can attribute to this signifier independently of the photograph. The cigarette and its dangling ash are in subtle dialogue with the fierce gaze, and give it an accent: the cigarette qualifies the meaning of the rest of the picture by requiring us to balance its meaning against that of the facial image. The ash-laden cigarette only has the meaning discussed above in this particular context, in this particular dialogue. It cannot be interpreted by reference to a 'dictionary' of semiotics.

There is a need for a theoretical approach to semiotics which will encompass the *poetic* function of signs as Barthes commented. Volosinov defines the work of poetry as 'a powerful condenser of unarticulated value judgements' (Volosinov, 1973:192). The conclusion of a drama may not be a *dénouement*, but an emotional moment which acts as a fitting ending. The narrative is closed by a return to a particular state of feeling rather than a final revelation of facts. Barthes appears to mean that a new sign is invested with *signifiance*, defying the attempt to classify and systematise all possible uses of signs. Saussurean semiotics cannot accommodate such a feature within any theory of codes.

Reaccentuation of the sign ensures that it never becomes permanently stable. Although the Bakhtinian sign has relative stability within its context of utterance, it can always be repositioned and used for other purposes as yet unanticipated. Walter Benjamin, for example, referred to this aspect of textuality as 'refunctioning'. Kristeva has identified dialogism with her concept of intertextuality, but this is misleading. Intertextuality as commonly practised does not take into account the vast range of texts – many of them not fictional or academic – which the sign may be in dialogue with. News reports and casual conversations may also feature. Intertextuality tends to examine only texts of the same kind as the original. It also tends to suggest that discovering a reference to another text is simultaneously discovering the meaning of a sign. If meaning is relational, however, then discovering an intertextual reference is only the beginning of an analysis. Dialogism looks to the new relations established between recognisable signs when they are juxtaposed.

The principle of multiaccentuality also enables an analysis which links formal relations with history. This is because the same sign can perform many functions simultaneously. Dialogism can broadly be distinguished as follows:

*Intra*textuality: where there is a dialogue within the text. This may be between two characters or between two elements of a text as envisaged by Barthes. This may be for other characters to overhear as the superaddressee.

*Extra*textuality: where the dialogues within the text are intended to be appreciated by the audience (the superaddressee) and therefore serve a function outside the text itself. In this case the drama-makers are communicating via the text with the audience.

*Inter*textuality: where the text's dialogue is a rejoinder to other texts (which may be other dramas or newspaper reports, or any forms of text). Parody is a good example of this. Intertextuality is not the same as the text's meaning since each reference to a prior text is a re-evaluation of it.

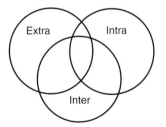

In the following examples of applying this methodology, we will see how the same signs can occur simultaneously in several dialogues.

According to Volosinov, the ruling class attempt to suppress the multiaccentuality of the sign and to give it an 'eternal character' (Volosinov, 1973:23). This denies the history which is implicit in the sign. The 'contradiction embedded in every ideological sign' only emerges in times of crisis', when the various dialogues in which the sign features become apparent. It is natural to focus on the one use of the sign with which we are concerned in our daily lives. This is why naturalism in television drama is so hard to penetrate at times. To return to the *Cracker* example, the ideological impact of this incident is not clear because it is cleverly designed to incorporate different ideological perspectives. Responsive understanding must involve the kind of consideration which is mentioned above. The required response is to evaluate the internal dialogue. The act of throwing the wine is a rejoinder, but does it signify a 'failure to communicate' (which might exonerate Fitz) or a rejection of masculine browbeating and special pleading? The question is one which it is not easy to answer but very productive to attempt. As Keyan Tomaselli argues in his passionate plea for a more political approach to semiotics, 'The media are a prime site of *struggle* (my emphasis) for the sign' (Tomaselli, 1996:45). It is essential to see this as a contested sign whose implications are not determinate. Volosinov argues against the notion of denotation and connotation on the grounds that they seem to be treated as if they came with the sign rather than the occasion of its use.

Semiotic Approaches to Television Drama

There are three main approaches to television drama in published studies of the subject at the time of writing, each of which assumes or states a semiotic theory on which it is based. These are the approaches adopted by Brandt, which is a more literary treatment, postmodernist thinkers such as Nelson and Baudrillard, and Tulloch, who stresses the struggle between various interested parties such as the author and the audience. In this section, the implications of each of these positions is outlined and the implications of the semiotic theory are discussed. The earliest and perhaps the simplest, is that of Brandt who chose to discuss 'authored' drama which had an obvious 'literary' content in his first collection of essays published in 1981. This approach relies heavily on the theoretical assumption that the author can dictate the meaning of the received text and that she or he is able to insert into the text content which is a set of valuable ideas. Charlotte Brunsden has pointed out that Brandt changed his approach considerably when the second version of this volume appeared (Brunsden, 1998). This appears to have been motivated at least in part by Brunsdon's criticisms of Brandt's choices of 'quality' drama. The now well-known argument focuses on what Brunsdon regards as 'uncontroversial signifiers of quality': literary source, the best of British acting, money spent and the Heritage aspect. The two exemplars chosen were *Brideshead Revisited* and *The Jewel in the Crown*.

Brandt defends his choice of drama vigorously, perhaps as a result of missing the point of Brunsdon's article. The significance of these elements is that they are generally regarded as indicators of quality, and this approach is also detectable in Brandt's work as well. This is not to say that they are always necessarily wrongly applied; some drama may correspond to these and still be regarded as of high quality. This is simply the standard view of the concerned parties. The interesting aspect of Brunsdon's criteria is that they are, with the possible exception of the acting, all extraneous to the actual content of the drama. The most important signs are those which signify something beyond the drama which smacks of a lavish ancestry. The unspoken belief behind this set of criteria is that good television drama mediates between Culture and the audience, yielding access to a storehouse of treasures denied to the general public.

The role of signs in such drama is to convey the ideas of the author and of the past in a conspicuously extravagant outlay on actors and production. Television drama of this kind is transparent, in that the signifiers themselves are forgotten as they allow the viewer to penetrate another realm which does not belong to them. The programme may be the crucial unit selected by Brandt, rather than the writer, but it remains true that the criteria favour dramas which mediate a world other than that which the viewers inhabit or know. While this is the case, the actual quality of the *production*, and the signs generated within it to complement, augment and undermine the main themes, will be overlooked as if television drama's only purpose is to be the poor relation of literature.

The single play is a writer's medium in that it is free from the commercial pressure to retain an audience which the serial or series suffers from. In the case of *The Tribe* by Stephen Poliakoff, the theme and the narrative are one and the same. In order to understand the structure of the drama, the audience have to grasp the fundamental authorial intention. Understanding here is not dialogue but acceptance of Poliakoff. This drama makes what Barthes calls 'the major sin in literary matters' of confusing 'ideological with semiological reality' (Barthes, 1978:136). Barthes goes on to say that 'One must deal with the writer's realism either as an ideological substance (Marxist themes in Brecht's work, for instance) or as a semiological value (the props, the actors, the music, the colours in Brechtian dramaturgy)'. The ideal would be to combine these two types of criticism, according to Barthes, but they cannot be identified automatically because an essential distinction exists in literature. Myth supervenes to sign-systems: it is a higher-level system which depends on existing semiotic values, and the signs are therefore arbitrary. The actual signifiers are irrelevant in establishing the kinds of conceptual relationships which Barthes identifies as mythology.

In more practical terms, therefore, Poliakoff's heavily criticised television play attempted to mediate between the writer's own ideas and the world which the audience were familiar with. The production took signs which have become familiar in the media: the cult, the run-down areas of London, the property developer, and attempted to create an artificial mythology. The created mythology was that a cult need not signify a group of people devoted to an obscure quasi-religious idea and endowed with mysterious powers. Instead, Poliakoff's drama proposes that the formation of a cult is an existential strategy to frighten off people and to create some *lebensraum* for personal development. It is a bluff which enables the tribe to live their own lives. Barthes' point about literature is that it continually aims at a highly individual use of language so that only these words in this poem can convey this meaning, but the mythologies which poetry depends on are independent of the actual words (or signs) used. In literary television drama such as *The Tribe*, there is such a distinction. We can discuss the idea of living an existentially 'free' life without necessarily discussing the signs which Poliakoff uses here. The semiotics of the drama are incidental to its theme. Only where, as in the *Cracker* example used in the introduction, the signs are intrinsic to the message, can we be said to have a 'poetic' television drama. In poetic uses of signs, the signs can only be further described and interpreted, they cannot be decoded because their use is original. In his review in the *Sunday Times* A. A. Gill wrote that the cast resembled, 'a new-ageish group of Pradaed-up pretty people who walked like an Alexander technique outing and gave away Psion organisers' (Gill, 1998). The very idea that these young people could look imposing and frighten off football thugs from a run-down suburb was not credible. Various shots attempted to make them look imposing by surmounting the brow of a hill, for example, but these attempts failed. The signifiers here were not up to the theme. Semiological reality did not correspond to ideological reality.

Dramas such as this become the embodiment of an idea in the writer's mind, a vehicle for his cleverness and not a means of mediating the reality which audiences know. Television drama's signs have to perform a function somewhat like T.S. Eliot's 'objective correlative' and be recognised for themselves rather than as the writer's self-expression. Ideally viewers recognise the signs and see them as intrinsic to the theme. Where a television drama does use familiar signs from the viewer's experience, semiology and ideology can coincide. As W. S. Gilbert says, 'Though it might be argued that our television drama would be more televisual were it not so, it remains the case that a writer's teleplay will be directed so as to realise the text' (Gilbert, 1980, p. 39). The signs used in a writerly drama attempt to realise a message which can be discussed without referring to the drama's visual text. If there is a constraint which the medium of television imposes on the creators of drama, it is that the signs should serve their thematic function: terrifying moments should seem terrifying and daunting characters appear to have the personality to carry off this role. Poetry has been described as 'memorable expression', and this implies that the specific words used are thought of as alone embodying a significant idea. In television drama, the equivalent would be to find the image, language and sound which correspond to a particular concept and are remembered as uniquely signifying that idea. The sight of Yosser saying 'Gissa job' embodies the concept of a man begging for the chance of dignity, and sums up much of the 1980s. This utterance is inseparable from its ideological inspiration.

In Poliakoff's drama, Jamie, a property developer, is sent to persuade a cult who live in a house in the inner city to sell their share. Jamie's boss wants to re-develop the entire area and they are the last remaining tenants. Jamie is literally seduced by the ambience and the nubile young people who inhabit the place. On meeting them and talking to them he finds that their weird style of dress and manner is in fact a bluff. They are ordinary people who are simply keeping the world at bay by seeming to hide a secret which the public fears. This is a rejoinder to the media coverage of 'doomsday' cults which preach apocalyptic fervour and which believe they are uniquely chosen. This drama presents the cult as a utopian group rather than a microcosm bent on

Armageddon. The cult's appearance is simply an existential strategy to preserve their independence. They do not exist in order to indulge in licentious sex, drugs or crime, although they do indulge their passions.

It transpires that some of the group have been saved from lives as prostitutes, for example, in order to establish themselves as creative artists. Jamie is asked to attend an Open Day and becomes one of them. Having slept with a woman from the tribe, played by Anna Friel, he is won over to the cause. Anna Friel plays the sex scene in the nude in a red room which signifies some kind of regression to infantile pleasures of the flesh. The casting of such a television personality helps to explain how he is easily sexually trapped. Jamie is then late for a presentation he has to give on re-developing the inner city and has not prepared. He is advised by the group's leader to 'Bullshit them; they won't know the difference'.

Jamie decides to do this and spontaneously adapts the Japanese term for bowler hat, which he learnt at the house, to inspire a 'new theory' of urban redevelopment. This is warmly received and implicitly endorses the tribe's stance towards the world. Bluff clearly works. In order to understand why Jamie adopts the policy of bluffing, we need to see that he has absorbed the principle upon which the commune and its leader survive. 'Yamatika Bushi', the bowler-hat principle illustrates how an audacious bluff can be more convincing than the most carefully-prepared presentation. Once this principle is made explicit, however, the leader cannot continue to exercise her charismatic hold over the members.

She usually leads the group past the chanting local thugs and uses her self-confidence as a shield. Her lack of fear usually convinces the locals that they must have a secret defence. When this eventually fails and there is a savage fight with the resentful locals, one group member dies. The bluff has been called and the principle is no longer infallible. One of the ironies of a charismatic cult such as this is that the leader preaches self-fulfillment but requires obedience. There is a semiotic parallel with Jamie's boss. If the members are inspired to realise themselves and acquire confidence then it follows that they will eventually go their own way. One decides to leave after the fight and the leader tries in vain to persuade her to return.

What follows is a rejoinder to the utopian movements. It is ironic that the tribe is sustained by gifts from a high-tech Japanese sympathiser who is clearly sexually fascinated by the leader. This is a sign that the tribe cannot sustain itself without selling the gadgets that he gives them. 'Do I share this revulsion with the modern life, with the urban world expressed by some of my characters?', Poliakoff asks in the introduction to his *Collected Plays*. 'The answer is a simple no. I am at heart a modernist'. The primary intertextual source for these ideas is none other than Poliakoff himself. In an earlier theatre play, *Strawberry Fields*, he criticises utopian hippies, and in the television drama series *Shooting the Past* he writes about the futility of the curators of a collection of photographs attempting to prevent their sale to a commercial company.

Nostalgic primitivism is not something which Poliakof endorses and *The Tribe* also shows this to be the case. Where the drama is concerned with the realisation of an intellectual idea rather than the creation of an idea in its own audio-visual terms, however, it is always possible as here that the drama will fail to make its point. The signs used in writerly drama are arbitrary and this means that they cannot act as effectively. There is no clear and efficient sign to denote the fact that a collective cannot be dedicated to individualism, for example, and this detracts from the drama. In the dramas selected for study which follow, the signs are not harnessed to express the ideas in the mind of the writer. Instead, the writer and creators of the drama express ideas through the shared social signs which they deploy to create meaning.

Unlike advertisements which many people can now read very acutely, television drama has not been subjected to such close attention. In authored drama the ideas of the dramatist obtrude: it is essential to grasp them, as we watch or the narrative falls flat and we will not understand it. The content or ideas and the narrative are one: the aim is not to see what the facts reveal, but to see what the dramatist has to say. It is didactic.

Television in general is often regarded as another example of postmodernism, and television drama has been subsumed in this phenomenon. Robin Nelson writes that 'Postmodern texts might be summarily characterised by a formal openness, a strategic refusal to close down meaning' (Nelson, 1997:246). Postmodern television drama would have no actual relation to reality because as an 'open' text, it generated no meaning which could be regarded as primary or context-bound. Any attempt at contextualising the drama would simply yield to further, endless meanings. In place of a strictly-determined meaning, the postmodern text has what Nelson calls, in a Peircean phrase, 'an endless process of semiosis'. It is ironic, of course, that television drama is actually thought of as a form of textuality which does not need much semiotic decoding but is instantly understood. Semiotics as outlined above may seem to do exactly what is alien to postmodernism in insisting that the text can be located within discourses and that it can refer to real events, and situations.

The postmodern argument can perhaps be summarised as follows. Any reference to 'reality' is naïve, because there is no reality independent of our means of representation, whether these be audio-visual or literary, for example. Once we realise that all perceptions of the real are, in fact, *constructions* from the available forms of representation, we should, according to postmodernism, cease to search for simple realism. Instead of aspiring to a perfect means of representing reality, we should acknowledge the many ways it can be dissected, framed and represented. Nelson calls this, 'pure textual practices' (Nelson, 1997 : 73). This is a process which, once begun, simply continues *ad infinitum*. Once we acknowledge the relative status of the postmodern construction of things, we should restrict ourselves to playing with the forms of representation rather than attempting to reach beyond to a real world which we cannot perceive. Television drama is often seen as a post-modern phenomenon where the pleasure is derived from the relationships between essentially vacuous images. Any attempt at social relevance is illusory.

Some theorists have argued that in discovering the constructedness of the postmodern world-view, we are, in fact liberating ourselves from the mythologies which a naïve realism may seem to present us with (Hutcheon, 1989). To see that the ideas we thought were simply perceptions of the real are, in fact, ways of superimposing meaning can reveal the possibility of rejecting them. The flexibility which theories of postmodernism allow for in interpretation make it a favoured theory for the writers who wish to emphasise the audience's ability to undermine ideology by exposing the artificial nature of representation. Television drama's preference for naturalism therefore only appears to perpetuate the myth that reality can be adequately or truthfully represented.

Baudrillard may have wished to distance himself from postmodernism but he has been included in the ranks of its prophets. His concept of the 'simulacrum' has a distinct relevance to television. Whereas the simulation pretends to have the same properties as reality but does not, the simulacrum goes one stage further and 'Bears no relation to any reality whatsoever: it is its own pure simulacrum' (Baudrillard 1986:170). As an example of a simulacrum, Baudrillard cites the film, *The China Syndrome* which he believes to be composed by amalgamating three real tragedies: Harrisburg, Watergate and Network (Baudrillard, 1994:54). Here the fictional disaster borrows so much from real events of the same kind, that it appears to be genuine. In truth, however, it merely looks sufficiently realistic to make an audience believe that it must, in fact, represent a genuine tragedy. In relation to the television drama, *Holocaust*, Baudrillard argues that it reveals the fact that television 'no longer carries any imaginary' (Baudrillard, 1994, p. 51). According to Baudrillard, audiences do not attempt to conceive of an imaginary because the television representation of the Holocaust is not recognised as an *image* (but is thought of as a report). There is nothing left to imagine. The aim of the broadcast is supposedly to act as a deterrent, but in doing so, it must present us with a screen filled with shocking reality. Television is taken to be real, because it resembles the events we believe to have taken place. The example of *The China Syndrome*, however, shows that when we respond to such things as televisual representation we might be deceived by a simulacrum: there is no guarantee that the seeming veracity of the drama bears any relation to reality. In fact, Baudrillard maintains that the simulacrum enters into what he calls, 'the hyperreal', a condition of the sign where a vacuous simulacrum is taken to be more realistic than real events of the same kind.

The two kinds of postmodern theory outlined above, however, come into conflict. If on the one hand a postmodern text is dissipated in a variety of possible readings, then how can it be taken so uncritically as a completely coherent simulacrum which does not stand in need of further explanation? The idea of the simulacrum cuts short the endless process of semiosis. This is one theory which helps to relegate television to the status of the lowest common denominator in culture which promulgates an unquestioning acceptance of that which it is easiest to absorb, sacrificing truth in the pursuit of pleasure. Moreover, the fact that simulacra are concocted from snatches of real events, makes them especially good examples of intertextuality, and what Jim Collins describes in an article on postmodern theories of television as the 'always already said'. The recycling of signs in postmodernism will therefore only allow us to quote ironically from a stock range of previous sayings. We cannot utter a cliché with sincerity. As Baudrillard says:

> The problem arises in the way that semiology operates: insofar as it immediately establishes a distinctive opposition between signifier and signified and between sign and referent etc; from the very first point of departure what semiology tries to do is to *domesticate* the sign. By comparison, in the world which I evoke, the one where illusion or magic thought plays a key role, the signs evolve, they concatenate and *produce themselves*, always one upon the other – so that there is absolutely no basic reference which can sustain them. Thus they do not refer to any sort of 'reality' or 'referent' or 'signified' whatsoever. (Baudrillard, 1993 :141)

The example of *Twin Peaks* clearly fits these descriptions. The search for the solution to the killing of Laura Palmer yields no satisfactory, final, ultimate meaning. The attempts which we make to connect the various signifiers simply proliferate without any conclusive outcome. There is a contradiction in the versions of postmodernism here: if postmodernism is reduced to quoting the already said, then it is hard to see how signs proliferate entirely by themselves without reference to prior states which exist in the world. Even *Twin Peaks* has to be seen in the context of the detective story, however much it changes the genre.

Baudrillard's theory of the simulacrum also conceals a theory of truth. Baudrillard argues that signs cannot have referents, hence they are empty and meaningless. This presupposes that only a sign which refers could be taken as real. This is the correspondence theory of truth: the view that a proposition can only be true if a state of affairs in the world corresponds to it. There is nothing in the real world which corresponds to the statement, 'Fitz is a psychologist', but it can be said to be a true statement, nonetheless. The postmodern argument is, therefore, that in television drama, signs only refer to each other and continue to create interrelationships of signs until they disappear into oblivion. Postmodernism can be seen as the *reductio ad absurdum* of the Saussurean claim that the relationship between signifier and signified is arbitrary. Because the particular signifier chosen to link with a signified could be substituted, it seems that the relationship is not based on any necessary features. This position has been extrapolated and taken to mean that there is a complete divorce between the system of representation through signs and the world represented. Put more starkly, the position is that drama, for example, is a fiction, which is, by definition, 'made up' and this cannot, therefore be in any sense about the real world. Saussure also asserts, however, that, 'The signifier, though to all appearances freely chosen with respect to the idea that it represents, is fixed, not free, with respect to the linguistic community that uses it' (Saussure, 1974:71). There are, therefore, social aspects which determine the range of signifiers which can be chosen if communication is the goal.

Bakhtinian thinking allows the sign to be infinitely flexible and open yet also to be linked to the social contexts in which it is produced. It reconciles the contradictory aspects of postmodernism which are mentioned above without adopting its nihilistic attitude. Edward Said (1978) distinguishes a critical opposition between Foucault on the one hand and Derrida on the other. The position he identifies, which takes the best from both of these thinkers, is very close to Bakhtin's. Whereas Foucault believes that texts are sites where the social 'strategies of control' exercise a hold over meaning, Derrida brings his critical powers to bear on a 'signifier freed from any obligation to a transcendental signified'. Whereas Foucault sees signs as determined by institutional power and struggling to escape it, Derrida, envisages signs as an endless, *mise en abime* where the sign is pursued endlessly without success. Said prefers to take what is best from both positions and to argue that 'a signifier occupying a place, signifying *in* place *is* – rather than *represents* – an act of will with ascertainable political and intellectual consequences and an act fulfilling a strategic desire to administer and comprehend a vast and *detailed* field of material'. Thus in the scene from *Cracker* we can read the scene as a failed attempt to delimit the meaning of a discourse. The words used cannot serve the speaker's purpose alone, but they do represent an act of willing that they should. The ramifications of the exchange are perhaps endless, but the social action can be understood. Said has grasped that some signs are positive gestures rather than representations.

Graham Pechey (1989) has pointed out the similarity between Bakhtin's theories and deconstruction, since the dialogues which Bakhtin identifies reverberate endlessly and cannot be contained theoretically. Since Bakhtin believes in the inter-connectedness of dialogues, the process of semiosis knows no natural boundary. Despite this, however, Bakhtin's approach to the sign also enables us to conceptualise it as a strategic move in a social practice to endow a signifier with new meaning and to manifest an intention and an evaluation. The nature of dialogism, however, is such an intricate web of inter-related meanings that the dialogic echoes rapidly escape any pre-conceived authorial control and extend into labyrinthine social processes. Thus it might be said that any dialogue created within an artistic practice such as television drama is an attempt to pin meaning down, a wilful *action* which may or may not succeed in creating a social meaning for a sign. Recognition of the purposeful *act* need not compel us to accept a fixed meaning for the sign. Gary Genosko observes that Baudrillard's belief that signs evolve and produce themselves is not entirely at odds with the Peircean view even though Baudrillard's aims are rather different' (Genosko, 1994 : 56).

The difficulties which Baudrillard does place in the way of semiotic theory are based on the assumption that there has to be a one-to-one relationship between signs and referents. If the arbitrary nature of the signifier is taken literally, then it follows that it can be used in a number of ways, with different referents. It is possible to agree that signs are arbitrary in that there is no natural motivation which compels us to select the particular sound, image or word, yet also to maintain that signs can be effective in communicating. The fact that signs are arbitrary means that they have to be continually created *because* there is no natural connection to be relied upon. The fact that a sign is invented, therefore, gives no greater reason to suppose that the sign is disembodied and out of touch with reality. What needs to be studied is the process by which conventions are established, which involves a signalling of intention and a recognition by an addressee. The song 'Summertime' echoes throughout the episode of *Cracker* mentioned above. This use relies on incremental repetition, whereby the ironies and ambiguities in the song gradually emerge each time it is played to accompany a new scene. What emerges are comparisons between the final scene where the innocent man who is firstly accused of the murder is returned to his religious order. In part, the music signifies a consecration of the return to peace, which is only true within this particular drama in this combination of ideas. No convention can be appealed to identify the *specific* meaning here, but the active practice of incremental repetition is the socially-recognised fact which enables the audience to make such connections. Processes of sign-making are fairly conventional, but the signs which are used within them are often freely substituted.

There is an ambiguity in the verb 'to refer to', of course which conceals the problem of reference. Signs can make an allusion to reality or they can stand in place of a real object, acting as a perfect representative of that object. Baudrillard is using the term 'reference' in the way that the logician Frege distinguished between 'sense' and 'reference'. In Frege's usage, sense is the actual meaning attached to a word and reference the literal meaning. Hence the word 'snake' may be used to refer to a person who is untrustworthy. Here the connotations depend on the reference which is to the actual slithering creature. It must be true that any sign composed of three other signs has to be unreal, since it is constructed by definition. There is nothing to stop a sign composed from other signs of the real from invoking reality and making significant statements about it. Baudrillard calls this a ' silent analogy' which is very close to Bakhtin's dialogism. In a silent analogy, the similarity speaks for itself and it is the act of comparison which refers to the real (in the sense of alluding to it). In the following studies of particular television dramas, some signs are composite in the way that Baudrillard argues that *The China Syndrome* is, yet they nonetheless make powerful statements about current affairs. The transparency of their fabrication, in fact, prevents the audience from accepting them as simulacra. Many signs in television drama are composed of diverse fragments of news stories and national scandals to make a composite picture which resembles, but does not refer directly, to reality. Audiences do not necessarily believe that Flora Matlock is a real politician's wife.

In post poststructuralist semiotics, signs are open to multiple interpretations but they are nonetheless grounded in social practices which give them a provisional meaning. The analogy between the Bakhtinian sign and money is important here. Whilst the exchange value of a currency is determinate and fixed, the absolute value of a coin in one currency cannot be established. The exchange value, however, is an objective reality in its social context. Its existence does not prevent us from also saying that there is no ultimate value for money. In a similar way, although signs can be used in an infinite number of contexts, since their relation to one signified is not eternal, any use of a sign will take place at a moment in history when the sign has certain social functions which are determinate.

The position which I have been attempting to clarify in relation to media theory is that of interpretive semiotics. There is a distinction between the theory of signs as determinate meanings and the approach to signs as expressive of meaning which is open to interpretation. The anthropologist Geertz writes,

> I take culture to be those webs and the analysis of it to be therefore not an experimental science in search of a law but an interpretive one in search of meaning. It is explication I am after, construing social expressions on their surface enigmatical. (Geertz, 1974:5)

Saussurean semiotics and the anthropology of Levi-Strauss are examples of a search for a law which can be established scientifically. The concept of semiotics as a discipline which is about making meanings and interpreting signs has long been recognised but it is not conspicuous in the study of media texts. Interpretive semiotics can assimilate the principles of postmodernism without accepting its pessimistic conclusions. The sign-as-rejoinder is a social fact but not a reductive meaning.

The philosophical problem of universals is one which helps to clarify this distinction. There are two major theories of universals: words which designate general concepts such as 'justice' or 'canines' rather than particular things. Two major theories: the recurrence theory and the resemblance theory have been advanced to explain how this is possible. The recurrence theory suggests that the things which are all called by the same universal term share a common property, and the resemblance theory suggests that the range of items referred to by the same word are similar in some respect. The recurrence theory can be compared with Saussurean semiotics. In Saussurean semiology, the signified is clearly describable and recognisable. It is analogous to the idea that each item signified by a particular signifier has a common property. In fact, it may even be possible where this relationship is sufficiently strong, to engage in reverse signification: where the presentation of the signified calls to mind the signifier. Thus the opening of a detective drama set in Oxford may prompt the concept, 'Inspector Morse' without having to use the term.

The resemblance theory of universals is analogous to Peircean semiotics. The resemblance between things which are used to locate all items corresponding to a universal term can be compared with Peirce's interpretants. The resemblances may seem to be a feature of human judgement and therefore apparent to the mind. Possibly the best method of deciding whether there is such a resemblance is to seek a consensus. This approach can lead to pragmatism and the notion of interpretive communities such as those suggested by Stanley Fish or Habermas. If these are the only two acceptable positions, we are in a quandary. The two alternatives are, in philosophical terms, nominalism and realism. The realist is analogous to Saussure, who posits the existence of stable concepts called signifieds which are recognised each time a sign is deployed. The nominalist suggests that all that is common to the things which are signified by the same word or sign is that the same word or sign is used of them. This makes the category of the signified loose and arbitrary such as may be defined by an interpretive community according to whimsical choice. It is this kind of dichotomy which has seemed to present us with a choice between postmodernism (a version of the resemblance theory) and naïve realism (a version of the recurrence theory).

Hilary Staniland (1972) suggests that Wittgenstein differs from both the realist and the extreme nominalist. Nelson also employs this concept in his writing on television. Wittgenstein wants to deny the existence of abstract, general ideas, but he also wants to reject the view that there is absolutely nothing in common between universal things. Wittgenstein's notion of 'family resemblances' is the notion of a resemblance which can be based on different aspects of the items compared on each occasion. Thus there is no abstract notion of a recurrent resemblance to be explained. This could, of course, be equally arbitrary, but coupled with this is Wittgenstein's argument about private languages. If I base my use of the word ' horse' on the resemblance between all those animals with four legs, I will conflict with ordinary language. If I base my use on entirely arbitrary features no-one will be able to grasp my use of the word. The family resemblance has to be something which is both new and yet objectively recognisable. Moreover, it has to broach new ground set aside from that which existing language uses. Wittgenstein's concept of the link between the things which are referred to by the same word is, interestingly for the producers of audio-visual texts, a non-linguistic one. It may even be that we use words in different contexts on the basis of a visual analogy. The resemblance can be one which we designate personally, but the practice of naming has to be graspable by others. It is grasping that practice which consolidates the convention that in this case, ensures that signs have consistent meaning.

The concept of a family resemblance makes Bakhtin's approach to semiotics clearer. If we want to create a new sign, we have to make one which responds to the web of concepts already devised within our immediate culture. The sign must be recognisably rooted in the present, and also new. Fitz is a recognisable detective, yet the similarities and differences between him and other detectives are unique. The similarities ensure that his character is seen in its social context, but the differences ensure that his nature is endlessly open to debate and change. The Bakhtinian sign signifies a relationship between a sign user and a prior state of affairs. It is analogous to the family resemblance, in that the sign in use has to be understood as a new relationship between these two items which has a demonstrable basis for the onlookers. That relationship of similarity, however, may be based on different criteria on each occasion.

Interpretive semiotics, therefore, proposes a number of meanings for signs in available contexts but does not bind the meaning of such signs to these contexts. It is through the Bakhtinian process of recontextualisation that a sign can enter into an entirely new discourse and be regarded as having a new meaning.

At this point, the semiotic theory advance by John Tulloch may usefully be mentioned. In his own study of television drama, Tulloch attempts to reconcile the concepts of 'agency, audience and myth', as the sub-title of his book, *Television Drama* (1990), suggests. Tulloch deals extensively with politically committed drama and therefore recognises that authors do wish to impose certain semiotic values on their texts in order to make a political intervention. He also adopts ideas from Anthony Giddens, whose concept of 'structuration' reinstates the idea that individuals have some part to play in shaping their own lives.

> The analysis of complexly *contending* discourses (as a definition of genre) opens up, a systematic way to examine the ambiguating (as against socially controlling) aspect of TV drama. Potentially too, it restores human agency to drama-as-myth analysis, as particular audiences (Skirrow) and productive personnel (Winterbottom) take their place in the transformative *process* of genre. (Tulloch, 1990:75)

Tulloch recognises the authorial presence, but also acknowledges that the internal mythologies conflict and the audiences have to resist them to overcome dominant ideologies. Tulloch's work therefore paves the way for this study which aims to complement his undertaking. He recognises the existence of three contending forces: the author, ideology and audience in the struggle for meaning. The author has to expose the contradictions in everyday life in such a manner that the viewers will be able to actively disentangle them. The difficulty is that the notion of mythologies, as we have seen, is one which usually can only be resisted. The issues which Tulloch's study raise are how an audience can do anything more than merely oppose the existing ideologies as expressed in myths. As in so many theoretical approaches which derive from structuralism, the author and the audience are both restricted in their ability to shape ideologies and to generate them.

Robin Nelson argues that under the pressure to provide products for global markets, the political economy of television drama has tended to force the makers and sellers of the drama towards a postmodern position. 'A realism with contemporary referentiality is outmoded', he concludes (Nelson, 1997:84).

Authored drama and the single play which demand considerable interpretation are not such successful products in the global market as those which endlessly circulate internal meanings which are easily available to the viewers. Techniques drawn from advertising are used in highly commercial drama to 'situate' the viewer and establish an identity for them from the signifiers presented. Like the ubiquitous Coca-Cola advertisement, drama becomes a product designed to reflect lifestyles. Simulation is argued to be in the process of replacing realism, because simulations and viewers can be controlled more easily. If the study of signs in television drama can become as sophisticated as the analysis of advertisements is now, then there is hope that this trend may be reversed and that the viewers can engage in the process which Tulloch describes, of resisting ideology. This will not happen, however, without a detailed knowledge of semiosis.

Television Authorship: Samuel Beckett

In 1977, Samuel Beckett was asked to contribute to the BBC television series, *The Lively Arts*. His rejoinder was the sequence of three plays broadcast by BBC2 with the title *Shades*. Beckett is widely regarded as a post-modernist dramatist, hence to begin with his highly unusual television dramas illustrates how the theory of signs outlined so far can, in fact deal with innovatory practices where the drama bears little or no similarity to everyday life. The approach adopted here owes a great deal to the example offered by Fredric Jameson in his book, *Postmodernism, or the Cultural Logic of Late Capitalism* (1990), in which he demonstrates that even the most avant-garde experimental video does have its origins in social reality. The broadcast is, therefore, regarded as an utterance which is dialogically related to the series and to preceding television drama practices. This is an example of a rejoinder to a segment of the audience: those who are sufficiently conscious of the conventions of television drama to recognise when the rules are flouted.

Samuel Beckett asked that the television programme which featured his original television drama should be called *Shades*. This in itself is dialogically related to literature: Wordsworth's poem 'Ode on the Intimations of Immortality from Recollections of Earliest Childhood', for example, contains the lines, 'Shades of the prison-house begin to close/upon the growing boy'. The word itself contains the word 'Hades' to emphasise the purgatorial atmosphere of this drama. This allusion fits neatly with Beckett's lines such as 'we are born astride the grave/The light gleams an instant and is gone'. These television dramas might be seen as a rejoinder to Wordsworth's remark. The institution of television both records the phenomenon of the encroaching shades and represents it. Beckett's work can also be read as a rejoinder to the industry that suggested to him that he should provide them with a television drama. One genre to which the piece belongs is that of anti-drama: a genre which makes its point by virtue of its antagonistic relation to existing practices in this field. The following interpretation of the television broadcast is based on the premise that Beckett was making a typically terse rejoinder to the invitation. He wanted, in other words to offer a critique of, and a contribution to, television drama at the same time. The broadcasting of this programme is an historical gesture designed to add to the debate on television which was in progress. As Enoch Brater writes, 'the camera work, the voice-over and the sound effects point out its nature as a made-for-television thing, a manufactured drama which urges us to consider what video technology has to offer to the conventions of the theatre as we know them' (Brater, 1987:94).

'No form of semiotics', according to Julia Kristeva, 'can exist other than as a critique of semiotics. As the place where the sciences die, semiotics is both the knowledge of this death and the revival *with* this knowledge of the 'scientific' (Kristeva 1986:78). In other words, the practice of semiotics should continually re-examine its own foundations and subvert them. Semiotics should not merely challenge *what* signs are taken to mean but how signs create meaning at all. The avant-garde television drama of Samuel Beckett is here taken as an example of a signifying practice which illustrates how Kristeva's claims for semiotics can be fulfilled. Almost by definition, Beckett's work is a radically innovatory aspect of culture. Kristeva's statement implies that where existing semiotic practices break down, new practices take their place with a reinvigorated insight into the former tradition. Beckett's work can be seen as a critique of the contemporary television drama of 1977 which seeks to point out its assumptions and enliven its practices.

Mike Wooller's revision of Desmond Davis's book, *The Grammar of Television Production* was published in a third edition in 1974. This statement of the 'do's and don't's 'of television production was sponsored by the Society of Film and Television Arts. This book, therefore, represents the conventional wisdom of the profession at the time that Beckett was writing. The book is divided into conventions, rules and tips. The overall effect of the book can be summarised in two maxims: try to make the television producer's technique unobtrusive, and try to ensure that the viewer's curiosity is always immediately satisfied by the information which the camera provides. Any voice-over, according to this manual of production, should act as a metalanguage, and provide a means of establishing meaning clearly by commenting on the images on screen and specifying their meaning. This is a means of ensuring that there is no perceived disparity between the image and the commentary. Barthes call such a function *anchorage*. Beckett's innovative drama is a means of teaching us how signs can have a meaning by breaking conventions as well as conforming to them. In Bakhtin's terms, Beckett is revealing that the usual style of television drama is monologic: it appears to present us with information which emanates from one source which is taken as an absolute authority. Dialogical understanding, however, involves a recognition and rejection of this idea.

Beckett begins the drama *Ghost Trio* by showing us the scene in the bare room, reminiscent of a stage, for ten seconds before the commentator's voice is heard. This in itself violates one of the cardinal 'rules' of production as specified in Davis' book: 'never allow the picture to precede the sound'. The reason for this is that the picture alone remains mysterious and open to many possible

interpretations whereas a caption preceding a picture can anchor its meaning to the extent that the image no longer appears polysemic. Beckett's narrator introduces herself and speaks directly to the viewer. Here again the illusion is contaminated by a consideration which does not normally feature in drama. The voice not only directs our attention, she also commands our behaviour. The first order is to adjust the sound to take account of the low volume of her voice. The narrator offers at this point, a metalanguage, apparently explaining the scene we witness. This is in accordance with the maxim that television should immediately make its subject clear to the viewer and minimise ambiguity. At a more remote level, the language of the voice enters into the cultural dialogue in which Guy Debord states that 'Nowadays all information is an order'. In some circumstances the statement, 'Your garden is in need of weeding' is understood as an imperative: 'tend your garden'. Alternatively, it is a parody of the well-known injunction which followed a breakdown in transmission at the time, 'Do not adjust your set'. In Bakhtin's terms, this could be taken as a 'parodic-ironic-reaccentuation', an attempt to utter the words in a new context which adds a new inflection to an old sign.

Theodor Adorno criticises costume drama because everything is unified: in a romantic moment, for example, everything might be muted, the lighting, the two romantic characters' voices, the music, etc. The overall illusion is maintained because everything conforms to the prevailing mood. Bertolt Brecht, however, criticised 'the great struggle for supremacy' between words, music and production – which always brings up the question 'what is the pretext for what?' (Brecht, 1964 :37).

For Brecht, the aim of epic theatre was to achieve the 'separation of the elements', or the dis-integration of music, words and production. Beckett's drama gradually disentangles the elements by violating the conventional rules of television production as expressed in Davis. One such rule is that 'Any change of picture tends to attract the audience away from the subject matter and towards the technique, therefore never change it unless the next picture says something different that *has* to be said, something that emphasises a point or adds to the comprehension of the audience' (Davis, 1974:19). The female voice, or V then asks us to look at the same rectangular sample of wall, floor and window. Next the pallet, or bedroll is shown with the same rectangular shape. This clearly violates the 'rule' that the cut has to be made for a clearly discernible reason. The technique becomes content.

There are many other examples of ways in which this drama breaks the accepted rules of contemporary television drama. The overall style of naturalistic drama was one in which the various elements worked harmoniously together, so that televisual technique was not noticeable. Beckett favours the entirely unmotivated cut which transgresses all the 'rules' of contemporary television drama. One piece of advice given in a contemporary work on television practice is 'where there is virtually no movement, then cut for purely dramatic reasons, to favour the person who is speaking or for reaction or expected reaction' (Davis 1974:18). The first cut to the floor which is announced by Voice with the single word 'floor' is to give the audience sight of a section of floor which contributes nothing to their knowledge. Nonetheless, it is difficult to avoid staring at the section of floor on screen. Our passive viewing, continues compulsively.

The first section of the drama, the 'pre-action', then having toured the set, allows the camera to move slowly towards the one seated figure on the right of our screen. The camera draws closer as the music of Beethoven's Fifth piano trio, *The Ghost* begins faintly. The camera slowly draws close to the hunched figure of the man and then withdraws. The music stops. This again refuses to obey the accepted practice as Davis puts it: 'Fade out music only at the end of a musical cadence, never in the middle'. There is also no close-up of the man's face. Davis writes that audiences instinctively want to see what a new character looks like and that this desire should be satisfied with the close-up, but this again is denied here.

Beckett appears to be undermining the fundamental assumptions of contemporary television practice: that reality can be presented in such a way as to satisfy all curiosity, and answer all questions. As a postmodernist dramatist, he is famous for making the human condition eternally enigmatic. To accept the conventions of television drama is to suppress certain questions. What Beckett arguably achieves by refusing us the privileged knowledge of the television viewer is a reinvigorated perception of the most commonplace objects. The philosopher Wittgenstein's account of perception may help to explain this process. Wittgenstein's attitude towards perception is consonant with his theory of language. To perceive is not to apprehend certain sense-data and decode them. Husson, (1994) elaborates on the implications of Wittgenstein's views for semiotics. Wittgenstein takes the example of the following diagram as an illustration in a book.

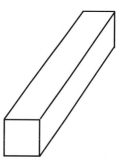

In the relevant text something different is in question every time: here a glass cube, there an inverted open box, there a wire frame of that shape, there three boards forming a solid angle. Each time the text supplies the interpretation of the illustration. But we can also *see* the illustration now as one thing now as another. So we interpret it, and *see* it as we interpret it. (Wittgenstein 1951 section xi:193)

Wittgenstein;'s argument can be applied to signs. Perhaps there are occasions when we do not see signs and decode them, since this implies that the signifier can be separated from the signified. Here the signifier simply *is* a box or whatever we see. The visual signs we encounter are also amenable to Wittgenstein's approach. What guarantees that we see a certain gesture from another person as a threat, for example, is not a rule, but the perception that the action belongs to the class of actions we learn to recognise as threats. There may be a 'family resemblance'. To perceive an action as threatening is not to decode it, but to see it as such. We know it to belong to this category because of our observation of human behaviour and the consequences of making such gestures. Threatening is a social practice we learn by acquaintance, not deduction. Similarly, Wittgenstein argues that to recognise something as a chair does not involve the ability to cite a vast number of 'rules' which govern the applicability of the word (see Wittgenstein, 1951, section 80). Beckett's narrator who asks the audience to contemplate the items such as the wall and floor which they have already 'seen as' both wall and floor is perhaps drawing attention to the phenomenon. Beckett's drama takes the mattress of the bed and invites us to see it as just another grey rectangle in a grey rectangular room. By refusing to use the conventions of contemporary television, Beckett encourages the viewer to look anew and to ask new questions. We have to contemplate our habit of 'seeing as' which can assimilate any television scene into an unexceptional domestic existence. This is defamiliarisation: making the everyday seem unusual.

This approach has also fulfilled Brecht's wish that the elements, which are comparable to Christian Metz's five channels, be separated. The music does not simply add to a prevailing mood, but instead sets up a dialogue between the music and the other sign-systems which we need to puzzle out. The effect of abandoning the 'rules' of television production is to establish a polyphonic dialogue between the diverse elements. *Signifiance* now takes over as the guiding principle in any interpretation. As Susan Petrilli writes, 'the instruments provided by decodification semiotics are inadequate for a convincing analysis of the distinguishing features of human communication such as plurilingualism, plurivocality, ambiguity, polysemy, dialogism, otherness: as such, verbal communication cannot be contained within the two poles of *langue* and *parole* as had been theorized by Saussure (Petrilli, 1994:104).

Signifiance lies somewhere between *langue* and *parole*. *Signifiance* is an example of a sign which communicates within its original context, but does not yet have universal recognition. Saussure seems to regard signs as either universally understood or not understood at all. In reality signs may originate in certain relatively marginal social practices such as innovatory television drama and then gradually extend into the *langue* itself, or they may remain a minority language game. Volosinov seems to be inconsistent on this score. As Volosinov says, ' everything that becomes a fact of grammar had once been a fact of style' (Volosinov, 1973:51). It follows that to make only grammatical utterances will not lead to any progress in communication: some signals must be originated. In

Volosinov's terms, *paroles* precede *langue* and *langue* is an abstraction from specific utterances. Kristeva's point is related to this position. In a television drama such as Beckett's *Ghost Trio*, the so-called 'grammar' of television is shown to be a habit rather than a set of inviolable rules. Some signs must exist objectively before they reach the stage of universal acceptance and enter into *la langue*. We cannot, therefore, dismiss anything as a mere signal merely because it is not recognised by an entire community.

The sign without a socially-agreed code, however, is attenuated to the status of what Volosinov calls a 'signal' – an agreement between individuals, or an isolated arrangement which does not impinge on the public codes of meaning. In *Marxism and the Philosophy of Language* the signal is described as 'an internally fixed, singular thing that does not in fact stand for anything else, or reflect or refract anything else but is simply a technical means for indicating this or that object' (Volosinov, 1973:68). The traffic lights are signs, but my wave to another driver signifying that he should go before me is a signal. It would not be recognised outside this context. Other signs can be used in its place. The signal does not feature in language, since its use is not governed by universal conventions, yet it is here defined as something which communicates successfully. As such it must form part of a theory of signification in general. Signals must not be dismissed simply because they cannot strictly form part of *language*, since signification subsumes language. To undermine a set of audience expectations is to reduce the status of certain signifiers from that of a code to that of a signal. Demonstrating that a certain televisual technique does not have a universal meaning shows that it cannot function as a sign, properly so called.

The next section, described as 'Action', shows the man getting up because as the narrator says, he thinks he hears an awaited woman: 'He will now think he hears her'. The man gets up, goes to the door, the window and looks for the woman who does not come. He then goes to the pallet, and examines his face in the mirror hanging above it. This draws an astonished gasp from the narrator. In the BBC production we see his face as if we are looking at him from the mirror. Contemporary televisual practice dictated that you should never let a performer look straight into the lens of the camera unless it is necessary to give the impression that he is speaking directly to the viewer personally (Davis, 1974:54).

Her next words are, 'Now to door', as if he will return to looking out of the door, but he goes back to his seat. The role of the narrator has been undermined here. Instead of acting as a metafictional voice which has total objectivity, she has been 'disobeyed'. The convention that in television a meta-narrative offers valuable true information to clarify and disambiguate the visual image, has also been subverted. In technical terms, we become conscious of a shift from the heterodiegetic narrator to an extradiegetic narrator (Stam *et al* 1992 : 97).

Our privileged opportunity to view the man examining himself in the mirror, is the closest that the production team can bring us to a similar shock. By gazing at the man from the mirror, we see him putting one finger to his lower eyelid as if examining his personal appearance. Faint music is now heard at the most distant point of the camera from the man, but at the command 'stop' from V, it ceases.

Critics of Beckett have been quick to treat the music as if it has a clear interpretative function and is meant to emphasise the emotions of the male actor. Poutney (1989:201) asserts that 'the music seems to be an externalisation of F's yearning for 'her'. This would seem to suggest that the music is non-diegetic, however, and is in the control of the unseen producers and V. It would also suggest a hierarchy of signifying systems is implicit in the drama with music only able to supplement a sign which is already clear. If, on the other hand, F himself controls the music from the cassette which we eventually see in his hands, then it signifies something else. When conventions such as those of television production are overturned, this does not mean that we are in entirely uncharted territory. The remaining social practice is that of drama. In this there is a fundamental expectation that we will be presented with an uncertain state of affairs and that the uncertainty will somehow be resolved.

Martin Esslin points out that structure is a signifier in drama too, and that the audience of *Waiting for Godot* only grasp the meaning of the play when they recognise that the second act has a structure which is identical to the first (Esslin, 1987:120). Drama, in other words, is a social practice which involves fulfilling some expectations such as those created by structure. The abandonment of codes does not make the text completely divorced from social reality. The drama stems from the relationship between the action and reaction. How is the man going to react when he learns that his waiting for the unseen woman is hopeless? What can we do when we have no reason to expect that our hopes will ever be fulfilled? Where does the answer to this question lie? Is the man himself the source of the answer, or can a philosophical argument be spun which does not involve his feelings? The drama of the piece perhaps lies in waiting to see whether the close-up can contain all the information needed to read the human condition in one face. At its most dramatic we wait to see the triumph of humanism, as if one face can tell us about us all. As John McGrath wrote in 1977, 'Since naturalism visually evolved from Hollywood film techniques, there is still retained a deep-rooted belief that the close-up of an actor's face somehow acts subjectively on the viewer' (McGrath, 1977:100).

In the third section, which is the reaction, a small boy dressed in oilskins comes to the door and is seen in the corridor faintly shaking his head. The negative sign can only confirm the unlikely arrival of the expected 'she'.

As the message is received, the man sits down again and we hear the remainder of the *largo* from Beethoven's *Ghost* Sonata, which reaches a crescendo and subsides dramatically with a sawing *decrescendo*. The precise source of the music is unclear and remains so throughout. In semiotic terms, this is an *acousmatic* sign as described by Stam *et al* (1992:61-2). and interpretation is an attempt at de-acousmaticisation, or the attribution of the music to one source. If the music was interpreting the action, then we might expect the *decrescendo* to be simultaneous with the discovery that the waiting is hopeless. In the BBC production, however, the final shot is a close-up of the man's face and a faint smile gradually spreads over it as he gazes at the camera. The smile would again seem to be inconsistent with disillusionment. In television drama, the accentuation of a dramatic text is often found in the director's actual presentation of the minimal *nebentext* in the original writing: '*boy turns and goes*'.

In the German production of this drama, for example, Beckett directed and had the small boy back slowly down the corridor when the man answered. Here the over-arching framework of human motivation establishes a dialogic relation between the man 's actions and appearance and the boy's reaction. The effect is also to evaluate the man's behaviour: if it is threatening or disturbing, it becomes less dignified and ritualised. Perhaps this signifies that the man is the ghost of the title. He is, after all, dressed in a long dark robe and walks stooped forwards as a ghost might.

The crucial aspect of such dialogical relations which come into being when conventions are abandoned, is that they require an imaginative response from an audience. Interpreting dialogism is not the same as understanding montage. Montage appeals to existing social conventions to make two consecutive images coherent, as Colin MacCabe has pointed out (MacCabe, 1981), whereas dialogism demands that audiences invent their interpretation within certain social practices. Montage amounts to perceiving a connection that already exists whilst dialogism involves creating a connection.

Beckett's 'theatre of the absurd' is celebrated as the prime example of de-contextualised signs which are deliberately presented without any historical or sociological origins evident. This is not to say, however, that the drama cannot be interpreted as a dialogic response to particular historical conditions. Beckett's exposure of the dubious philosophical premises of contemporary television drama – that everything is explicable and can be shown – is shown by a drama in which everything can be questioned.

The discovery that the man's cassette recorder is of the same rectangular shape as the other sections of the room we have been shown, is a further attempt to establish new dialogical relations. The music has been divided into excerpts and not allowed to flow uninterruptedly. The five-second cutting as the ritual of waiting and expectation is played out becomes a predictable rhythm much like the beat of a musical bar. These signs begin to converge, suggesting perhaps, that all art here is aspiring towards the condition of music. The various interpretations of the piece tend to suggest that there is a dialogue about the arts. As Robert Samuels suggests, music is an art where the signifier is created in the act of listening (Samuels, 1995:15), but in this piece, all the other signifiers are generated by the viewing and listening process. Metz's notion of the 'imaginary signifier' is one where the Saussurean process of identifying both the sign-vehicle and then the signified associated with it, does not take place because the signifier is itself imagined. As Barthes argues in *Mythologies*, the most effective way to undermine traditional signification is to subvert the meaning attached to the signifier, to 'change the object itself' rather than the connection between object and concept.

Beckett's television drama foregrounds style and plays down content. Like the tableau, it has 'a meaning, not a subject' (Barthes, 1977:75). Our first concern with drama such as this is the internal relations of the scene, and not what it may represent. Barthes, for example, writes:

> Are there other messages without a code? At first sight, yes: precisely the whole range of analogical reproductions of reality – drawings, paintings, cinema, theatre. In fact, however, each of those messages develops in an immediate and obvious way a supplementary message, in addition to the analogical content itself (scene, object, landscape), which is commonly called the *style* of the reproduction. (Barthes, 1977:17)

The style of the tableau is itself a message. The most difficult question to answer in Beckett's work, of course is just what message we are meant to receive. If semiotics is about objectively verifiable communication, then our means of objectively verifying the transmission of a message here are very limited. The 'trio' of the title can be construed in several ways:

Voice/man/woman
man/woman/ us
audience /voice/man
audience/performer /playwright
F. /Boy / V.

This multiple ambiguity haunts the viewer from the outset and makes the drama itself a polysemous signifier. It could be argued,for example, that the piece shows us that in all the triadic relationships above, there is an inevitable ghost, or absence. Someone must always lie behind the spectacle, out of sight and in command of the proceedings, a 'ghost in the machine': the author, or the narrator or the composer. Also for the sign, there must always be an absence, something which we do not see, or signification would not take place at all. Absence is necessary in order to enable a haunting piece of music to work at all. Absence is, in this sense, the price we pay for the sublime emotion of music. This means that the final smile on the face of F., may mean that music has sublimated his emotions and that as Beckett says, the desire to express even a hopeless situation has to be fulfilled. This interpretation would lead to the view that the man was reconciled to the absence of the female by virtue of acknowledging the nature of art and signification itself. Without a human longing, music could not have its emotional effect. This might explain the final accentuation of the close-up of the man's face as he finally accepts his lot. The aim of Beckett's drama is perhaps not to communicate a clear meaning so much as to generate the kind of critical thinking in which we are now engaged. This is the 'desired response' of which Bakhtin speaks.

Dennis Potter, however was infuriated by this piece and asked in the *Sunday Times* whether 'the Jews on the way to the gas chamber would have understood?' (Fletcher, 1978:210). The drama can be read as a philosophy of quietism: that once futility is recognised all we can do is dwell on the poignancy of the futility itself as the only course of action left. The issue which this raises is that the pregnant moment does not arise. At no point is there a Brechtian gest which constitutes a direct rejoinder to contemporary society comparable to that of *Mother Courage*. This leads to the charge that the drama is a futile exploration of formal relationships: it is a fascinating structure like a mandala which simply generates many ways of viewing it and legitimates them all.

It may be that the text itself cannot be accused of ideological futility. Susan Sonntag took Beckett's *Waiting for Godot* to Sarajevo, and the play was performed in San Quentin prison in the Unites States to great acclaim in both cases. Perhaps the combination of text and context is needed to develop a sense of the pregnant moment. In his essay, 'Musica Practica' Barthes pays particular attention to Beethoven's music. Barthes traces a unique historical moment in Beethoven which is analogous to the transition from a writerly to a readerly literature. The nineteenth-century Beethoven is 'the first man of music to be *free*' (Barthes, 1977:150). Beethoven enables the Romantic composer to break with convention and to begin to trace his own struggles and inner life in his music. The later Beethoven, however, is the composer who does not give to hear but give to *write*. The music is no longer representational and instead demands an audience that can structure it, according to Barthes. Thus there is not a signified behind the music which is the writer's life, but we have to impose meaning upon the music. The man in Beckett's drama is therefore possibly struggling to achieve a 'breakthrough'. This is a term which comes from Adorno and which Samuels (1995) applies to Mahler's music where a theme tries to intrude several times before it finally bursts into full prominence and continues unabated. Perhaps, then, the answer to Brecht's qustion here is that the music does not interpret the man's situation. The drama is a pretext for the music and the man finally celebrates his ability to read into the music his own struggles and inner life. If the breakthrough is read as the moment when the listener 'writes' the music, then it may be seen as a liberating and empowering one with a historical dimension of great importance.

The word 'shades' also occurs at the very end of Yeats' poem, 'The Tower' to which Beckett's second television drama screened in this broadcast 'refers'. The phrase ' … but the clouds', is a direct quotation from Yeats's poem, which is a meditation on ageing and its effects on the speaker. Dwelling on the sensual memories of the past which he can recall, the lyrical speaker of Yeats's poem finds himself searching 'in the grave' for conclusions and perceptions to sustain him. So far in discussing *Ghost Trio* we have been considering what Barthes would call the *studium*, or the cognitive intentions behind the drama: its theoretical assumptions. The *punctum*, however, is the emotional effect of the piece which may be unrelated to the theory. As Barthes says, 'In order to perceive the *punctum*, no analysis would be of any use to me' (Barthes, 1980: 42). In a dialogue with himself, the speaker bids his reflective being to bring to light those truths which have been long buried. In particular, the price paid for loving and losing women is one piece of information which the speaker searches his own mind to discover.

The most pertinent question for Beckett's play seems to be:

> Does the imagination dwell the most
> Upon a woman won or woman lost?
> (Yeats, 1971 : 222).

In response to his own thought, the speaker remarks that if it is the woman that the man has lost who provokes his imagination the most, then he should admit the personal failings which cause this loss, or the memory could blight the day and turn everything to darkness. It is unbearable, in other words, to recall the loss of a loved one who was lost because of one's own fault, hence it is best not to bemoan the inability to imagine her image. The poetic image Yeats uses is that the sun will be 'blotted out' if the memory of a failed relationship recurs. Successful envisioning of the departed woman will lead to a failure. At the very end of the poem, however, the contradictions inherent in this process of thought assemble. The speaker strives to concentrate on 'a learned school', or rational thought and to make the images of past lovers:

> Seem but the clouds of the sky
> When the horizon fades;
> Or a bird's sleepy cry
> Among the deepening shades.
> (Yeats, 1971:225)

Ironically, of course, the process of articulating the poem has begun the very danger which it warns of: the day is darkening as the recollection of the woman is indulged in. The attempt to make the memories no more than the familiar sights and sounds of twilight, which signify loss and an imminent revival of the day, are futile. The familiar sights and sounds of twilight are now permanently tinged with sadness. Has the speaker's strategy worked or failed? The conclusion is open.

The poem, therefore, in the manner of 'High Art' attempts to generate a universal law. Admittedly the contradictions undermine the law *stated* in the poem, but this only reinforces the feeling that we are learning something about human nature. This is the social practice of High Art against which Beckett constructs a piece of television. The expectation is that the 'human condition' will be appealed to and this rhetorical appeal will instruct us in the trials and consolations of being human.

It seems, however, that Beckett is bent on exposing the final contradiction rather than leaving the impression that some comfort can be gained as Yeats's poem does. The television piece begins with the voice of the one male character speaking the line, 'When I thought of her it was always night. I came in.' The voice then corrects himself and says, 'when she appeared it was always night. I came in.' The expectation generated by televisual codes is that the voice is a metacommentary and that the action will now exemplify the process he has referred to. The ritual of coming in and advancing eastwards, towards the closet, westwards now dressed in 'robe and skull', and finally disappears northwards into what he calls 'my little *sanctum*' in order to beg the deceased woman of his dreams to appear to him. The man who has been walking the roads all day is a typical Beckettian character : he resembles a tramp and has no identity.

The only stage direction is that the lighting should create a bright circle at the centre with shadows all around. In an interesting technical experiment, Beckett has no camera movements at all: the scenes are simply presented in sequence. This is the nearest equivalent to the 'mind's eye'. The bright circle can be seen as a metaphor for consciousness. This would justify the lack of overt televisual technique, since the purpose of the drama is to re-enact the processes of memory and attention should not be drawn to the television apparatus. The commentators on this drama have largely referred to the content in a familiar manner, but what has often been overlooked is the utterance itself. The speaker is not simply attempting to recapture the image of the departed woman, he is trying to recapture the *act* of capturing it. He is not simply telling us what happened, he is also going through the same motions. This is why the ritual of coming in and moving in each direction before finally disappearing to the inner sanctum is repeated to 'get it right'. The ritual itself is regarded as the means of evoking the spectre of the dead woman. The television aesthetic in drama is that the drama should offer us all that it is possible to see. We have privileged access to the domestic and private spheres of life in conventional television drama in order that we can piece together the whole narrative. In this case, we also literally 'see' what the character sees when the woman's image reappears to his mind.

Ritual, in semiotic terms, 'does not introduce any order into a chaotic world – it invents an order' (Lindgren and Knaak, 1997 : 124). The ritual walking back and forth is repeated as rituals must be, in order to evoke the image. The ritual appears to be a kind of homage. In place of communication, which promises a definitive process of tranmission of facts, the ritual method of communication simply acts out a meaning. Beckett is constantly wavering between communication and ritual. His characters seem to promise meaning but often deviate towards ritual repetition. The television ritual might seem a way of reclaiming a face from the past and re-enacting memories, but this is a myth.

When the man's voice decides to go through the ritual for a third time, it has become a sign. Within this drama, the ritual has now acquired a specific meaning for the viewers. Wittgenstein gives the example of an elemental language-game involving builders:

> -But when I call "slab!", then what I want is, *that he should bring me a slab!*_____Certainly , but does 'wanting this' consist in thinking in some form or other a different sentence from the one you utter?____
> (Wittgenstein 1951: section 19:9).

The point which is addressed here is that the concept of meaning is embedded in a social practice. Builders call for fresh materials from their under-labourers when they are required, and orders have to be issued. Grasping the meaning of the command means acting accordingly and bringing the slab. This social action is all that is needed to justify the claim that the builder's under-labourer has comprehended the meaning of the command. He does not need to translate the words further. If he obeys, we could not withhold the claim that he understands on the grounds that he cannot produce a translation of the command as a sentence, for example. As Wittgenstein says, 'explanations come to an end somewhere', and he ends the explanation at the point where 'forms of life' are reached.

Bringing the slab – participating in the form of life we describe as ' building as a team' – is sufficient to demonstrate understanding of this command. The single act of taking the slab to the builder might not be sufficient in itself to convince us that the addressee understood, but once the addressee has successfully assisted in the building, we can be as sure as possible. This leads Wittgenstein to assert that language is not a rule-governed activity. There is no rule which enables the meaning of the word 'slab' to be inferred here, only a social practice which can be observed:

> ...(by, for example, watching other builders at work), and imitated. The command, if it is first used by these participants, may be nothing more than a signal at this stage, but it may nonetheless succeed in indicating something to someone. As Wittgenstein says, 'obeying a rule' is a practice. (Wittgenstein, 1951 section 202 : 81)

The invention of a new social practice, with its attendant signs, is, however, dependent on existing practices as Barthes suggests. The builders example above is one that we comprehend because building is well understood. The link between signifier and signified, however, is not firmly established by such practices. It is within a social practice such as this that we can understand a new sign because we know the purpose of such activities. The rational aim of building is a fundamental fact which assists us to imagine what a builder would require of helpers. This sounds as if we depend on existing practices and cannot develop any completely original ones, but here I am only offering an explanation of why the example is cogent. It is perfectly possible to invent a new social practice. 'Voguing' is a social practice begun in America in which young people meet socially to flaunt their extravagant personal style in dress and adornment in order to impress on a competitive basis. It is original, but it is analogous to other forms of human activity and its rational purpose can be transferred analogically, from one area of human life to another. It is a hybrid activity formed by merging the activities of the fashion show and competitive sport. The importance of this example is that the purpose of the activity is different, yet discernible from our existing knowledge. Signs, therefore, may need to be understood in originating contexts where no clear precedent exists to enable decoding. The social practice does not determine the meaning of individual signs, rather it determines the *kind* of meaning which can be attributed.

The myth which it enacts is that which Yeats writes about. Will the act of regarding the image of the woman seem to become an evanescent impression of the fading twilight if he treats it in this manner? The speaker distinguishes three possibilities: the image is called upon and disappears; the image is called upon and lingers; or the image is called upon and the woman appears to be mouthing the words of Yeats's poem which the title alludes to. The speaker then bitterly recalls that the most common case was when the image did not come at all and he busied himself with cognitive, abstract things such as 'cube roots' in his frustration. Ritual enacts myth, and the myth enacted here is that the contemplation of what Yeats calls 'learned schools' will prevent the pain of memory. Rather than dispelling the image of the dead woman, the words have been endowed with a certain ritual function which inevitably recalls her. Even the woman herself seems to mouth the words which suggest that she should be regarded as inconsequential: 'but the clouds in the sky'. The piece ends with the man repeating the words as if they will bring the woman's image back. Beckett is uttering a rejoinder to Yeats's rather sanguine account of how to tolerate loss.

The irony is that in attempting to use his rational powers to make the image of the dead woman seem nothing more than the clouds at twilight, the man has, in fact, endowed the clouds at twilight with a special poignancy. When the woman's face reappears to him, it seems to be mouthing the words of Yeats's poem and it is forever associated now with those words. The words which are meant to dispel the image now have the effect of haunting the speaker with their associated beauty. The process of indulging in rational thought to dismiss emotions is based on a myth: the emotions cannot be banished so easily. When finally the man succeeds in summoning her image at will, he then speaks the lines as if the incantation will rid himself of the problem emotions. By now, of course, the myth has been exposed. We can see that the image does not recur without an association with the very idea of trying to rid oneself of the image.

If Beckett was trying to satirise the naturalistic practices of contemporary television, then he does not replace them with a drama which avoids a claustrophobic focus on the intimate feelings of an isolated individual much like naturalistic theatre. The drama relies almost entirely on a rhetorical appeal to our notion of 'the human', and for many viewers this seems to fail. Dennis Potter's outrage on behalf of the Jews is an example of this. The semiotic reading above, however, takes the dramas as strategies in the practice of representing humanity in a mediated form. The effect on viewers and drama-makers may be to avoid the representations of the Holocaust which seem to present Human Nature as always on the verge of redemption. The very savage criticisms of representations of the Holocaust may be avoided by a careful study of Beckett's television work. As Raymond

Williams wrote, the naturalistic emphases were seen as 'internal properties of the medium itself, when in fact they were a selection of some of its properties according to the dominant structure of feeling' (Williams, 1974:56). Beckett at least illustrates that naturalism does not have to be regarded as television's aesthetic foundation. Other strategies can be used, but the effect is to ask much more of the viewer.

'A hypothesis within a recognition': the naturalism debate

Emile Zola made a distinction in his essay on 'Naturalism in the Theatre', published in 1881, between 'metaphysical man, the abstraction who had to be satisfied with his three walls in tragedy – whereas the physiological man in our modern works is asking more and more compellingly to be determined by his setting, by the environment that produced him' (Bentley, 1968:370). As a reaction against 'metaphysical' tragedies, naturalism in the theatre was a progressive influence which sought to counter the view that 'Man' could transcend his material environment completely. Raymond Williams wrote that, 'With the coming of television as a majority service... It was possible to transmit performances of an orthodox theatrical kind, and it could be argued that the television play was the ultimate realisation of the original naturalist convention: the drama of the small enclosed room, in which a few characters lived out their private experience of an unseen public world' (Williams, 1974:56). Beckett's *Ghost Trio* perhaps parodies this idea by drawing aesthetic attention to the idea of watching a box within a box. As so often happens, however, naturalism took the diametrically opposed view to that of the Romantic generation which often espoused the absolute autonomy of the individual. In the scientific atmosphere of the new positivism which derived from thinkers such as Auguste Comte, human behaviour was not determined from within but from without. In addition, all representation in art could be traced to provable scientific facts about Man. Raymond Williams argues that by the 1920s the naturalist play was beginning to *include* the social determinants which its characters had formerly only alluded to. Naturalist television drama therefore moved easily between the private room and the social world which governed the behaviour of its occupants, often establishing the relationship between the two. Man was the product of an inescapable scientific determinism.

Although Naturalism might seem to be suited to a Marxist approach with its emphasis on the determination of social behaviour, the Marxist critic Georg

Lukács, wrote that 'Naturalism, socialist or otherwise, deprives life of its poetry, reduces all to prose' (Lukács, 1963:78). Naturalism, in other words, tends to make individuals representative of a social force at the expense of their individuality. The strict determinism which makes every action and sign traceable to a social origin, deprives the individual of any ability to act in a unique fashion. In addition, the 'poetry' of the individual's existence cannot be explored because a self-conscious treatment of such things would detract from the naturalistic style which requires us to believe in the illusion with which we are presented. Naturalism is a transparent medium through which the social structure can be perceived, and to focus on the poetic nature of the medium itself, would cloud this transparency.

Brecht wrote that 'What the film really demands is external action and not individual psychology' (Brecht, 1964:50). This statement may seem to assimilate naturalism with materialism. Film in many ways is the ideal medium for the materialist, since it permits an artist to display the determining forces of society as they are at work. On the other hand, Brecht also writes in the same essay that 'Great areas of ideology are destroyed when capitalism concentrates on external action, dissolves everything into processes, abandons the hero as the vehicle for everything and mankind as the measure, and thereby smashes the introspective psychology of the bourgeois novel' (Brecht, 1964:50). The dangerous tendency in naturalism is that it conceals the individual voice in its attempt to reveal the links between society and behaviour. As Brecht states, shortly after this, 'As soon as the human being appears as an object the causal connections become decisive'. This is another way of stating that once it is clear that the main object of interest is the individual, any causal link which determines their behaviour is seen as some kind of universal law. As Roland Barthes put it, 'Photography cannot signify (aim at a generality) except by assuming a mask. It is this word which Calvino correctly uses to designate what makes a face into the product of a society and its history' (Barthes, 1980:34).

Raymond Williams suggests that Strindberg's experiments with theatrical expressionism as in the *DreamPlay* are the precursors of some televisual practices. The representation of inner reality need not be a denial of materialism, but can also show how social reality impinges on the individual and is reinterpreted internally.

It is not surprising, therefore that television dramatists with socialist inclinations tend to have an ambivalent relationship with naturalism. Although they often use this style. they also condemn it. Dennis Potter complained of 'the prevailing, unexamined "naturalism" of the medium as a whole' (Potter, 1984:30). John McGrath described naturalism in television drama as 'this makeshift bastard born of the theatre' (McGrath, 1977:100). As a rejoinder to metaphysical Romanticism, naturalism was a major advance, but as a form of television, McGrath denounces it. The fundamental objection is clear: television is the medium for reporting facts. Once we use a naturalistic setting, the presentation of any situation in what looks like an authentic context, tends to make an audience assume that they are watching what really happens: what Brecht called 'society's causal network'. Moreover, the individuality of any character is soon swallowed up in the general principle which she or he is supposed to illustrate. The more authentic the drama, the more firmly causal relationships are established. Potter complained of the Marxists, structuralists and semiologists who had moved away from the singular or the individual towards the 'universal and systematic' (Potter, 1984:26). Analysis and evaluation also tended to accept the naturalist doctrine and reduce the television drama to its component social features. In thorough-going naturalism social being did not determine consciousness as Marx claimed, it *was* consciousness itself. Thus a drama could be written which would show characters' emotions succeeding one another as if there was a law of the emotions common to all people in the same situation. John McGrath also complained that a new type of drama was needed which showed that things could change (see McGrath, 1977) rather than offering a world where what was shown was inevitable.

As an ardent socialist, McGrath wanted to depict a world in which human action could bring about revolutionary change. In naturalistic television drama, McGrath detected the influence of Hollywood and the Actors' Studio as directed by Lee Strasberg. The Actors' Studio was dedicated to Method Acting which employed the techniques of Stanislavsky who is the leading figure of naturalistic acting. In Stanislavsky's approach to acting, the performer recalls a situation from their own 'emotional memory' which made them feel a particular emotion in order to act that emotion. It is also causal in that if a cause (an emotional experience) can be remembered, then the effect (an appropriate performance) can result. When performers demonstrated such techniques on camera, McGrath criticised the Hollywood style of filming which appeared to suggest that a close-up acts subjectively on the viewer. All this engages the viewer without ever presenting the ultimate cause of the emotions we witness. McGrath is really objecting to the expression theory of art which is implicit in the naturalism he describes. The expression theory suggests that the creator makes a work in which their emotions can be reproduced through the effects on the audience. McGrath speaks of the naturalist's intention to 'involve the viewer emotionally in the character's predicament'. The work, in other words, causes the same emotion in the audience as the creator originally experienced. In nineteenth-century naturalism, Ruskin compelled his art students to dig holes in the ground so that they could examine flowers at eye level and depict them authentically. The televisual equivalent is the close-up.

McGrath's argument is still one of the most persuasive attacks on this aesthetic, over twenty years later. However, is a somewhat confused mixture of positions he attacks the notion that naturalism on television should contain everything in a closed system of relationships and focus on the characters' verbal dialogues. It seems that this is because it is trying to signify a social reality through the mediation of a small band of realistic performers. The use of a character who loses his job to signify that many people are losing their jobs is what McGrath calls mediating social reality 'to the point of triviality'. McGrath really wants to be able to make his views felt in a didactic fashion, rather than relying on what he disparagingly calls 'symbolism' (which may well be intended here to include signs). The essay argues that the controversial drama series *Days of Hope* would never have been screened if it had stated explicitly what its position was, because 'the naturalistic form allowed it to imply but never to *say* what it meant' (McGrath 1977:105). The theatrical tradition which characterised much of the early television drama of the 1960s, foregrounded the verbal relationships because theatre had done so, whereas the televisual medium had other potential resources. Television, unlike cinema, is taking much longer to liberate itself fully from the traditions of the theatre.

The attack on naturalism from a Brechtian perspective is predictable and consistent. The emotional engagement with characters who emote rather than present a case for rational debate is a dangerous example of the response to the classical theatre which Brecht warns us of. McGrath opts instead for a more overtly rational approach in which the viewer is engaged in contemplating a problem. He would prefer to carry the story forward with a montage style that 'quickens the imagination' rather than dwelling on the emotions. At times it appears that it is most important to follow the narrative. On the other hand, McGrath also quotes Troy Kennedy Martin with approval as he describes the new television drama which will take over from naturalism:

> The new drama will be based on story rather than plot... It will be more personal in style; it will compress information, emphasise fluidity, free the camera from photographing faces, and free the structure from the naturalistic tyrany of time... Through stream of consciousness and diary form it will lead to interior thought, interior characterisation. (McGrath 1977)

If the clasic objection to naturalism is that its determinist foundation presents an inescapable fate, then it was essential to render a psychic life which could exist despite the conditions of existence and could formulate the revolutionary alternative. The description of a 'new' television drama, however, fits Beckett's work which is not hailed as a socially progressive alternative. The 'new' television drama is still a distant prospect. McGrath himself interestingly reveals that he subscribes to the television practices which Davis cites in his 'grammar' of television: 'Stylistically, I went for one rigid rule: no camera move, no cut, until the next piece of story was to be revealed' (McGrath, 1977: 103)

McGrath's objections to naturalism derive from a pioneering account of the televisual aesthetic. He cites three characteristics of the television image: it 'lacks sensuality'; it has 'objectivity'; and 'it is conditioned by all the other images that have preceded it'. Whereas the cinematic image can overwhelm us, the television image is 'at best nice'. This may be a feature which new technologies are beginnning to eliminate, of course, with the advent of wide screen and surround sound televisions in the digital age. With advances in technology such as the ability to enlarge a screen image at home and simply turn the lights off, technology may eventually remove any distinction between television and cinematic aesthetics. The point remains, however, that it is harder to be overcome by the image and to surrender to its effects. This is partly due to the scale of television which always reduces images to less that life size. 'Objectivity' is used by McGrath to mean that the television image established a certain aesthetic distance by virtue of the medium in which it exists. The television set is constantly visible in front of us; it is a piece of furniture, and usually is seen in lighted conditions. We cannot be seduced as in the cinema into identification. Bazin wrote that Tarzan was only possible in the cinema because only in the cinema could we identify with a character we knew we could not resemble. In the dark, we can forget that we are watching a film. In the theatre, for example, Bazin argued that the physical presence of the actor always serves as a barrier to psychic identification. The television set plays the same role: it can serve as a constant reminder that the image is transmitted and not an 'imaginary signifier'. If Beckett's drama is an attempt to make television images take on the characteristics of cinema, it is because they can make us ask *what* we are looking at, and not accept the conventional signifiers without question. Television images, however, foreground codes initially: they usually demand not to be construed but to be *recognised*. This is where McGrath's third point is relevant. The image is recognised by virtue of its similarity to others. This is comparable to Bakhtin's point that all signs have meaning by participating in existing dialogues. The ability to detect a family resemblance which may arise when a character is made up from features of several different real people, for example, is crucial to the function of signs. Character is foregrounded in naturalistic television drama because its scale means that it tends to focus on the actions of individuals and small groups rather than large-scale social action which would not affect us as deeply as in the cinema. Television drama rarely if ever attempts to show a scene such as Eisenstein's famous depiction of a crowd of people mowed down by soldiers like cattle in the film *Strike*.

From these fundamental aesthetic features, McGrath draws the conclusion that naturalism's attempts to establish empathy through close ups of emotional moments is futile. Instead he advocates an emphasis on narrative, 'on seeing what happens rather than being drawn into the emotions of the characters'. In Brechtian fashion, his own television drama can tell a story powerfully by unconventional means which owe little or nothing to naturalism and authenticity. This fits neatly with Brecht's disapproval of the classical theatre's attempt to engender sympathy rather than rational reflection.

McGrath's other comments on the failure of television dramatists to use the full 'language' of television and his approval of Troy Kennedy Martin's remarks, imply that he does see the importance of representing the emotions of individual characters and attempting to reveal the inner reality of the mind. This cannot be achieved by narrative alone. The error in the reasoning here is that the fact that the television image retains a certain aesthetic distance all the time, does not mean that it cannot create empathy with a character. The classic example of *Cathy Come Home* is one where it can be argued that the very distancing of the audience from the characters' plight is exactly what created empathy. It was not necessary to identify with them to feel their anguish at the loss of their home. The empathy here was, however, based on a rational disapproval of the social policy which gave rise to the situation. Emotions and reason were allies. There is an elision of the two processes of identification and empathy which produces a challengeable conclusion in McGrath's article.

The television image can be distinguished not by its ontology but its semiology. The television image in naturalism is one which is a tripartite sign: it encompasses all three functions of icon, index and symbol, but it can only be seen as one at any one time. Witgenstein calls the sudden perception that a line-drawing can be seen as two things, both a duck and a rabbit, for example, as the 'dawning of an aspect'. Furthermore he states that, 'The expression of a change of aspect is the expression of a *new* aspect and at the same time of the perception's being unchanged' (Wittgenstein, 1951:196). This would help to explain Bakhtin's concept of 'reaccentuation' where the same sign can be given an entirely different meaning. The semiotic functions here are analogous to the 'aspects ' of visual perception which Wittgenstein describes.

The image is iconic by definition. As a piece of naturalism, it must resemble reality. It is indexical in that it shows one set of people but their conditions of existence can be generalised to apply to a larger section of the population. The wives of all philandering Conservative MP's are partly characterised by Paula Milne's drama. Thirdly, the image, as argued above, is often also symbolic at the same time as apparently offering no more than a simple copy of reality. The symbolic dimensions are really semiotic aspects: the three meanings defined by Barthes all apply to the semiotic function of naturalistic images. Such images either signify something by reference to a code, or signify within the drama that a certain aspect of the plot has unfolded, or compose an entirely new sign which locates and highlights a new meaning. Each of these three aspects implies a certain critical distance on the part of the viewer rather than the passive approach which has been argued to describe much television. The iconic image is at least compared with reality and can be criticised for any departure from naturalism. The indexical or metonymic image can be criticised if it appears too difficult to abstract a generalisation about a wider social group from this one example. The symbolic aspects are, of course, subject to various debates and varieties of interpretation.

When John McGrath somewhat cynically remarked to an audience at Cambridge that 'television watching is a frame of mind' (McGrath, 1981:110), he was referring to the uncritical attitude which viewers might take to the images they are presented with. In fact, television drama viewing might well be a frame of mind, in that it is a particular aesthetic attitude. The attitude which ensures that a drama is viewed as communication of messages, rather than a simple portrayal of reality, is the attitude which remains conscious of the triple sign. This position, however, is not without its theoretical issues. As Erdinast-Vulcan (1995) remarks, the problem with Bakhtin's theory of signs is that it presupposes a subject who is the ultimate manipulator of the signifying systems and is not constituted by them, a transcendent subject. How the subject can do this is a contested matter.

Robin Nelson, for example, cites a number of characteristics which would give the appearance of naturalism but not necessarily the consequences which McGrath describes.

(1) uncensored imitation of human behaviour.
(2) telescoping of events and other manipulations of plot.
(3) the conveying of information by implicit as well as by explicit means, entailing slow development.
(4) a style of acting and production which does not overtly acknowledge the presence of the audience.
(5) inclusion of the trivial, the commonplace,the inessential, the irrelevant. detail, employed to further the illusion that the audience is seeing life and not an artefact.
(6) dialogue written in the way people really speak.
(7) the reproduction on stage of real locations.
(8) the employment of real properties and the wearing of authentic costumes.
(9) representative characterisation which, by economic deployment of detail, implies individual life. (Nelson, 1997:105)

The above characteristics do not necessarily imply that a television drama will automatically adopt an extreme determinist position. It is inevitable, however, that a naturalistic production will use the style to make aspects of social determination clear. Brecht himself did not denounce Stanislavski's methods out of hand. In fact he gave a list of features of Stanislavski's naturalistic acting which he endorsed, including, 'the representation of reality as full of contradictions' (Brecht, 1964:237). The epitome of McGrath's 'new drama' for television was *The Cheviot, the Stag and the Black, Black Oil* (1977), which, in Brechtian fashion, mixes naturalistic performances with factual offerings about the exploitation of the Highlands by the English. The problem of confusing the naturalistic actor with a social factor is avoided by separating the functions of informing and acting. McGrath's complaint that in naturalism, 'every statement is mediated through the situation of the character speaking, mediated to the point of triviality', is a condemnation of the way in which an individual is meant to bear symbolic significance. His solution was to divorce individuals from the primary role of mediating reality.

John Caughie wrote some time ago, 'But naturalism in any kind of historical sense is something more than a form, a mere absence of style, or a looseness of narrative: it has served within a politics of radical humanism to introduce into the social histories of theatre and literature, at certain points in their histories, an element (the working class, women, social justice) which had previously been excluded' (Bennett *et al* eds, 1981:338). Naturalism established itself as a concept and a style which dealt in revelation. Since the days of *Cathy Come Home* the expectations aroused by the genre are that an untold history or an unspoken problem will be exposed. This has little to do with the fundamental *concept* of naturalism and more to do with its use in British television practice.

Raymond Williams describes 'critical naturalism' as 'an inherently critical form' because 'it showed the world as unacceptable by showing directly what it was like, and then how impossible it was when people really tried to live in it' (Williams, 1973:393). Williams is here echoing the views of Bertolt Brecht in whose *The Messingkauf Dialogues* the dramaturg says,

> ...certain social movements did have their roots in naturalism and it works. The audience was brought to see a whole lot of social conditions that couldn't be tolerated – to feel that they were intolerable, I mean. Teaching in state schools, the restrictions preventing women from gaining their independence, hypocrisy in sexual matters – these things and many more were held up to criticism. (Brecht, 1965:24)

The conventions of naturalism are often not apparent to an audience that sees it as transparent, but Williams maintains that both realism and naturalism are reducible to sets of conventions at any one historical moment. There is no especial virtue in either form. Where a naturalistic drama takes a familiar situation and explores its possible future ramifications, it can easily be accused of a lack of realism, but the potent social criticism of realism is just as possible in the naturalist form. Both Brecht and Williams argued that the noble aim of drama was 'to tell the truth'. McGrath has, however, produced a list of features which he argues should be manifest in any serious writer of television drama, and this challenge is still not taken up by contemporary examples – whether that is because of the demands of the television authorities who require quick financial returns, or because the list is too daunting, is a matter for debate:

> 1. analyse the real nature of television communication and the processes of material and ideological production.

> 2. intervene in the situation in order to challenge the stifling 'TV naturalist' form which reduces the world either to a small bowl of emotional stew, handed out in weekly dollops, or to a series of criminal acts, performed by deviants who end up shot by our hero, or led off weeping to the loony-bin.

> 3. re-assert the possibility of forms in television which do allow a small degree of theoretical thinking into the act of creation and communication, which allow for a world-picture that involves the working of the human mind rather than the automatic operation of convenient prejudice.

> 4. create vigorously and well, with an awareness of the limitations of the medium, in such a way as to command a deeper response from a popular audience.

> 5. use words, images, ideas with a historical awareness as well as an awareness of the audience.

6. create a world where events have reasons, where the past determinations of the present are shown in all their complexity, and the present's determination of the future is seen as a series of human choices.

7. enrich the audience's awareness of the possibilities of humanity, through play and imagination as well as through work, through communication and community, as well as through solitary achievement. (McGrath, 1981:114)

This is a programme for a materialist television, and many of its commendable insights can be demonstrated in the following study.

Part Two

Textual Analysis

The Politician's Wife: A hypothesis within a recognition

In *The Politician's Wife* the use of naturalistic techniques demonstrates vividly how sexual hypocrisy and the repression of women's independence can be shown. The drama won a BAFTA award and this was undoubtedly in part because it is clearly a rejoinder to current events which introduces the viewers to a dialogue. The first half of the drama is a rejoinder to current events in the news, and the second is a *counterfactual* which is thereby recognised as a hypothetical extension of the situation characterised in the first. The second half asks, 'what if...?'. This is in keeping with the theatrical practice of Stanislavski, who encouraged naturalistic actors to arouse certain emotions and to speculate on how they would react. The first half of the drama is a pastiche of various Tory ministers and their scandals which remains within the boundaries of a recognisable naturalism, and the second half shows the consequences of a situation we have not previously encountered. Overall, the drama is an utterance with a specific intention, which is to call into question the behaviour of contemporary Conservative politicians and to address the passivity of their wives. At the time of writing, the first example of a wife of a famous politician standing for government has occurred in the United States in the person of Elizabeth Dole. Hilary Clinton has also begun an independent political career. These facts illustrate how Greenblatt's 'circulation of culture' operates.

Uncritical naturalism was simply the faithful, photographic reproduction of reality, with no underlying sense of purpose discernible to the audience. As Brecht's figure, the Philosopher remarks in *The Messingkauf Dialogues*, when it comes to the 'laws which decide how the process of life develops, 'These laws can't be spotted by the camera' (Brecht, 1952:27). In other words, the underlying social forces cannot be represented in the shot alone. Content analysis cannot reveal realism at work, since it relies on a particular relation to reality and formal criticism of a faithful reproduction of reality will not detect this.

103

In 1992 David Mellor, who was then responsible for the Conservative government's policy on the media, including newspapers, was discovered to be having an affair with an actress. In response to the press coverage, he agreed to pose with his children, his parents-in-law and, of course, his wife at a five-barred gate at the entrance to 'Thistle Cottage' in order to present an image of solidarity and to counter rumours that his marriage was in difficulties. The scandal was the first of many such cases which were hailed by the press as example of 'sleaze', or moral corruption. The Tory MP Alan Clarke's wife appeared on television during this period to discuss her husband's much-publicised infidelities and to explain her resentment and toleration. She also defended her husband and spoke movingly of her loyalty to him even under the most publicly-humiliating circumstances. The wives of many disgraced Tory politicians during the last Conservative government remained loyal to their husbands and so saved their careers. This and many other aspects of the Conservative government's behaviour is alluded to by Paula Milne's *The Politician's Wife*.

The first part of the drama acts as a rejoinder in that it represents the political image-makers as cynical and conniving. The drama is a perfect example of a simulacrum in that it could almost be a factual account of the life and morals of a conservative minister, although it is, of course, fictitious. The first half of the drama is composed from various news stories about unfaithful Conservative Ministers. This tactic ensures that we recognise the veracity of the representation we see. The second half, however, speculates on what might happen if a Conservative wife chose to fight back, which has not happened as yet. In this sense the second half is suggesting what if something had happened which we know did *not* happen at the time. The fact that the second half is counterfactual and we know this to be the case, means that it can propose a radical alternative to the current state of affairs where Conservative wives stand by their husbands and subordinate their own needs to his career. This is the 'hypothesis within a recognition' as Williams terms it. What is of great interest in the drama is the process by which the cynical manipulation of the news leads to a resurgence of integrity and dynamism by the wronged wife.

The Politician's Wife begins with a paradigm example of dialogism which is, moreover, accentuated by the production. The opening of the drama presents a television screen on which the politician's wife is speaking about her first meeting with her husband at Cambridge where he was speaking on penal reform. She is wearing a drab brown plaid outfit with a long skirt which comes down to her ankles and a hairband. These clothes connote a highly conservative personality and conform well with the outmoded style of many Conservative politicians. The grainy image signifies that we are watching her on television. A self-satisfied smile also signifies that she relishes telling the story of her first encounter with her husband. The camera then moves to one side and we see that the screen is, in fact, a monitor on a camera in an actual television studio. The politician's wife is speaking to young people in one of the familiar television programmes where celebrities answer questions from a studio audience. Soon the camera zooms out to show us the studio where the discussion is taking place and eventually the camera where the crew are monitoring the screen image which is broadcast. In positivist semiotics, the zoom out signifies context, which is true here (see Cowdery and Selby, 1995) but it also has the function of revealing a fundamentally important aspect of the plot. The essence of the appeal of this type of interview is the frankness and intimacy which it generates. The wife is attempting to present a monologic voice in Bakhtin's terms. The monologic voice gives the impression that it is the sole source of authority which can speak on the subject. Thus when a woman speaks about her first meeting with her husband, for example, it must appear that she is the sole source of knowledge and her words cannot be challenged. Monologic utterances conceal their dialogic aspect, however, in Bakhtinian theory. The camera moves smoothly between the wife's three audiences for her words: the television public; the studio audience of young people; and the television professionals in the studio. As it does so, the sequence of shots reminds us that she is addressing three audiences simultaneously. She must appear sincere to the audience, professional to the studio and reliable and endearing to the public.

The primary dialogue is between the wife and the children. We, the audience(s) are the superaddressee: we are the real intended hearers of this conversation. Bakhtin's theory of communication is that in speaking to another person we are really speaking for the benefit of a third person who may overhear the dialogue, the superaddressee. In listening to the wife's ways of dealing with innocent questions we hear evidence of her sincerity and professionalism. The camera moves back, however, to incorporate the frame surrounding this image and to emphasise its grainy quality. Then the signified is that we are watching a television programme. We occupy the position of three types of audience: the naturalistic audience for a politician's wife on television; the studio audience of young people; and the media professionals who are appraising her performance. We are reminded of the constructedness of the television performance when, in a separate brief shot, the director signals that the show has to be 'wound up'. The final fleeting image is of the wife sitting in the studio at a distance with the television screen displaying her image in close up beside her. The relatively large size of the screen image as against her studio person, is also a sign: the ultimate persona she is adopting here is, perhaps, the media figure she creates and not her 'true' self.

This analysis reflects what McGrath states when he argues that in naturalism 'every meaning is implicit and ambivalent' (McGrath, 1977). The reliance on semiotics here to emphasise the theme of the drama is seen by McGrath as a difficulty, partly perhaps, because it does not permit the didactic introduction of facts counter to the naturalistic style. It may be, however, that an increasingly media-literate age will come to identify the function of these signs and to follow naturalistic drama by incorporating their understanding of signs into the overall pattern of discourse. It is the signs which demand an active and creative viewer, whose role is to do more than decode. Decoding can be a mechanical process involving audience activity but little independent thought. As Barthes says of Eisenstein's films, they are not polysemic: the meaning is always the revolution. Decoding Eisenstein's montage is largely a question of divining his intentions. It has become commonplace in media theory to contrast the active viewer who has to puzzle out montage from the passive viewer who does not question the pattern of signs offered to them. In reality, however, signs such as these enable naturalism to maintain its style and yet to problematise its meaning in a way which requires thoughtful consideration. Whereas the politician speaks his mind and reveals his most intimate motives in his behaviour, the wife is often inscrutable and silent. The wife's subjectivity is represented in more than words, since she also participates in a number of scenes where the actions she performs are, as McGrath says, 'ambivalent'. It is at these semiotic moments that the drama creates an imaginary: a further realm beyond that which is shown to us which we can only conceive of. In this case, we are never absolutely sure what is happening to Flora Matlock and we have to construct our own version of her motives in order to derive a coherent narrative.

Perhaps the most revealing part of this brief opening dialogue is the claim she makes that the wife was attracted to her husband by his 'moral base'. This is clearly preparing her for a shock when news of her husband's infidelity reaches the national press. It is clear that at this stage she regards herself as the willing helper of her husband who is prepared to subordinate her own needs to his. This is a very conventional relationship where the husband is credited with all the insight and vision and the wife's purpose in life is to serve him. Flora Matlock, does indicate that she is not entirely passive, however, when she reveals that she did originally correct her husband's address to the Cambridge Union on one or two factual points.

The opening is followed by a short scene where the camera is hand-held and follows Duncan Matlock's aides as they race through the parliamentary office to deal with a crisis. Flora is alerted by telephone that Duncan is coming home to his country house unexpectedly. The press are hounding the family. The hand-held camera is a device taken from documentary, which as John Caughie says, gives the impression that we are watching factual television.

Duncan Matlock returns to his country home with his chief aide. They discuss the cynical manipulation of the press and it is clear that their sole intention is to play down the story of Duncan's affair with another woman which has just broken. The aide shows the politician a *Mail on Sunday* story where his wife was interviewed on the possibility of her husband's unfaithfulness. We see a newspaper picture of Flora which instantly recalls her television appearance. As he comments, 'Thank God one knows better than to believe everything one reads in the papers'. The media persona of Flora Matlock will be exposed as suffering from a delusion, but her husband pays scant regard to the effect on her image or her feelings. The scenes which follow the opening establish a clear internal dialogue between Flora's public statements and the reality. The structure of the drama has been established as the relationship between these two themes.

Duncan Matlock confesses to his wife that he had an affair at the party conference, and she is distraught. The minister is thoroughly determined to suppress the story and to avoid any serious consequences for his career. He is 'Minister for the Family'. One feature of the many revelations which challenged the last Conservative government in Britain was the dignified silence which many wives kept when the news of their husband's unfaithfulness was announced. Wives generally did not indulge in soul-searching in the media. It is made clear that Flora's compliance is essential to the successful manipulation of the press campaign in defence of Duncan Matlock. The ultimate impression will be that the family has experienced a painful moment but has not suffered any great damage. In the drama, we see how the male members of the cast successfully manipulate Flora by appealing to her conscience. The facts we know (the silence of the wives) are explained by a coherent set of motives which are invented for the fiction. Flora's father counsels her to accept that infidelity is the price that she has to pay for marrying a man of her husband's distinction and that she is the key to his future. Flora and Duncan take a photo-call reminiscent of David Mellor's. This moral blackmail is bitterly resented by Flora, but she succumbs to the pressure and agrees to present a public image of family solidarity. There is agreement that if Flora 'holds fast' then the public relations battle for Duncan's reputation and career can be won.

As the party chairman's wife telephones to offer moral support, plaintive music begins. The music acts as a sign that the theme of the drama is echoed again. It underscores the re-appearance of the politician's unfaithfulness. The naturalistic evidence begins to mount that Flora recognises the dependency which others have on her. She has always answered her husband's letters to constituents and her father expected her to be part of the victory when Duncan became party leader.

Flora is not naturally inclined towards self-sacrifice, but she allows her altruism to be manipulated. Shortly after this, Flora unbuttons her night-dress and examines her breasts as she kneels in front of the fire. This is a sign, but one which needs to be interpreted in the light of the drama. The sign may imply that she is considering and evaluating her own sexuality, which has been denigrated. The symbolic value of this action encompasses many of her anxieties about her role as a woman and illustrates how fundamentally troubled she is. This action comes shortly after her father says that he is not sure where she gets her strength to endure these trials from. The action of regarding her own breasts can also be read as a dialogically-related sign. It is Flora's answer to this remark. The strength derives from her nature as a woman and her love for her family, including the children who were nourished by her breasts. It is only later that we learn that she and Duncan had made love in front of the fire shortly before the scandal of his affair broke. This endows the sign with retrospective significance. Within the drama, the sign signifies a questioning of the nature of their sexual relationship.

As the narrative proceeds, however, we see Flora listen to the tapes of telephone conversations between Duncan and his lover. These reveal the fact that he is lying. Duncan's parliamentary colleagues assert that he has told the truth, which enables Flora to see the depth of their lies. It seems to be inevitable, however, that Flora has to accept rather more than a subsidiary role. Not only does she have to resign herself to maintaining a pretence, she also has to remain quiet while she is blamed for 'marital problems'. We are not given any insight into the reasons why Flora chooses to endure this burden once she realises its full extent, yet she does accept the role of faithful wife. In order to comprehend the narrative we have to imagine her motives. The use of signs to signify Flora's internal state call for an imaginative reponse by the audience. A woman smoking a cigar, for example, is not a sign which we automatically refer to any detailed code. It may mean many things, but here it seems to signify that Flora is assuming her husband's position and 'masculine' behaviour. Television drama can incorporate an imaginary element such as this because it does not explain such moments, but instead leaves us with an unencoded sign, an example of *signifiance*, that needs to be interpreted in the dramatic context. The women who attend her husband's parliamentary surgery to ask for the nursery to remain open, bring Flora a bunch of flowers which the children have grown. This is again a sign of their sympathy for Flora which is dismissed by Duncan Matlock as a cynical attempt to get what they want.

Duncan's lover appears on television to discuss the affair in a programme which is reminiscent of 'Richard and Judy'. Here she reveals some details of Duncan's sexual proclivities. This is a direct allusion to similar examples from the real Tory Party. David Mellor, for example, became a laughing-stock because it was claimed that he liked to make love wearing Chelsea football kit. In Duncan's case, he likes to play a submissive role in bed. The lover blames this on his wife's inclination to be submissive in sexual matters. The lover also makes it clear that she believes the sexual relationship in marriage is all the more intense the greater the love between the partners. This is public humiliation for Flora. When she and Duncan are next in bed, she mounts him and hits him wildly. Duncan is aroused by her frenzied activity and grasps her firmly. He then makes love to her from behind in a passionate declaration of love, during which he seizes her breasts. Immediately after this incident, a tousled Flora attempts to open one of the minister's parliamentary red boxes, but cannot. Instead she takes a cigar from a smaller wooden box, allowing her wedding ring to be foregrounded in the shot, and smokes it quite naturally as if she has always smoked cigars.

Whereas the Politician's feelings and motives are always expressed verbally, Flora's inner turmoil has to be understood through signs. In the context of the drama, these signs develop a poetic significance, in that they become metaphors for certain attitudes and situations. When Flora smokes a cigar, she is clearly asserting her attempt to adopt or usurp the masculine role. Post-coital smoking may be a sign of detachment from the sexual act which she has taken part in so vigorously. Such signs are not examples of positivist semiotics where they signify a social fact. Instead, they respond dialogically to other previous signs within the drama, to show that character has changed. In Barthes' narratology, indices are signs of character, and the nature of the sign is determined by the character type. Character, in other words, is pre-determined. In *The Politician's Wife*, character changes as Flora adapts to the situation. The signs we see determine our understanding of her character rather than interpreting an already-formed character. In this drama the poetic semiotic narrative permits change within a naturalistic mode of delivery.

Duncan is able to demonstrate how unreliable words alone are. In his speech to the Conservative Association for the Family, Duncan gives a superb example of 'spin-doctoring 'when he presents a marvellously rhetorical speech defending himself. Words give no sure indication of character because they can so easily be adapted to create a rhetorical effect. As Marx once said, we do not judge a man by what he says of himself. The insincerity of Duncan's speech is signified by the cut to his two aides who are watching anxiously from the wings as he addresses the association.

The second episode opens with another television interview with Flora Matlock. On this occasion, we see three monitors with two images of Flora and one of her interviewer. Flora is answering questions about her reactions to her husband's affair in a very direct and frank manner. The opening scene again pans slowly through the studio to show the actual setting for the interview, but on this occasion, we see only one person speaking with Flora. This is dialogically related to the opening of the first episode. It invites a direct comparison in order to construct a symbolic reminder of how the poetic narrative of Flora's personal development has continued. Here Flora is seen to be much more honest. The conversation is addressed to one speaker only, but its dialogical relations are far more extensive. Her husband is seen watching the programme and expressing his admiration for her staunch defence of him. The very fact that Flora is speaking by herself and not as a member of a team, however signifies her growing independence. When she alone is framed in the television shot, it has come to signify that she is not now attempting to satisfy a number of audiences simultaneously. She may be defending her husband but she does so on her own terms. In addition she is issuing a rejoinder to Jennifer Caird, her husband's lover, by arguing that her husband's affair was the result of extreme stress and was not an emotional involvement at all. This directly contradicts Jennifer's statement on television earlier that the quality of a sexual relationship reflected the quality of an emotional commitment.

When Flora encounters Jennifer in the toilets at a restaurant in the House of Commons, she asks her whether she believes that what separates humans from animals is that humans have a conscience. Jennifer retaliates by arguing that perhaps the distinction is that animals do not repress their primal urges. The debate here is of direct relevance to naturalism. Flora answers that conscience could also be a primal urge.

Flora is attacking the idea that the sexual relationship between her husband and this woman could be construed as the satisfaction of natural instincts, and whether her own moral inhibitions are, in fact, sexual inhibitions. Naturalism would tend to suggest that such sexual liaisons are the inevitable product of circumstances such as extreme work pressure and close proximity to temptation. Flora herself has, in fact argued this on television. If so, however, then all moral anxiety is futile. Naturalism tends to make morality seem redundant. Such things will happen. Flora retaliates that perhaps conscience is also genetically determined and that one day scientists might isolate it and enable all of us to have a conscience. Then, she says to Jennifer, 'We will be equal'. The rejoinder to Jennifer's statement is that if she is determined by uncontrollable factors to express her sexual nature without restraint, many other women are not and that those who have a conscience are also determined by nature but on a higher plane. To have no conscience gives this woman an unfair advantage in seeking sexual satisfaction. This is a reminder to the alert viewer that we should not find the naturalism of the drama to provide a complete exoneration of the adulterers. What one woman's nature dictates is not thereby a universal law for all women. Here the dialogue foregrounds a debate which could have taken place between the writer and a producer, for example, and almost becomes a metafictional comment. Whether Flora means that the addition of a conscience would bring Jennifer up to her level or enable her to compete for Duncan with Jennifer on equal terms is an ambiguity which is left open. Audience reactions to this are not predictable as in montage. Life is unbearable for Flora because she is made to bear the blame for a situation which was not of her making, and guilt follows.

Paula Milne, has spoken of the attempt to avoid 'agit prop' in her writing (Day-Lewis, 1998:111) by not clearly espousing a partisan viewpoint. Flora is someone we are intended to sympathise with whilst realising that she is a 'dyed-in-the-wool Tory'. Her politics are irrelevant at the early stage of the drama. The realist process which Paula Milne states that she was trying to represent was the one whereby women's 'sexual anger becomes political'. Although much of this drama is subject to the criticism which John McGrath made of television naturalism, it does not seem to be radically undermined by this. McGrath is concerned mainly with naturalism's inability to make the didactic elements of drama explicit. The supposed passivity of an audience may mean that the drama therefore becomes entertainment but not education and McGrath's Brechtian mission fails. The television drama aesthetic, however, does entail an element of the imaginary. The audience can be supposed to be familiar with recent current affairs by virtue of being a television audience. This means that they can be presented with the fragments which are known about a public scandal and will recognise them. The television drama is able sometimes to make the known facts coherent by filling in the gaps with the private events which explain them. Thus television drama's aesthetic is to make our public world more coherent by explaining its consequences for individuals and groups which remain hidden from the public. To do so with a didactic message is to invite obedient reactions, but to do so with an ambivalent figure such as Flora is to leave open the question of whether the representation is accurate. We, the audience, have to imagine whether the private lives of such individuals are as they appear on screen. It is not the naturalistic details on screen which we evaluate, these always look convincing. Instead it is the relations between the private and the public moments which we judge. Would Flora have been a sexually repressed woman who took pleasure in becoming a more assertive lover? The relation between sexual aspects of the personality and public behaviour is dialogical and therefore remains open for us to reflect upon.

When Flora Matlock discovers an item of black lace lingerie in her husband's filing cabinet at their London flat, she is clearly moved, but this does not provoke a strong reaction. What does create the 'pregnant moment' is when she discovers that her husband has failed to table an item for the council agenda on the closure of a local nursery as planned. Flora's reaction is here dialogically related to her personal feelings, as the women campaigning for the support of the nursery have shown her a gesture of personal kindness. When Flora was suffering from the indignity of the press revelation of her husband's infidelity, they brought her a small posy. It later transpires after Flora asks that the children have picked the flowers from the nursery garden. Flora phones her husband and asks to speak to him but is told that he cannot answer any calls. She informs the respondent that it is his wife but the woman tells Flora that there are 'no exceptions'. Flora has braved all the humiliation so far for Duncan, but when she passes on the message that it is 'urgent constituency business' and is ignored, this is the turning point.

Flora has agreed to swallow her pride to act in the best interests of the party, but when her husband refuses to acknowledge her valuable role as his advisor on constituency matters and fails in a moral duty as well, she cannot forgive him. The absences, 'memories, lessons, promises,' as Barthes calls them have clearly determined this action. The hypothesis of which Raymond Williams speaks, is given here: treated in such a manner, this is how the wives will react? Flora tolerates Duncan's faithlessness because she believes in the values of the party, but when Duncan cannot even live up to the moral integrity she says she married him for, then this is the time that she can no longer justify her own self-denial. There is a brief cut just between the moment when Flora receives the refusal to answer her call and her decision to call the press. At this point, from Flora's perspective, we see a wheelchair campaigner in the front line of the demonstration against the nursery closure. Her immediate reaction is to phone the local paper with a story for them. News of Duncan's failure to save the nursery as promised hits the headlines. The change of heart seems to be precipitated by the courage and commitment of the campaigners which is callously betrayed for political ambitions. The brief montage provides a further moral justification.

With this action Flora takes sides against her husband. This is the beginning of a treacherous campaign which is just as devious as Duncan's. The pregnant moment is the one where she will not accept the indignity of having her contribution to the party treated as if it were worthless. This recalls all her past treatment and looks forward to her future behaviour as a Machiavellian political figure. Flora is called upon to address the Conservative Christian Wives association, and in doing so confronts many of the women who opposed her husband's continuation as an MP.

In a superb rhetorical flourish which again shows the power of words on television is not to be underestimated, she sways the meeting to her side. Her argument is that she has had to set aside her personal feelings for the sake of the party and so should the women present. The solid defence of the party, she argues, is what matters most. The argument recalls Duncan's speech on the Family and even echoes many of his phrases and strategies. The action becomes a sign that Flora can deceive just as well as her husband. Within the drama, it has a unique meaning which has numerous echoes.

Flora's motives are not articulated, nor does she 'emote' incoherently as McGrath describes the action of many naturalistic dramas. She plans a deliberate campaign to shame her husband into acknowledging his moral duty. Her state of mind is shown in a number of signs which the audience cannot decode but must interpret imaginatively. Dressed in a new outfit, she listens to the tapes of her husband's conversations with his mistress and seems self-possessed. At one point, however, as she dresses in a much more careful manner she seems to be considering her personal attractiveness. As she looks into the mirror, in anguish, she smears her lipstick over the reflection of her lips. This sign is multi-accented, but seems primarily to signify her distaste for the superficial manner she has to present to the external world as she plots her campaign. The act of smearing the lipstick on the mirror can mean that she does not wish to wear the disguise herself and externalises it: she finds the act of 'dressing up' repugnant. Her new-found political behaviour involves deception and appearances. The action also partly suggests that she has been made to feel that she needs to imitate her husband's mistress. She cannot wear the lingerie he finds arousing without becoming like Jennifer Caird. It is an act of bad faith, and therefore prevents her from attempting to rekindle passion for her husband by this means.

Following the story of the nursery, Flora encourages her father to buy a large house called Pangbourne Manor. This results in another scandal as Duncan is blamed for selling the house to a member of his family at a knock-down price via one of his companies, Onshaw Insurance. This appears to be a compromising position from which Duncan cannot escape, but in a speech to the House of Commons, he asserts that the purchase of the house was to provide a nursery for the people of his constituency. Flora, assisted by Duncan's personal assistant, who leaked news of his affair to Flora, sets out to catch Duncan in a final plot. Duncan is planning a piece of legislation which will eliminate Child Benefit and privatise the service. Again, this could be seen as a pr-emptive rejoinder to existing Conservative legislation by the writer. It is an opportunity to debate a move which was certainly possible at the time of this administration, and to discredit it.

Flora deceives her husband into believing that if he dropped his bill on the abolition of State child benefit, he will be given a Cabinet post. She also tells Sir Donald, the leading Conservative that she 'can't reach him' when she asks for his compliance in dropping the Bill. The same phrase is used by Flora when she is speaking informally with the women who run the threatened nursery: 'I just can't reach him'. This ambiguous sentence is repeated to signify that she is assimilating her personal relationship with her husband and her political dealings with him. In both cases he is too egocentric to comprehend what Flora puts to him. Meanwhile she invites Jennifer Caird to stay at a nearby hotel to discuss the lifting of parliamentary exclusions against her. This is a trap, as the Press are then invited to photograph what is represented as another secret liaison between Duncan and Jennifer. This is the final nail in Duncan's political coffin and a divorce ensues when Flora reveals that she has leaked the information to the press.

Throughout the drama, the atmosphere of the piece is one of judgement. The viewing audience are continually aware of a moral question and are enabled to take up a position on that question. Colleagues and students who watched the drama on its first screening were highly conscious of its condemnatory rejoinder to the behaviour of men such as Duncan. As with many obvious rejoinders, however, its evaluative aspect is not clear. This is where the audience have some freedom to consider Flora's behaviour within the parameters defined by the writer and the production's utterance of them. This drama is not didactic as Eisenstein's films are, nor does it disappear into a morass of openness where all manner of interpretations become feasible. It is a calculated response to a well-defined situation which means that interpreting it as a rejoinder may be up to the audience, but only within certain rational limits. Is it advocating Flora's behaviour or demonstrating how she too is corrupted? Alternatively, is is really above this question of blame and attempting to make a more elevated moral point about the virtue of responding to justified anger? Is it a means of interpellating women to act as their consciences dictate and not in bad faith? Is it a seditious onslaught in preparation for what was then the forthcoming general election? The possibilities outlined above belong to various practices which can be recognised within our uses of television: agit-prop, preaching, moral philosophy, for example. The semiotic approach which has been outlined above argues that only within these recognised practices and in relation to the historically-identified situation can any valid interpretation be made. Even if we accept these constraints, however, there are still many ways of interpreting the ideological inclination of the rejoinder. Is Flora's behaviour preferable to allowing Duncan to continue? The question cannot be answered definitively, but it is clearly opened and the audience tend to have a clear opinion.

This is a drama which does encourage the viewers to overcome any initial prejudice established along party lines and to focus on the issues. It shows the possibility of changing the situation in which a woman finds herself by decisive action. New possibilities are opened up. In cultural terms, however, this is

British drama and Paula Milne refused the opportunity to produce an American version on the grounds that it was too rooted in British political life which an American audience might not understand. This fact demonstrates how closely the naturalism is related to its context.

Critical Naturalism:
Big Women

*B*ig *Women* is a historical account of the Women's Movement based on the lives of a group of feminists from the early 1970s to the present. It is a television version of the book published in 1998 with the sub-title *Big Girls Don't Cry*. This pop song title from the sixties is an ironic reflection on the history which the drama relates. As Brand points out, 'Drama provides a context in which we can judge what music is 'saying' (Brand, 1998:9). Originally written to mean that women should not indulge in frivolous behaviour, after seeing the drama, it signifies that the high-profile women of the sixties and beyond were remorseless in their pursuit of their goals. The drama was produced by Tariq Ali. He is, therefore able to remember the early days of organised feminism in its revival in the late 1960s.

The drama begins with a naturalistic montage of 1970s life: flared jeans, tight-fitting t-shirts, the mini-skirt and the mini-car. The characters are dressed to recall an authentic impression of 1970s 'taste'. Music from the period is used to add an ironic reflection on what we see. The major social event mentioned is the *Oz* trial which the Australian visitor, the clean-cut Brian, stops to read about while visiting a typical 1970s bazaar. The Oz trial took place in the summer of 1971. This was a trial for obscenity of an 'underground' magazine which featured a cartoon of Rupert Bear having sexual intercourse. This trial was second only to the Lady Chatterley trial in the history of obscenity actions. As the philosopher, Richard Wollheim, then Grote Professor of the Philosophy of Mind and Logic at the University of London, and an expert witness, argued, it was really a lifestyle that was on trial. Unlike today when moral pluralism seems to be regarded as a fact of life, such developments as feminism were subject to close moral scrutiny. It is difficult in the contemporary world to imagine some accepted positions were regarded as so extreme that the debates were about whether women had any right to live this way at all.

Brian remarks that the two main female characters 'don't even walk like women'. The rhythm of the opening scenes is a bouncy and fast-moving pace which is reflected in the way that the women walk purposefully to their next destination. The music, 'Power to the People' gives the scene a buoyant momentum which signifies that they are engaged in a socially progressive movement. Layla and Stephanie, the two women featured in the opening scenes, are seen fly-posting the slogan 'A woman needs a man like a fish needs a bicycle'. This is again an authentic allusion to this period which was familiar at the time. The Australian couple, Brian and Nancy who are visiting England on a back-packing holiday, are used as a device to allow us to hear the contemporary views of the non-political members of society. Naturalism manoeuvres the narrative conveniently so that vital contextual information is conveyed without conspicuously drawing attention to the fact.

The women's meeting gathers: Layla (described by Fay Weldon as a 'liberal'), Stephanie who works in advertising, Alice the intellectual, and Zoe, a graduate, wife and mother. Zoe is openly chastised by Layla for her lack of revolutionary zeal. Zoe replies that 'I have a point but you won't listen. I have a degree in Sociology'. Zoe signifies the kind of woman who was not a separatist feminist, but who wanted her marriage to 'Bull' to survive and improve. There were, broadly speaking, three main kinds of feminists at this period: Radical Feminists who wanted to live without men; Marxist Feminists who wanted to liberate the working-class and everyone else; and liberals who wanted equality with men, not to exclude them. In the friction between Layla and Zoe we see the divisions within the Women's Movement. Zoe as a liberal feminist, is looked down upon by her sisters who are more radical and also oppressed by her husband who has no notion at all of women's equality. She is marginalised and silenced. Layla, however, is also a heterosexual woman who has affairs with men and is not a separatist. In ideological terms, she is represented as a liberal because she is concerned about her own pleasure. She is a liberal in that her own interests as an individual come first. She despises Zoe for a lack of self-centredness. The gathering is what was called at the time a 'consciousness raising' (Fay Weldon, 1998:24) where the women who attended would be encouraged to come to conclusions about the nature of their oppression. The intention was to enable all present to achieve the same degree of enlightened feminism.

This is where the contradictions in the women's behaviour begin to show. Alice states that the voices of women have been silenced and enjoins the group to 'speak out', but when Daffy protests that she cannot speak in front of men, without developing a high voice, she is rebuked. This demonstrates a contradiction: they protest about the silencing of women's voices but they do not allow each other to speak. The result is that Daffy, who likes men, goes to bed with Hamish, the husband of Stephanie while the women meet downstairs. Layla next shouts at Zoe's child, asking her to shut up and asks why the child is there at all. This is a particularly misguided remark for a woman who is attempting to understand the plight of women in general, of course. Retrospectively, this will be seen as a sign of Layla's gross insensitivity, since the child in question, Saffron, grows up to be a 'big woman' in publishing herself.

The editing of the scenes at the beginning is crucial in signifying the nature of the rejoinder. The technique used to foreground the contradictions is overlapping dialogue. Alice, the theoretical thinker of the group is giving a lecture on Marx's concept of praxis. The voice of Alice, which is deliberately teacherly and somewhat patronising, is heard as Daffy and Hamish embrace and undress. The irony is that as Alice speaks of theory and practice coming together, Daffy and Hamish are having sex.

If 'praxis' means orgasm in Victorian pornography then both meanings are illustrated here. The editing makes Alice's words doubly ironic: the theory is that women achieve solidarity, but in practice some follow their own desires. The divorce between theory and practice is signified, since Daffy believes in sisterhood, but acts otherwise.

Intercut with these scenes where Daffy 'betrays' her sister feminist, however, are shots of Brian and Nancy the Australian couple in the youth hostel. Nancy is singing 'Greensleeves', a romantic ballad, but Brian dismisses this as 'a cat's chorus'. Here we see what Alice meant: Brian is silencing a woman in the way that Alice describes. In a Brechtian gest which conveys the male attitude of an entire generation, he hands his socks to Nancy, holding them at the toes like a pair of fish and tells her to wash them as he will need them in the morning. This act of giving the distasteful garments to the woman he professes to love, provides the essential motivation behind the scene. The editing here signifies 'balance'. If the previous scene made the Women's Movement appear ridiculous, this one redresses the situation by showing the kinds of male behaviour which provoked women to act.

When Nancy asks Brian to sleep with her and behaves seductively, he refuses and argues that only 'bad girls' have sex and go on the pill. He believes in the traditional gender stereotypes and tells Nancy that men are the predators and women the prey. This statement is again a contradiction, since Brian does not show a predatory streak. He has placed the onus on Nancy to subscribe to the ideal he believes in. Instead of attempting to seduce Nancy, he wishes to retain her 'virtue'. It is at this point that Nancy concludes to herself after repeating the slogan that 'a woman needs a man like a fish needs a bicycle', that she will leave Brian. Nancy has used the slogan to liberate herself from an unsatisfactory relationship, and this balances the implicit criticism of the Women's Movement in the previous scene with Daffy. This is a small but significant 'pregnant moment' in which we see the beneficial effects for Nancy of recollecting what she has seen and looking forward to a life of her own. The moment of decision crystallises the problem and focuses on its solution.

Layla is contemptuous of the women who are not as aggressive as her. She argues that they want role models or 'big women' in the movement to show others what is possible. This title is dialogically related to the novel *Little Women* by Louisa M. Alcott, and draws attention to the historical changes in women's history. In this sense the drama does attempt to show the human potential for changing circumstances. Fay Weldon does not simply want to attack the Women's Movement. On the official Fay Weldon Homepage on the internet, Weldon says that she is not making fun of the movement, merely 'telling what happened'. The rejoinder here is aimed at a specific audience who may be able to recognise such contradictory behaviour. Whereas *The Politician's Wife* assumes only a knowledge of current affairs in the media, and therefore addresses a potentially vast audience, *Big Women* requires some knowledge of the events we see parodied. If the two types of behaviour: one stern and theoretical, the other passionate and devious are both recognised as naturalistic in that they did actually happen, then the contradiction is evident and the dialogue entered into is one between the writer and the knowledgeable viewers.

Alice states the contemporary orthodoxy that 'men own the means of production', in an attempt to marry Feminism and Marxism. Fay Weldon has written a number of provocative articles in which she has expressed the view that men should be pitied in the wake of the feminist changes which have taken place in the time span of this drama. In an article entitled, 'Pity Poor Men' (*The Guardian* Tuesday 9 December 1997), she expresses the view that women were indeed cruelly treated until the Women's Movement began to create a reaction. The tables have turned, she argues, and that it is men who are now unable to prevent themselves from becoming victims. Weldon almost responds to her own character when she writes, 'It is true that men own and control what used to be called "the means of production", but the glass ceiling begins to shatter below the age of 40'. Barriers to promotion, in other words, are beginning to disappear.

The author argues that the Women's Movement was not about vengeance but justice. In this sense she aligns herself with the ideological position taken by Zoe. Layla's cruel taunts against her sisters are clearly designed to be an ideological criticism of women who attempted to argue for some form of rapprochement with men. Zoe is ridiculed for suggesting that swearing alienates males. In an apparent attempt to turn a cultural tide begun by the politically active women of her generation, Fay Weldon famously stated in *The Times* in June 1998 that 'Rape isn't the worst thing that can happen to a woman', and was roundly condemned for suggesting this. To many women, she became a 'Mandela' figure: someone who had led the revolution but then sold out and became a charlatan. A further article in *The Independent* was needed to apologise for the vitriol that was stirred up and to confess that the author did not have any clear intention. Weldon's rejoinder is more of a rhetorical posture, asking the question whether women used the feminist movement for their own ends. In trying to understand the precise nature of the rejoinder to feminism, we are perhaps sifting the evidence she has provided rather than exploring a clear denunciation.

The events of the drama seem comic now, but Weldon claims that she is not laughing at the pioneers of the Women's Movement. It may be the fate of all pioneers in any struggle to be extreme and ridiculous with the benefit of hindsight. Hence we have the comic scene where Alice is describing praxis when at that very moment we see Daffy and Hamish in bed. The editing here is clearly intended to draw a parallel between the two events. Hamish says, 'Feminism will never work because all women are traitors'. Stephie storms out of the house when she finds Daffy has been treacherous to her with her husband. She does so stark naked to signify that she takes nothing of her old relationship with her. Later Layla sleeps with Hamish betraying two sisters and reverting to the very attitude which she attacked Daffy for in the first place. Alice says 'Oppression has made sisters of us all' just as the editing shows us Layla discovered in bed with Hamish. This shows that there is no loyalty amongst these women and undermines what Alice is claiming. Feminism didn't succeed in creating solidarity amongst all these women against the 'common enemy': man.

It is not only the feminists who are funny, however. Brian the Australian is also hilarious. He represents the most conservative viewpoint of the day. Nancy decides to leave him just after we hear him say that men are the predators and women the prey. In fact, he has refused to sleep with Nancy which contradicts his vision of men as 'predators'. He is full of contradictions. If men are predators yet he wants women to be virgins when they marry, this does not seem to be realisable. Nancy leaves at the moment that we hear this contradictory statement. This is an example of the way in which naturalism can present us with more then one view of the causes of human behaviour. The precise reason why Nancy goes is not given. We have to imagine a reason for her, although the causes are clear. This shows that McGrath's statement that naturalism defends the *status quo* need not be true. Weldon believes that she is only 'presenting what happened' and allowing people to make up their own minds, not showing a causal sequence which we accept uncritically. This is therefore a criticism of men's attitudes at the time, although it is not made absolutely clear.

The womens' decision to form a women's publishing house is celebrated by dancing naked and drinking. Layla initiates this naked dance by stripping off her clothes to celebrate her nature as 'woman' and enjoining the others to follow suit. This is an allusion to the ancient Greek playwright Euripides' and the myth of the rites of the Bacchae, women who held orgies of naked sex and wine at which one man was torn to shreds by his mother for spying on them. Bull appears to claim his wife Zoe, and is outraged at the goings-on. This man is not attacked by the women, but the consequences for his own life which follow in future episodes are catastrophic. By alluding to the Maenads, the women demons, the contrast with the actual women's movement is made clear. These modern women are toothless and nowhere near as dangerous. Men do not escape the blame, however. Bull is a pig if ever there was one and his actions are unforgiveable.

The example of the public controversy about Fay Weldon's statements on rape, shows that the accentuation of an utterance can be misunderstood both by the writer and the audience. In the case of the statement on rape, Weldon's retraction shows that the semiotic power of the statement exceeded her intentions: whatever she wanted it to mean, society dictated what its effect was. As a rejoinder to the complaints about rape, it seemed heartless, not progressive. The scene with the women dancing naked was an example of how the paratext of a television drama can focus on controversial elements to create publicity. Jon Dugdale in *The Guardian* (Tuesday 30 June 1998) wrote that he found it 'troubling' that Daniella Nardini who played a highly assertive woman in the television drama, *This Life* should be asked to appear naked. He felt that this casting might simply be a cynical attempt to appeal to sexual motives. The pre-publicity which advertised this fact enabled viewers to dwell on prurient reasons for watching the drama, instead of understanding its dialogues. The practice of television drama created another dialogue between the programmers and their publicists and the viewers, in which the sign of Daniella Nardini naked is simply the gratification of prurience. Fay Weldon might have been exploited for this end. Ever since the days of *The Wednesday Play* on television in the 1960s, television drama has served one ulterior purpose which is to be in the vanguard of moral change. Nowadays there is a very heated dialogue about sex on television which seems to be about the right of television companies to exploit sexually stimulating shows.

Layla is a woman who espouses individualism under the auspices of feminism, and the drama shows how her selfishness is gradually realised as nothing more than this. The nude scene is one where the precise accentuation might be easy to misunderstand. The publishing house which the women plan to create on this evening is very similar to Virago, the feminist publisher which followed a comparable path. Virago also decide to publish the classics of women's writing which had disappeared. Carmen Callil, the woman who led the establishment of Virago, however, has been quoted as saying that she took no offence at Weldon's portrayal of her comparable character however, and that such events did not take place. In terms of naturalism, then, this episode is not meant to reproduce the historical events of the 1970s so much as use them to establish a hypothesis. The hypothesis is about the long-term effects of Layla's type of self-indulgence. Fay Weldon is well-known as a television dramatist for *The Lifes and Loves of a She-Devil* and this genre is quite unusual, since it was a fantasy, close to 'magic realism'. The revenge of a slighted wife was powerfully presented in a non-naturalistic manner as the wife transformed into a devil. The drama is a sympathetic rejoinder to the women who have suffered rejection like the central character, and acknowledges the existence of their anger. It is a means of externalising an emotion common to many women which has not otherwise been made quite so public. The central character therefore displays real emotions in an unreal narrative. Other historical narrative dramas such as *Our Friends in the North* have taken an allegorical style. The final reconciliation between man and woman signifies perhaps the growing strength of women in New Labour. *Big Women*, however, is not allegorical: its characters do not correspond to characters who actually existed. Instead they signify extreme types who are recognisable and the series dramatises the consequences of the stances these types adopt.

Layla can be read as moving subtly from a naturalistic figure to a symbolic one. As such she has to compete with other female icons in contemporary television drama. One other significant female character is Ally McBeal, the eponymous young lawyer of the series, whom Weldon describes as 'a powerful self-righteous, whimpering bitch'. Ally McBeal seems to represent the epitome of extreme liberal feminism, in that she believes in self-fulfillment at any cost, but also appears to be exploiting a 'girlish' manner. She is an amalgam of some of the most potent ideas of feminism and what Weldon calls, 'sadomasochistic male fantasy'. She is vulnerable to a degree, but her independence can seem to require a callous response to men's emotions. She can demand justice yet live to be exploited, thereby neutering any valid aspect of her political posture. Self-respect, it seems is the price of her self-realisation, and this is a desperately cynical conclusion. It is a calculated guess that Fay Weldon prefers Layla to Ally McBeal.

This is the existing dialogue on the contemporary woman who has lived through feminism and has negotiated her own position within society to incorporate it. Layla is powerful and self-righteous, but does not exploit femininity in order to achieve her ends. She may be an unrepentant individualist, but she at least has the courage to defend this stance. As such she is distinct from both the she-devil, who is pure revenge, and Ally McBeal who is a commercial compromise designed to appeal to both male and female viewers. Layla is discovered in bed with Hamish by Daffy, and both Daffy and Stephanie demand that she be 'excommunicated'.

It is a sign that Hamish is wielding a chain when he is first seen. The chain is used to make the pine tables he sells look older. Alice quotes Rousseau (believing it to be Marxist) when she says that 'Men are born free but everywhere they are in chains'. Hamish protests that there are more important things than feminism. He is tied to a harsh proletarian job. The problem for the feminism shown here is that finding independence only began women's problems. What do you do with freedom and how do you avoid exploiting others when you have it? These are the questions which the drama poses for the social dialogues of the day. Fay Weldon has become famous for speaking out about what she believes is the harm done to men by feminism.

Fay Weldon, however may believe in 'the end of ideology', the view that there are no longer any ideologies such as Marxism or Feminism which explain everything and which we can live by. The pregnant moment which is pivotal to the narrative of the whole drama is the suicide of Zoe in the second episode. Zoe has written a book on the plight of the graduate housewife, but Bull is adamantly opposed to her writing and her involvement with the Medusa collective. He is also convinced that her work has no value. When Stephanie phones to say that Medusa is interested in publishing the book, Bull lies to Zoe and tells her that they do not want to publish it. He then burns the manuscript despite Zoe's desperate pleas. History can be seen as comprehensible in the light of this action. Such an action does not reflect a genuine event, and therefore constitutes a rejoinder to the historical situation. It expresses what the women in Zoe's position felt like: how they were equally frustrated but unable to win the sympathy of either their husbands or their allies in feminism. The action is a complex sign which also signifies that a certain strand in feminism was silenced. It creates a response rather than reflecting what was happening.

Thus when Zoe kills herself, to avoid showing only one reason, the drama has everyone quite naturalistically, (but unrealistically) offering an explanation for Zoe's suicide at the funeral. Layla arrives late after having been to bed with Hamish and interrupts the ceremony to give a short paean to Zoe, the 'bright star'. Layla, however, blames Zoe for being weak. Stephanie continues, however, by blaming patriarchy for the suicide and exonerating Zoe completely. It is said that her husband 'diminished her'. Daffy, however, continues the dialogue by arguing that the Medusa Collective was responsible for not publishing Zoe's book and for alerting Bull, her husband to the fact that she was writing. Bull leaves at this point signifying, perhaps, that he does not wish his guilt in this matter to be revealed, and the priest objects to the interruptions. Nancy, has a different viewpoint: she claims that Zoe was caught in a double-bind, unable to leave Bull because of the children and her inability to earn very much, yet deeply unhappy. Alice then takes up the cause and argues that Zoe was weak. Her gender prevented her from fulfilling her proper place in society, yet she could not struggle against this. Alice wants Zoe to become a source of righteous anger to 'shape the world'. The final interruption comes from an anonymous woman who confesses to having had an affair with Bull which caused Zoe's suicide.

Each person present gives a reason why Zoe killed herself which conforms to their personal ideology: Layla's individualism, Stephanie's feminism, Daffy's essentialist arguments for the inescapable nature of women, Alice's revolutionary Marxism, and the anonymous woman's simple jealousy. All seem plausible enough. It may even be possible to regard all the explanations as credible, but irreconcilable in practice. This event in the narrative signifies that a pluralist explanation is ruled out by the ideologies prevailing at the time. A monocausal approach to Zoe's death is avoided and no one explanation is offered as the most likely. This approach has its historical precedents. Strindberg wrote in the preface to *Miss Julie*,

> The motivation of my plays is not simple and real life is seen from more than one viewpoint. An incident in real life is usually the result of a whole series of deep-buried motives but the spectator usually settles for the one he finds most easy to understand, Someone commits suicide. 'Bad business', says the businessman. 'Unrequited love' say the ladies 'Bodily illness', says the invalid. 'Shattered hopes' says the man who is a failure. (Strindberg, 1888, republished in 1976 : 93)

Naturalism avoids the uncritical representation of the *status quo*, yet it does remain within character. Even when naturalistic events take an unprecedented turn as in the suicide of Zoe, they must do so in keeping with the character so far established. As Aristotle remarked, even inconsistency in character must be consistently inconsistent.

The naturalistic approach which presents a number of shocks of recognition in conflict, ensures that McGrath's criticism of naturalism that it presents the current state of affairs as inevitable, offers a very strong case. The next event where the characters have the chance to exercise their choice in determining their future is when the Medusa Board meet to discuss their future. When naturalistic drama wants to represent the process of choice, it finds a naturalistic moment when motives and reasoning are spelt out. In episode three, set in 1983, Saffron, Zoe's daughter, has shown herself to be one of Thatcher's children by developing an entrepreneurial approach to life in general and she becomes the editor of a women's journal. Her manner is abrupt and decisive. She brooks no dissent and she is ruthless in her plans to modernise the traditional journal by eliminating aspects such as the embroidery page. Saffron does not do this for ideological reasons, however, but because it is better business. She is, however, emotionally involved with Medusa since she recollects the establishment of the enterprise. When she recollects the nude dancing scene it is shown through a fish-eye lens and tinted in the colour saffron to signify that we are seeing her perspective. Layla's harsh words are also remembered. Each character now develops into an alternative fashionable stance on political events. Alice, the Marxist philosopher becomes an 'earth-goddess'; an alternative belief system sustains her.

The next pregnant moment comes when Medusa discusses the action to take over their financial problems. The two alternatives are to sell the publishing house to a male millionaire or to find a replacement for Layla. Layla proceeds to pronounce a brutally frank judgement on the remaining members of the board which makes it clear that they are not capable of following in her footsteps. Layla is a 'big woman': she alone had the determination and vision to maintain a small publishing house, whatever her personal characteristics. Through devious means she and Zoe collaborate to acquire 51 per cent of the shares from men friends and vote in favour of selling, which is in their financial interests. The existing women members vote against the sale but Layla and Saffron between them have the advantage and the sale goes ahead.

The drama as a whole has as its theme the consequences of feminism for the contemporary generation. It is an utterance which is a rejoinder to the contemporary women who have lived through the same circumstances of having been born, like Saffron, out of them. The social practice is one of self-justification in that Fay Weldon is making her views seem all the more credible by dramatising the origins of them. The text's narrative plays out the long-term consequences as Fay Weldon sees them. Saffron is pictured briefly in a news photograph with Peter Mandelson: she has something of the spirit of 'Blair's Babes' about her, and this is an up-to-date allusion to successful career women. What is crucial, however, is to assess the accentuation of this concept.

As Saffron enters Medusa, she collects a copy of her late mother's book, *Lost Women*. This is perhaps a prophetic title, but the fact that Saffron shows this amount of interest signifies some emotional attachment. Her motive for taking over the publishing house may not be entirely mercenary. As Layla is cruelly deriding the talents of the other board members, Saffron is seen to have a faint smile which seems to be a look of admiration. Thematically, this is highly significant in that if this is the accentuation we read into the sign, then Saffron, the successful career woman of today, is identified with Layla's brand of self-interested individualism. This is a damning comment on the legacy of feminism if it is taken in this manner.

The character of Layla, however, is that of a 'big woman'. The phrase resounds with meaning. It is dialogically related to the emergence of prominent women in society whose motives may be questionable, but whose presence is not ignored. The second episode is contextualised with a poster of Margaret Thatcher and her unforgettable line, 'the lady's not for turning'. In semiotic terms, there is no code for the precise phrase ' big women', but the series has shown what it takes to become such a person: it has created a signified. The term ' big' is not neutral but it does not condone or condemn the women. 'Great women', for example, would have been too emphatic. 'Large women' might have sounded too pejorative. The signified of the phrase 'big women' is of a woman whose presence obtrudes on her social scene whether she is admired or not. 'Big women', like Margaret Thatcher are known for their personality first and foremost. The phrase taken in dialogue with the drama has identified a new aspect of our culture more carefully. Layla is not taken from a stock range of signs which constitute 'contemporary women'. The sixties pop song, *Big Girls Don't Cry* concludes each episode and emphasises another aspect of Layla's character: she is unrepentant about what she has done, who she has upset, her inability to have children and her lack of a permanent relationship with a man. She does not regret what it has taken to achieve what she wants. All the other women on the board do cry. Layla's absence of regret is also a sign. The character of Layla has a touch of the Nietzschean drive to self-determination, however, in that she has learn to succeed by apparently taking control of herself.

'Morse Code' and its Successors: *Morse*, *Cracker* and *Fitz*

Morse

In the episode, 'The Wench is Dead', Morse is ill in hospital and cannot go to work. He displays a natural passion for justice in his attempt to solve a murder which happened in the nineteenth century to while away the time. The allusion to Marlowe's play, *The Jew of Malta*, where the lines 'but that was in another country, and besides the whore is dead', occur, signifies that the expected reaction would be that the murder is not worth investigating. The issue of gender is also raised here, since Morse's detection often involves a negative attitude towards women. The passion for detection is assimilated with a passion for justice, but the innocent dead woman receives little consideration. His instinctive wisdom is driven by a desire to see wrongs righted, although the drama does not end with a posthumous pardon for the innocent men who were hanged, but the detection of the actual murderer, as if this concludes Morse's interest. At a convention on the history of crime, Morse reveals to the author of an academic historical work on crime in the nineteenth-century that he knows exactly who the last man to be hanged in Oxford was and the date: 1863. Furthermore, he becomes convinced that Dr Van Buren, the woman who has written the book, is wrong in her assumption that the men hanged were the murderers. The camera shows us a Victorian toy in which a small figure of a man is hanged inside a model jail just as this exchange takes place. As a sign this both echoes the talk of the Oxford Canal Murders and also presages Morse's sudden illness which follows.

Morse's trade could almost be described as forensic semiotics: he is adept at understanding what apparently unrelated clues signify. Morse's approach, however, is humanistic in that he solves the murder by continually questioning his suspects' motives. His approach is to piece together the actions of the participants in terms of their rationality until the entire event is reconstructed. His ability to construe human motives acts as a moral lesson to all those around him, especially his new police assistant, the graduate trainee, Kershaw, who also has a degree in History from Oxford. The drama as a whole can be construed as a rejoinder to those who would reduce the human to a set of statistics or probabilities such as might happen in a historical account or in offender profiling. When Dr Van Buren muses that the Victorians were probably better judges of human nature than us, Morse disputes this. The ability to solve a crime so remote in history is a test of the universality of human nature and vindicates Morse's method in general. It is proof to him that fundamentally, everyone acts for the same kinds of reasons. He also states that Oxford has too many academics and not enough policemen, which shows clearly that he has a fundamental antagonism towards the academic community.

Whereas the signs within the text are all highly conventional and would easily conform to an analysis by signifier and signified, the actual status of the text as an utterance makes the significance of the drama much more complex and debatable. This is how the apparently unambiguous 'Morse code' can be shown to be more complex. As Shaw and Vanacker write, 'In opposition to real life, the detective's world is semiotically fully determined; every clue is significant, pointing towards the eventual discovery of the criminal and the exculpation of the innocent' (Shaw and Vanacker, 1991:15.) The fact that even the music is acknowledged by the composer, Barrington Pheloung, to contain clues, is a further sign that everything has a definitive meaning determined by the drama-makers, which in this case includes the composer. The social practice in which Morse is engaged now is a vindication of 'common sense'. As Shaw and Vanacker comment, 'In the classical detective novel of the inter-war period, the hitherto passive reader is invited to search along with the sleuth: democracy comes to the detective story' (Shaw and Vanacker, 1991 :15). The series is to some extent dated in that it constructs the viewer as someone who can apply the same intelligence as Morse himself and thereby vindicate the same principle.

The Oxford Canal Murder was the case of the killing of a woman identified as Joanna Franks while she was travelling from Coventry to London on a barge to join her husband. The body of the woman was found in the river. Witnesses saw an unidentified man walking along the riverbank, but the man called Don Favant was never found. There were four people on the boat: three men and a boy, but only the three men were charged with murder and two executed. Morse checks the price of travel by the stagecoach and discovers that the barge represented very little saving and took far longer. The history of the incident also recounts that Joanna alighted from the boat at one point to complain about the lewdness and drunkenness of the men on the boat to an official of the company. Despite this, however, she returned to the boat and continued to drink with the men. As Morse muses on these anomalies, the historical scene is interposed and we see a recreation of the events of the murder. This re-enactment is accompanied by plaintive violin music which then signifies that we are seeing the past each time it recurs.

Although the drama appears to the viewer to be monologic in that it presents and justifies the opinions and values of Morse alone, it operates in two principal ways. On the one hand we have the words and insights of Morse himself, and on the other we have the visual re-enactment to compare with his guesswork. As the drama proceeds, the alert viewer can see how Morse's theories are confirmed. Despite the authoritarian stance of Morse, some gaps remain to allow the audience the pleasure of participation in the reconstruction.

Morse is puzzled, for example by the fact that a charge of rape was dropped against the men. Kershaw manages to locate Joanna's actual trunk in an archive in Oxford and her 'drawers' are found in it. The undergarment has been cut in an apparent attempt to 'gain entry'. With the help of a forensic scientist, however, Morse discovers that this cut seems to have been deliberately made with a knife rather than as the result of a tear. He formulates the hypothesis that the boy on board had been offered a deal to testify against the men and that he had stolen from Joanna and therefore wanted to keep this quiet. The scene on the barge allows us to see what actually happened. At one point the boy is seen emerging from the hold where the woman is sleeping and he is asked by one of the men ' have you been havin' her?'. It transpires that Joanna, as we later see, has probably seduced the boy and has asked him not to tell about her. She secretly disappears from the boat one night unknown to the other men on board. Morse is therefore not quite right in his supposition and we, the audience are enabled to see how a clever hypothesis is not entirely accurate. There is a dialogue between the re-enactment and Morse's words: they do not fit perfectly together, and this makes us the 'superaddressee' in Bakhtin's terms, the third party who overhears a dialogue between two others and appreciates the combined meaning of statement and response. In this case we appreciate the distinction which Todorov finds in his analysis of the detective story between the two elements: the story of the crime and the discovery of the culprit. These two narratives are distinguishable and enter into dialogue with each other. The pleasure associated with this genre, therefore, lies partly in the fact that we are not merely overwhelmed by Morse, but also in a superior position of knowledge where we can evaluate the characters and their surmises.

Shaw and Vanacker refer to a 'semiotic hierarchy' in the classical detective story where there are several cadres of agents trying with increasing degrees of success to solve the crime. At the lowest level are the historical characters who blunder into executing the wrong men. Next in the hierarchy is Dr Van Buren who makes a more sophisticated defence of this conclusion. Morse is above her with a superior conclusion and we and the authors of the drama finally see how all the characters have fared in the act of detection. This means that the viewers are enabled to participate in the dialogue of forensic semiotics which Morse plays out. The satisfaction may well come not from guessing the solution so much as feeling at one with the process and understanding it fully.

One surmise which Morse uses to good effect in solving the crime, however, is that of the sexual behaviour of 'woman'. One of the questions which he asks is why a 'respectable' woman would return to the boat and continue drinking with the men. We see an image of Joanna drinking and holding the bottle high up in a clumsy manner to drain every drop. This immediately corroborates Morse's suspicions, since it signifies a lack of 'respectability'. The fundamental premise behind Morse's thinking is that the murder displayed signs of being a woman of low virtue, but this is never stated openly. He does, however, state that 'the key to the whole mystery is what kind of woman was Joanna Franks'. The title of the episode recalls the play, *The Jew of Malta* and a very similar quotation is used by T.S. Eliot at the beginning of his poem, 'A Portrait of a Lady'. Dr Van Buren accuses Morse of using his instinct in the case and even his ' sexual instinct'. This is a dialogic interchange which exhibits the way in which a formal property of the text can be multi-accented. The dialogic meaning of this rejoinder to Morse is that he may be relying on an outdated view of women's morality. This relates directly to a modern audience for whom a notion of womanly virtue such as this would be vastly out of date. At one level it is an intra-textual rejoinder to Morse's antiquated gender politics. In terms of the genre of detective fiction in history, however, this is a rejoinder to the various 'rules' written by practitioners of detective fiction in the 'golden age' of democracy. One of the foremost rules was that there should be no reliance on intuition or coincidences or any leap of imagination which could not be reached by the audience. This extra-textual dialogue temporarily casts doubt on Morse's method and raises the issue of his contemporary relevance. When Morse's reference to women's morality is ultimately shown to lead to the detection of the crime, however, he is vindicated and the audience can share in a certain smugness that Morse is able to think beyond contemporary ideology. From our position which we share with Morse in the semiotic hierarchy, we are able to see the short-sightedness of a contemporary opinion. The real viewer is the superaddressee here and is encouraged to comprehend a further dialogic meaning which is concerned with the naïvety of Morse's critics.

By searching the records of the insurance companies with the aid of Kershaw, Morse discovers that Joanna had taken out a life insurance policy which her tearful husband cashed for a large sum. The solution to the murder is that Joanna's husband had murdered another woman and once her corpse was discoloured, he had dumped the body in Joanna's dress in the river. To the witnesses it appeared that Joanna had been killed but she had swum ashore and disappeared. The man seen at the crime scene was her husband waiting for her. The boy had been seduced and sworn to secrecy. The other major clue was that her shoes were left behind on the boat as if she had left unwillingly but they did not fit the corpse. Morse explains his theory to Dr Van Buren but she remains unconvinced and unable to exhume the body, he is forced to give up.

It is sometime later that Morse suddenly realises who the woman was. In her trunk an old music-hall poster was found advertising the stage show of a music-hall magician, The Great Donavan to whom she was previously married. When Kershaw visits the Oxford archive where the trunk Joanna carried is still kept, he finds the initials 'FTD' inscribed on it. It is at this point that Barrington

Pheloung begins to lay clues in the music he has provided. As we know from interviews with him, the composer 'lets the audience know in some sort of musical code who the killer is' (Brand, 1998 : 60). The initial few bars of the plaintive violin music consists of nine notes which are all given the same accentuation: no one note is emphasised any more than the others. The name Don Favant, also contains nine letters. As the music is played over the scene of opening the trunk, however, the phrasing changes to emphasise the first, fourth, and the ninth notes. The violin stresses these notes much more forcibly. These notes correspond to the nine letters of Don Favant's name and draw attention to D, F and T. Morse is completing a crossword clue to which the answer is 'Don' when the realisation of the name-swapping strikes him. In this scene the poster found in Joanna's trunk advertising The Great Donavan is shown on the wall and the music playing again emphasises the notes at the same points. Charles Franks, Don Favant, and FT Donavan were the same man. This is a moment of perceptive intuition.

Morse travels to Bertnaghboy Bay where he discovers that the coffin of The Great Donavan was, in fact, empty and had been weighted down with stones. The scene immediately changes to a flashback. In a music hall where Donavan the magician is performing, he is locking his wife, the woman assumed to be Joanna Franks, in a large wooden box only for her to escape. Morse infers that the man and his wife collected insurance money on two occasions: when Joanna was supposedly murdered and when Donavan supposedly died. Dr Van Buren has previously told Morse that she feels he has a lively imagination and should write novels. A detective, she tells him, like Dickens, is 'a great conjuror'. Both Morse and Donavan have, therefore, been competing to offer the world an interpretation of the facts which are public. Both men wish to have public acceptance of their interpretation.

When Morse has the grave of FT Donavan dug up, he opens a wooden box and appeals rhetorically to his audience, his partner, to accept that he has solved a mystery. Just as a conjuror reveals his trick to a sceptical audience and can only rely on their credulity, so too Morse can only be satisfied with the knowledge that he was probably right. The instinctive detective cannot ultimately convince the determined empiricist in the shape of the historian who will demand conclusive evidence. Although there is a sense of closure in the narrative, Morse's supposition remains a hypothesis which can still be doubted.

One curious example of *significance* is the fact that as the grave of Donavan is exhumed, Morse has to buy whisky for the diggers. The camera takes in these three full bottles which feature prominently in the scene as the grave is dug. The camera frames the bottle briefly to establish their status as signifiers. Although there are two diggers, there are three bottles, which also makes them significant due to the excess of meaning. The number three is perhaps intended as a poignant reminder of the three men who were executed for the murder. This sign echoes the whisky which Morse is given by his male boss in hospital, but is not allowed to drink by the nurses. Dr Van Buren also refuses to give

Morse alcohol. It is also related dialogically to the drink which 'Joanna Franks' consumes aboard the barge. The feeling expressed by Lyn Thomas that 'Morse, despite his appearance, is breaking through boundaries of gender and genre' (Thomas, 1995 : 9) is perhaps emphasised here. The women in the drama are opposed to drink, which has connotations of Dionysus and intuition through intoxication. Morse's 'feminine' intuition is seemingly enhanced by strong drink. Alcohol as a sign is found in many scenes and as Barthes says of the third meaning, it 'structures the film differently without subverting it' (Barthes, 1977 : 64). The fact that Morse pays in whisky to solve the murder aligns him with the men who were condemned because drunkenness was a sign of immorality amongst bargemen. This sign associates Morse with the very people he has tried to judge at a distance and estranges him from the women in the drama who attempt to keep alcohol beyond his reach. Such small details illustrate that the code can be broken in the sense that it can also be opened up to semiotic analysis in its cultural context. Morse both crosses a gender divide by adopting an intuitive approach and also reinforces it by creating a new difference. This does not overturn the main narrative, but it introduces a new strand of gender definition and sexual antagonism. Dr Van Buren is perhaps correct when she accuses Morse of using his 'sexual intuition', yet the fact that he appears to solve the crime 'justifies' his sexism.

Cracker: Reflective naturalism

John Simons points out that the factual accounts of forensic police work which have been published share many of the characteristics of detective fiction (Simons, 1990). The character of Fitz in *Cracker* is based on a real forensic psychologist, Ian Stephen, who actually works with convicted murderers and makes predictions of the kind which Fitz attempts. Stephen describes how his technique involves empathy, or sharing feeling with the perpetrator, but that he also refuses to avoid condemning the horror of the crime (See Crace, 1994). Robbie Coltrane had extensive consultation with Stephen and they even wrote an article published in *The Psychologist*. Ian Stephen felt that the collaboration helped to raise the image of the profession. The naturalistic approach to the drama involved making sure that the actual details of the forensic method were followed so that the drama seemed authentic. The police advisor, meanwhile, threatened to leave when Fitz was allowed to interview a suspect and browbeat him, since this was against the Police and Criminal Evidence Act which governs the interviewing of suspects.

Fitz, has a body of specialist knowledge to bring to the solution of the crimes he is involved with which the public could not possibly be in possession of. His art is in applying this knowledge to come to conclusions which are evident to the public but which they could not reach independently. As in semiotic analysis, the results can be clear once reached, but the method is specialised. In one sense, therefore, the detective figure has apparently reverted to an earlier age when the detective was superior to the audience. *Cracker* also confronts the human but with the phenomenon of offender profiling very much in mind. This is a much more effective means of establishing guilt and it does not necessarily need to refer to motives. Motives emerge as the means of 'cracking' the suspect and gaining a confession, not arriving at his guilt. The contradiction in *Cracker* is that the practice of offender profiling seems to rely on objective factors such as statistics which imply that the offender can be characterised by the social circumstances which formed him, yet the actual cases are always located in a much more personal cause. The social practice which the *Cracker* series participates in might be called 'collective therapy'. When particularly traumatic incidents occur such as vicious murders, the actual public reaction is one of horror. Explanation of the cause fulfils the need to enter into dialogue about the incident as in trauma therapy and the need to express feelings. It also serves the purpose of reassurance that the incident was caused by an abnormal psychology and that such dangers do not lurk inside every person or every home.

The curious aspect of an *Inspector Morse* drama is the fact that we see very little sympathy for the victims: the two innocent men who were hanged and the murdered woman. Barthes uses the terms *studium* and *punctum* to distinguish between the intellectual recognition of the artist's intentions and the emotional effect of a small detail. The *punctum* is absent in both *Morse* and many other contemporary detective dramas which are concerned only with catching the culprit. The *punctum* 'pricks' the viewer: it provokes an emotional reaction which is difficult to account for or identify. In studying photographs, Barthes observes that some details strike him with a deep significance but he struggles to put this into words. As he writes, 'The *studium* is always ultimately coded, the *punctum* is not' (Barthes, 1993 : 51) The *punctum* often derives from a small incidental detail which signifies some deeply personal emotion that cannot now be clearly identified. In this drama, an example of a small detail which could be described as a *punctum* is perhaps the Victorian toy which, when activated, stages a hanging outside a model of a Victorian prison. The small wooden figure is shown in close focus as he plunges through the trapdoor to his symbolic execution. This is a disturbing sequence and one which has no clear convention to decode it. In what Barthes terms 'the blind field', the unseen events which must precede or follow the image, someone has activated the machine for the amusement of the guests. The lives of the men were considered to be of little value because boatmen had a bad reputation, but they were not exactly executed on a whim. Some aspect of the savagery of execution, however, is conveyed by this. It is also possible to read this as the trivialisation of the hanging. In a detective story it becomes a mere detail of no great significance.

The *Cracker* episode, 'To Be a Somebody', is an example of a drama which does disturb the viewer and demands that the issue of murder be confronted *as a murder* and not merely a problem to be solved. The final murder is a protracted affair which is harrowing to watch. The sociological function of collective therapy here is merged with a debate about social justice. A series of murders is committed by a man who is seeking to avenge the deaths of innocent people in the Hillsborough football stadium disaster. The social practice of therapy is linked with the familiar practice of protest at the alleged refusal of the authorities to accept blame for the disaster. This drama surpasses critical naturalism as it has been described by asking whether we can excuse any behaviour by the victims of unbearable circumstances in society. If a situation is found to be unbearable, then what next? How should we respond? We not only see how a certain person was driven to extreme behaviour, we also see his justification for a vengeful response deconstructed. In the *Cracker* series, we have an ideological stance adopted which suggests the political theory of communitarianism: the individual is partly determined by environment and partly free to choose how to respond to it. The individual has both rights and social duties. Showing how his views and behaviour are formed does not excuse them. This is something more than critical naturalism, in that it not only proposes a hypothesis about how the righteous feelings of trauma survivors might be perverted, but it also enters into a dialogue about the morality of their hypothetical response.

Inspector Morse, for example, shows only the process of detection and is satisfied with an ending once that is completed. The *Cracker* series is based on the ordinariness of the criminal and the need for human motives to be considered. Whereas offender profiling regards individual motives as almost irrelevant, in the *Cracker* dramas. motive is everything. Fitz is fascinated by people's motives. 'Motive' for Fitz, however, does not mean 'reason'. In *Cracker*, the motive is not just a desire for material gain, and therefore a reason for committing the crime, but a psychological justification: the deep causes of the perpetrator's need to seek this kind of gratification. Offender profiling reveals many serial killers to be very ordinary people who are attempting to aggrandise themselves, to turn themselves into a social sign by committing a crime for which they become famous.

This drama is a variety of protest at social injustice, namely the tragedy at the Hillsborough football stadium in 1989 at which 96 people lost their lives. The writer of the *Cracker* series, Jimmy McGovern also wrote a docu-drama simply called *Hillsborough* in 1996 in which the families of the victims expressed their outrage at the tragedy both during and after the incident. This drama was broadcast at a time when the families were fighting a campaign for the police officer allegedly responsible for herding the fans into an already-overcrowded enclosure, to be held responsible for the deaths. The broadcast coincided with the campaign to have the inquest verdict recorded as unlawful killing. As Derek Paget observes, 'Transmission of *Hillsborough* occasioned a renewal of the debate about compensation for the families of victims' (Paget, 1998 : 207). The drama *Hillsborough* dramatises the inquest and the personal consequences for the families of the dead. It is a harrowing experience to watch this drama and its success has been acknowledged with a number of television awards. The broadcast therefore was an utterance in the campaign against the refusal by the authorities to accept blame. In an interview for *The Sunday Times* Jimmy McGovern is reported as saying that the drama was 'a challenge to the perceived view of the tragedy, questioning the role of the police and the manner in which previous enquiries had been conducted' ('Getting into Hot Water', *The Sunday Times Magazine* Sunday 7 September 1997 p 56-58)

Albie, the anti-hero of this drama, is therefore not simply another serial killer. In this drama he acquires a new significance. He is also the bitter spirit of vengeance which may have infiltrated the families and others in their anger. The intention of the drama seems to be to show how people might behave if they are treated in this manner but also to warn that this does not justify taking revenge. It is a rejoinder to the police response which expands on the possible social consequences of allowing this kind of anger to build up. The rejoinder might be put in simple language as 'by denying justice you may create more crime'. The rejoinder may have several different audiences, however: the police, the families of the dead, people in general, and even the writer with himself. It is by revealing the ways in which various kinds of rejoinders may be construed that we can deny the view that naturalism is a genre which presents us with unquestioning acceptance of the *status quo*.

The genre of the detective story has certain assumptions built into it, which need to be described. As Michael Westlake puts it, (Alvarado and Thompson eds 1990 : 248), the public sympathy 'lies with the criminal while it condemns the crime'. As Westlake states, the detective is like the censor who must 'know the inadmissible thought in order to deem it unsuitable'. This factor has bred generations of detectives whose personal lives are subject to great difficulties such as broken marriages and drinking. Fitz is created at a particular moment in History when Jimmy McGovern notes the need for a return to a kind of humanism. Jimmy McGovern refers to the 1980s when the Berlin Wall was destroyed and, as he put it, 'at a time when I was feeling utterly fucked up by the destruction of things I believed in and I now perceive as lies. 'Fitz is therefore able to examine motives which formerly people might have not wanted to acknowledge. He is not inhibited by political correctness. When a young woman is attacked, he can recreate the murderer's mind and his sexual desire for her. 'Post-Hillsborough man', as Cracker has been described (*The Sunday Times, Culture*, 15 October 1995), has earnt the right to be cynical and to attack the sacred cows of left-wing ideology which has failed him. He has seen his very humanity denied in an incident when people whose voices were not heard as they screamed for their lives, apparently because football fans were not regarded as human beings. The fact that death on this scale can be officially explained away and that journalists from the *Sun* could famously accuse the living fans of urinating on the dead, were the supreme moments of political cynicism. Fitz is a working-class intellectual who has finally renounced intellectual pretensions and has, in McGovern's words, come to believe ' the only thing that matters is not the ideology you espouse, the slogans you chant, but what you actually feel deep down in your heart and soul' (Sean Day-Lewis, 1998 : 59).

This is illustrated in Fitz's dialogue with his wife, Judith. There is a possible reference to Judith and Holofernes in mythology, here. Fitz believes that we are all governed by motives and that the fashionable ideologies of the day were inspired by ulterior motives. He attacks his wife and her ideologies he now regards as archaic, for concealing her own selfishness. For Fitz it is better to act out of compassion than self-interest masquerading as political respectability. Judith, however, retaliates by accusing him of being bourgeois, and accusing him of never feeling anything. She knows that this will hurt him the most. The anger she feels at his accusation makes her resort to defending herself and her love of her job as a social worker.

She admits to doing the job because she like it and it makes her feel good to help someone. At this moment what happens is that she displays the very thing which Fitz has accused her of lacking: passion. His response is to ask her to go to bed with him. He wins the argument without his adversary having to concede intellectually. This exchange between Judith and Fitz is later paralleled by the interrogation of Albie in the police station by Fitz. There is a 'poetic' dialogue between this kind of browbeating which compels someone to return to their most natural behaviour and the questioning of the criminal. He is subjected to the same process and the narrative is only fully understood if the similarity between these two incidents is recognised. Just as a metaphor is not announced as such, but must be 'seen', so too this applies to the recurrence of themes in the drama.

Just like Albie, however, Fitz has experienced a struggle when he looks into his own self and attempts to ground his own self-respect. He is a compulsive gambler whose marriage is in trouble, who drinks heavily and who neglects his son. He also begins an affair with the woman police officer, Penhaligon. The fact that he is also physically very large makes Fitz a sign of unquenched appetites. He is almost a Gargantua figure. As Westlake states, the detective must 'enter into the realm of the repressed' and know the temptations which beset the criminal as well as he does. By plumbing the 'lower depths', ironically, Fitz can also make a living as a forensic psychologist and reinforce his behaviour. Fitz is prone to indulging all his appetites, but his defence against sinking into vice is that he is aware of his motives. His interrogations of criminals always expose their self-deception, and refuse them a comfortable mythology with which they can justify themselves. This perception of his own desires is what stops him endorsing his fundamental drives as if they were fundamentally good. When Penhaligon complains that he has failed to meet her for a romantic assignation, Fitz answers that he did not do so because it would be easy to fall in love with her. This is an example of his moral restraint.

In many ways Fitz personifies Gargantua, one of the main characters invented by Rabelais to illustrate the role of the bodily appetites in society. Bakhtin, however, was aware that the problem with naturalism was that it tended to align characters with particular tendencies such as appetite, and restrict any further significance. Fitz actually signifies much more than this. Naturalism tends to make us ignore any further dialogic meaning. Studying television drama can reawaken the dialogues, and make the text ambiguous and multiaccented rather than a simple polemic.

Fitz is therefore capable of making mistakes and does not pronounce infallibly on the basis of 'common sense' like Inspector Morse. Fitz is clearly a development of the detective role and very different from Morse, but he also owes a great deal to the tradition from which Morse emanates. Both have a colourful personality and a keen ability to see that others have acted on prejudice. They are both able to perceive the truth. Both characters have personal difficulties with women and a sexually adventurous nature, although Morse is middle-class and restrained in his personal life. As John Sutherland remarked in *The Guardian* when he was discussing the American dramas which feature characters from different series working together, 'Morse would no more co-operate with Cracker than dog would mate with cat' ('Inspector Morse? Meet Cracker...' *The Guardian* Monday 26 April 1999). Whereas Morse is detached and stands outside the crime, observing and commenting objectively however, Fitz is unsettling and requires us to take a radically different view of society and ourselves to understand it. In *Inspector Morse*, everything returns to normal once the crime has been solved: detection is the ritual purgation of society whereas for *Cracker* it does not remove all social problems. Although Fitz is relentless in forcing people to confront their motives, Robbie Coltrane has said in a magazine interview, 'We want to know the forces driving the killer and what, if anything, society has to do with that terror' (*Emergency Television*, Issue 2 November 1996 :19). Morse detects individuals who are themselves responsible for evil.

Morse's faults are really blemishes on a highly respectable career, whereas Fitz is definitely flawed and often contradictory. In the episode under discussion he make serious mistakes as well as shrewd insights. Fitz does not cast out demons, he lives with them and inflicts them on all about him.

Michael Westlake however, points out that the TV detective 'at once offers an identity that is secure, competent and "individual" and that can rely upon the support, trust, affection of his/her colleagues. Individuality plus community.' (Alvarado and Thompson eds 1990 : 250). To watch an episode of *Inspector Morse* is to be reassured that a return to psychological wholeness is possible, whereas *Cracker* presents us with the eternal 'split subject' of psychoanalysis. The murderer in *To Be a Somebody* is both a mouthpiece of McGovern's frustration at what he perceives to be the injustices of Hillsborough and also a figure we can denounce as misguided and self-aggrandising. If we can identify with something, it is surely the act of uttering these ambivalent feelings towards such an incident. Whereas in classical cinema we might need to gain a coherent image of a character to identify easily with them, television drama may only succeed in making further 'splits' of this kind to develop our personalities as we view.

To 'open up' the dramatic text to interpretation, we need to find the various kinds of rejoinders which this drama is making to various groups and dialogues in society. Is it responding to the police, the families, to the would-be killers, or is it even a dialogue which the writer is having with himself? The drama constructs dialogic relations between the murderer and the detective to emphasise their comparison, For example, as Albie is having trouble scraping up 4p, we see Fitz gambling in a casino placing large bets on the table. Implicitly, this editing establishes a negative evaluation of Fitz and approval of Albie, to confuse us further when Albie commits an apparently racist crime. This drama, however, attempts to transcend racism and sexism briefly by finding causes which lie deeper still.

By choosing the detective genre, the makers of this drama have implicitly evaluated the crime. Detective dramas concern antisocial acts such as murder: they cannot be condoned. By linking it with the documentary of protest, however, we have a new hybrid genre which implicitly condones the protest, if not its form of expression. There is therefore an ambivalence about the drama's evaluation which has to be explored by an active audience. The notion that the audience for a television drama is active if they have to piece together a creator's intentions, is not necessarily coherent. In some cases, the writer may have a clear didactic intention which the 'ideal viewer' of the drama will detect and follow. This, however, is not empowering the audience to participate in social debates. It is merely encouraging them to work harder to grasp a clear intention. We know, therefore that the choice of genre has implications for the moral evaluation of the crime. If the anthropological function of detective drama is an exploration of our own guilt and suspicion caused by violent crimes, then we have to search for an answer here.

Albie, whose father was at Hillsborough but died later of cancer cannot pay the full price for a *Guardian* and a packet of tea bags at the corner shop and is refused 4p credit by the Asian storekeeper. In a fit of rage he goes home, shaves off all his hair and returns with the money. He also deliberately brings his father's wartime bayonet and stabs the elderly shopkeeper. He tells the shopkeeper that he may as well act violently because he is regarded as a nobody. In fact we see him at work in a factory where he is able to answer crossword clues. He is evidently intelligent as reading *The Guardian* signifies, but this coded sign has to be seen in the light of the entire utterance. It may be an ironic jibe at the readers of that newspaper in that the choice of any other newspaper would have condemned a certain readership as potential murderers. The enlightened readership of *The Guardian* represent the very middle-class ideologue that Fitz is so fond of attacking. Later Albie attacks and murders the university professor who has dared to offer a psychological profile of him. In the wake of his killings, Albie leaves a long number. It is Fitz who deciphers this number as signifying that he is going to kill 96 people to avenge the dead at Hillsborough in 1989.

The social reaction to extremely violent murders or serial killers is often to ask why and how such things could happen. Albie's tactic is to make other people know how he feels. He believes himself to be misjudged and misunderstood and in his assault on DCI Bilborough's wife, therefore, he makes her 'feel like nothing'. The implication of this statement which has dialogic relations with Albie's own words, is that Mrs Bilborough feels like Albie. There is a tendency in some detective drama to ignore the horror of the crime and to suppress one's feelings. As Janet Wolff (1993) has pointed out, semiotics can be accused of turning corpses of women particularly into mere signs and ignoring the horrific crime which resulted in death. If we use classical semiotic theory the corpse has to be encoded as a sign of a manoeuvre in the genre, and not a tragedy. McGovern's writing and the television production, however, is designed to engage the viewers' emotions.

In *Cracker* we are meant to experience the *punctum*. DCI Bilborough's death is long-drawn out and extremely harrowing. We see his wife reacting and the resulting tragedy is emphasised. This is not just another murder, but a tragedy. Even the police who were 'guilty' of failing to prevent the deaths at Hillsborough are also human beings who deserve to live. In another echo of the tragedy, Albie leads DCI Bilborough into the alleyways around his home to his death. The dull brown brick walls are eerily reminiscent of the Leppings Lane entrance to the Hillsborough stadium where the tragedy occurred. This is an ironic echo of the way in which the police herded the football fans into Hillsborough to their deaths. It is all the more painful for this.

We are made to feel Albie's anger and the sadness he causes. He has left his wife after hurting her because she did not experience the same tragedy as him. She admits to guilt as she was 'out with the girls'. This is a familiar feature of tragedies and several divorces occurred as a result of Hillsborough. The tragedy caused untold alienation between people who believed they could no longer be understood and those who loved them and claimed to. The enormous gulf between the survivors and those who were not there is also echoed in the title. The ambiguity is that Albie both wants to be someone for egotistical reasons (ie he wants to be an important person) and also simply to be recognised as a human being, rather than an anonymous number in a mass accident.

Fitz intends to explore this ambiguity in attacking Albie's state of mind to 'crack' him and make him reveal the other murders he has committed. The practice of offender profiling is in a sense, a tribute to naturalism: it selects certain environmental factors such as poorly-paid jobs and credits these with the ability to help create a serial killer. The causal relationship between the circumstances and the crime is evidence that the philosophy underlying naturalism is true. In discovering why Albie committed the crime, however, Fitz has to explore his motives, which are not derived from the circumstances, but only exist within his mind. Here there is a chance to show that the same circumstances are not always reacted to in the same way by all people. Since the drama opposes glib ideological positions, it does not show someone who is a simple product of circumstances, since this would be to subscribe to a determinist ideology. Our interest is in why Cracker, for example, does not give into temptation whereas the murderer does. Just as Bakhtin's theories of signs betray a belief in a subject who organises signs over and above the system which s/he uses, so too, Fitz shows a belief in the human subject manipulating circumstances and having an ability to change his life. The final interrogation, therefore, is a test of Fitz's ability to probe into the human mind. As in the Conservative Association for the Family speech in *The Politician's Wife*, language is very important here and when we are probing the mind of a killer, we cannot do so effectively with images.

Albie has to face the fact that his motives were wrong, that he wanted glory, not justice. Fitz is able to break him by exposing this fact. The final interrogation scene, however, is not without some setbacks for Fitz. Albie accuses him, with some justification, of attempting to impress Penhaligon, and Fitz loses his temper. At first, Albie refuses to enter into dialogue with Fitz and simply repeats football chants. This has the effect of creating what Bakhtin calls 'zero-degree dialogic relations': there is no communication with Fitz. The aim must be to engage Albie in conversation. When Albie does begin to speak, he asserts that the people he killed deserved to die for 'assuming things' such as his class and intelligence. Fitz's technique is to provoke him by ridicule: 'So that's Albie's law? People who assumes things have to die? At this point Fitz utters the remark about sentimentality which is later repeated verbatim in the American series, *Fitz*. He accuses Albie and 'all the murderers he has ever known 'of sentimentality which makes him sick. Albie's rejoinder is to tell him that a fourth body is buried on his allotment. The dialogic relations here are important and might easily be missed. Fitz's technique reveals the truth he wants to know because Albie wants to prove that his feelings are not restricted to trivial matters and he also wants revenge. The technique which is fully successful, however is achieving empathy. This is based on Ian Stephen's real accounts of his interviews with psychopathic offenders:

> Empathy is one of the most effective forms of communication with an offender. I don't pretend to know exactly how a person feels, but I try to let him know that I have an understanding of what might be going on in him. (Crace, 1994 : 49)

The strategy used is that Fitz talks about his own father' s death and how they finally had little to say to each other as it drew near. Albie despises him for using his personal life, but when the 'cracker' speaks in the dramatic present and conjures up the scenario with the father disillusioned with football, and soon to die he asks Albie: 'What's left (to speak about)?' and Albie replies 'Nothing'. This is a breakthrough because it is the first genuine dialogue between the two men. Fitz reminds him that his father would not want revenge but Albie asserts that *he* does. This is said with an emotive evaluation which suggests that revenge is still possible. In a moment of intuition which characterises all detectives, Fitz grasps the fact that Albie has planted a bomb. The fact that revenge was still a possibility meant that this was the only way it could be achieved. One bomb is discovered, but Fitz forgets the possibility if another and a journalist from *The Sun* is caught in a final blast. This is perhaps the one concession to the author's feelings about the newspaper which wrongly reported that the fans urinated on the dead at Hillsborough. The drama does not, therefore, conclude with a comforting message that we can easily discover the truth. Fitz uses his intuition rather than an ideology, and is wrong. The way in which we can find the truth in post-ideological world is left as an open question.

Fitz

Dan Glaister (in '*Cracker* Lite Proves Thin on Danger', *The Guardian* Monday 25 August 1997) argues that 'The grime and grit of Granada's original are gone' in the American adaptation of *Cracker*. In particular, Robert Pastorelli who plays the part of Fitz is criticised for not matching the screen persona of Robbie Coltrane. The episode of the American *Cracker*, simply called *Fitz*, does not have in the American scene a set of people of the kind that the English *Cracker* attacks for their ideological self-deception. The bombast of the English Cracker is not such a potent weapon in the hands of Pastorelli, who, it is argued, lacks the presence to seem sufficiently threatening when he attacks people verbally. What America does have, of course, is a concern for abnormal psychology and the media stars who exhibit such features. As the American Fitz is berating David Roberge, played by Coltrane he tells him,'You're the new O.J.', referring to O.J. Simpson who, like Coltrane's screen character also attempted to mount an elaborate defence using the media and was destroyed, or so it would seem, by fame. In the episode of *Fitz* screened in England, Robbie Coltrane is cast in the role of the villain, David Roberge, a movie producer who hires Fitz to assist his defence. This drama, therefore, takes part in the social practice of self-justification as the producer of the drama attempts to show that Pastorelli can give a convincing performance in 'cracking' Coltrane's character and thereby proving that he has the acting ability to carry off the role. This is what Robert Stam and his co-authors describe as 'celebrity intertextuality' (Stam *et al*, 1992:207).

In the John Sutherland *Guardian*, piece, he discusses the latest twist in this phenomenon practised by David E. Kelley who writes both *Ally McBeal* and *The Practice*. Kelley's newest idea is to feature characters from *The Practice* in *Ally McBeal*. The appearance of Coltrane in *Fitz* works surprisingly well, and can perhaps be related to postmodernist theories of the sign. The 'always already said' refers to the view that signs in postmodernism are endlessly recycled and can be recognised as repetition. Performers would certainly fit into this theory and since they too are 'endlessly recycled' in new roles, this phenomenon should not prove surprising. The appearance of performers in such contexts creates a sense of a 'fictional universe' where identities proliferate. The use of Coltrane, however, must be seen as 'ironic casting', in which an ulterior motive dictates the choice and not his immediate suitability for the part.

Robbie Coltrane plays David Roberge, a film producer who is seen welcoming a mother and daughter to his casting party. The attractive young daughter, Devon, is encouraged by her mother to regard Roberge as someone who can 'do a lot for her career' and she is last seen being shown around his palatial home by Roberge. The final shot shows her entering the bedroom where there is a rocking horse and Roberge declares that this is where reputations are made. The rocking horse signifies that she is really a child and emphasises the moral disgust in the scene. Devon is found dead in the fish pool the next morning.

There is a brief cut to Roberge in bed with his eyes wide open, staring manically before him as the body is discovered. This sign of extreme anxiety points clearly in the direction of his guilt but without offering any proof or explanation. The audience therefore have a privileged insight into the crime. If guilt has already been suggested, however, then the emphasis of the drama is on motive.

While the party is in progress, however, Fitz is drinking at a wake in honour of a dead policewoman. The two events clearly establish a dialogical contract between the two men at the outset of the drama. He becomes drunk and abuses the other policemen, calling them 'buffoons' and blaming their incompetence for the policewoman's death. He accuses the lieutenant of 'worshipping at the altar of his career', and acting out of a fear of the consequences for his job. This foregrounds the theme of the episode which is the effect of a career on one's self-respect. Once a career has ensured that someone has a reputation, they will act dishonourably to protect it. This is a modern mythology. The 'poetic' narrative which emerges through metaphors continues with Fitz asking the lieutenant whether he knows the 'dilemma of sacrifice'. Fitz states that the dilemma is that the act of sacrifice is intended to be worthy but the victim is sacred, therefore there is a contradiction in the act: a sacred person must be harmed. The metaphorical link with the notion of the career as an 'altar' signifies that a career is designed to offer such sacrifices, which are intrinsic to it. When Fitz's father visits, he is an ex-soldier who is desperately keen for his grandson to have a similar career. He berates Fitz for the fact that his son is not yet clear about his career plans, and is 'slovenly', but Fitz retaliates by saying 'I am not bringing up soldiers here dad'.

Ironically, of course, Fitz'z own failures are ascribable to his father who is now blaming him for bringing up his grandson wrongly. Fitz does not believe in forcing his son to take up a career too early. David Roberge, however, has been a child star, which he recognises has distorted his life. The mother of Devon is also forcing her daughter to play the role of a media performer even though she is only 15. When Roberge is suspected of the killing, he hires Fitz to assist him in his defence. He argues plausibly that he does not need to kill to obtain sex, as it is freely available in the circles he mixes in. Fitz actually takes part in a television programme in which he supports Roberge's case and describes Devon as 'a young woman not uncomfortable in the presence of men'. It is at this point that Fitz's father describes him as a 'fraud'.

In conversation with Roberge, Fitz discovers that he values the Koi pool in his grounds because the fish are a symbol of freedom and their name actually means long life. He also uses a metaphor to express his feelings for his career. Roberge distinguishes between the rose which is a sign of beauty co-existing with thorns, and the century plant which blossoms spectacularly once in a hundred years. 'Life may be a like a century plant but we've got to fight it', he declares. This signifies his attitude towards his career: he must not allow his talent to succeed only once.

When the mother of the victim withdraws her statement that she slept with the security guard on the night of the murder, the guard is arrested and incriminating clothing is found at his home. This arouses Fitz's suspicions and he visits her to ask why she changed her story. In typical 'Cracker' style he breaks down her resolve by using a metaphor about the mother-daughter relationship. He compares her attitude towards Devon's film career with a mother holding on to her daughter as they spin round on a merry-go-round. She lets the daughter lean out further and further until she is finally pushing her in encouragement and she ends up dead on the floor. The mother breaks down at this and confesses that she was paid to change her story and promised, 'she would be made for life'. Once again a career has been given priority.

Fitz goes to see Roberge, armed with the mother's confession and announces that he no longer works for him. He then proceeds to question Roberge to get at the truth. Fitz's technique is based on the premise that sometimes the perpetrators he interrogates 'don't even know themselves'. The moments at which he 'cracks' the suspects are the points at which they are compelled to acknowledge a truth about themselves which they had repressed. Earlier Roberge had explained his fascination with goldfish to Fitz. As a child he had sympathised with the goldfish he saw in a bowl because they were expected to perform for others and had no privacy. He had begged his mother to enable him to put the goldfish in a pool. The Koi followed later. Fitz tells Roberge that it was the fact that the body was dumped in the fishpond that gave him away as the murderer. The pool signified freedom to him, a refuge from the media spotlight, and Fitz describes his placing of the body in the pool as a gesture of remorse. The sign here means that she is left with the free creatures who signify an escape from a lifelong showbusiness career to Roberge. Roberge breaks down at this point and explains that a bondage sex game had gone wrong and he was unable to save her from drowning because his hands were tied when she slumped into the water suffering from an excess of valium and alcohol.

At this point, Fitz condemns Roberge as 'sentimental, 'just like every killer I've ever met'. For viewers of the British series *Cracker*, this will be recognised as a direct quotation from the interrogation of Albie in 'To be a Somebody' inspired ultimately by Coltrane's acquaintance with Ian Stephen. The implication is that the man who attaches enormous importance to cherishing and protecting his own feelings will be much more liable to find it necessary to sacrifice others to protect his sensitivities. The dialogic rejoinder also signifies that this is an example of a role reversal for Coltrane. This is a good example of a dialogic interchange which is extratextual and is aimed at the contemporary audience. Fits insists that Roberge's followers do not honour his sensitivity, however, but instead 'flock to the throne of arrogance'. As a rejoinder, this drama participates in the practice of justification by staging a reversal of the role which Robbie Coltrane popularised. The repeated lines are here an example of re-accentuation, where the same words have a different value in a different context. Fitz accuses Roberge of 're-staging the ending', or deliberately re-constructing the plot as if life were a movie. The scene is also a powerful example of a rejoinder directed at the actions of media stars such as O.J. Simpson. The motive is that fame is too attractive and desirable to ever give it up by confessing to a killing. As Pam Thaler puts it in *The Spectacle: The Media and the Making of the O.J. Simpson Case*, 'The fight is for credibility' (Thaler, 1997 : 57). Once this idea has infected a star, it remains with him in all contexts.

The theme of the drama is woven into the plot in a similar manner to *ER* and *NYPD Blue*. The theme is concluded at the same time as the plot but they are not parallel throughout. The theme is actually one where Fitz's work philosophy and personal life coincide: he is shown to be a successful man in avoiding the dilemmas which he accuses others of in the end. Unlike the British *Cracker*, Fitz is fully vindicated by the plot in which he renounces the temptation to seek career advancement by taking Roberge's money and avoids transmitting this mentality to his son. The British Fitz is far less unified and would find no lasting benefit to his own life in solving such a case.

A further distinction between the two dramas which explains their differences lies in their attitude towards ideology. Geertz distinguishes between the interest and the strain theory:

> For the first (interest theory), ideology is a mask and a weapon; for the second, a symptom and a remedy. In the interest theory, ideological pronouncements are seen against the background of a universal struggle for advantage; in the strain theory against the background of a chronic effort to correct socio-psychological disequilibrium. In the one men pursue power; in the other they flee anxiety. (Geertz, 1974 : 201)

Albie in *To Be a Somebody*, as the title suggests, presents himself heroically as pursuing power for the underdog, but in order to do so he hides from himself that his anger is motivated by a longing to fulfil his personal desires. Fitz is able to break him when he detects that Albie is disguising his personal socio-psychological anxieties as the search for power for a dispossessed minority. When Fitz realises that Albie actually wants to become his father to assuage his grief, he also realises that Albie has falsely identified with the Hillsborough disaster which was not responsible for his father's death. Geertz points out the function of metaphor and social symbolism in creating ideological connections between events. In this case, the reference Albie makes to 'treating us like animals' refers initially to the herding of football fans into the Hillsborough stadium, but is generalised to mean that his entire social class is subjected to inhuman treatment. The justification of his search for power by sacrificing 96 people to claim revenge and publicise the Hillsborough tragedy is therefore revealed as a personal trauma disguised as a noble cause. The exposure of a personal anxiety masquerading as a political stance is characteristic of the *Cracker* drama series and conforms with McGovern's view that in a society which has largely abandoned ideology, the tendency is to fall back on personal feeling as a guide to moral action. When Fitz declares that sentimentality lies at the heart of every murderer he has encountered, therefore, in the British *Cracker*, this is accented in performance as a remark born of frustration and not a personal condemnation of Albie. In the British version, Fitz is referring to a common psychological condition of self-deception. The American Fitz is directly condemning Roberge for his self-indulgence which is clearly motivated by self-interest. In the land where ideology is often geared to defending the freedom of the individual, self-fulfillment is a political goal.

ER: The semiotic unconscious

It is the case that 'caring' dramas such as *ER* and *Casualty* form an identifiable genre, but like the many police series, such as *NYPD Blue*, they are founded on an intimate knowledge of specialized procedures which are unfamiliar to the general public. Performers spend time with real doctors, observing their procedures and the official MGM internet site even contains a glossary of medical terms for devotees of the drama. A recurrent feature of the genre is that it incorporates discrete micro-narratives of individual clients and issues, but also establish recurrent personal themes which are maintained in each episode. In the case of these dramas it might at first appear that naturalism is meant to initiate us into professional worlds where the public image is rarely supplemented by knowledge of the private concerns which exist behind appearances. *This Life* gave British viewers a chance to see what the domestic lives of young solicitors might be like. *ER* is an American product which has established itself as both a popular and highly regarded drama, but it may seem as if its appeal is that it delivers a glimpse behind the scenes which satisfies curiosity rather than empowering the audience to articulate responses in a continuing dialogue.

As in *Big Women*, however, the naturalism is engineered to produce a number of perspectives on the same issue, as well as continuing the personal life-stories of the medical staff, although this is difficult to grasp as the events move at speed. The theme of the episode, 'The Miracle Worker' is the role of the doctor in society. The successive patients each present the doctors with the opportunity to adopt a differing professional attitude. It is Christmas Eve and the atmosphere is jovial, but tragedy is even more deeply felt at this time. Dr Mark Greene's first patient is playing the part of an elf for Father Christmas and has a recurrent condition. He informs the doctor that 500 units of treatment always restores him to health, but Greene insists on starting with 200 and only finally works up to 500 whereupon the patient recovers. During this time the patient shouts angrily at Greene and berates him for not taking his advice. Greene explains to a colleague that he was not sure that such a large dosage would not cause an adverse reaction. In this brief incident we understand the temptation to please the patient and to see this as the ultimate goal. Professionalism, however, means reaching the right result by the right procedure for the right reasons. It is never simple expediency.

The first exchange between Kerry Weaver and Mark Greene results in Mark being offered a little homespun wisdom. Kerry's grandmother used to say that smiles are infectious. Mark recalls this advice and attempts to put this into practice with his next patient. His unusually cheerful demeanour attracts attention and he states that he is attempting to transmit his own cheerfulness. This simple approach to the 'bedside manner' is based on the fundamental view that the role of the doctor is to make the patient happy. Mark's first patient, however, turns out to be an irascible elderly woman who interprets his cheerfulness as a sign that he is using expensive drugs unnecessarily. She is still shouting as he walks away.

Although Mark has failed to communicate his happiness, the audience can see that he was wrong to think that there was such an easy solution to the doctor-patient relationship. Despite the anger he caused, he had to prescribe the treatments which he mentioned: professional ethics demanded that he be firm in the face of bitter recriminations. Pleasing the patient is seen as the easy way out. Medical mistakes might occur. The MGM website mentions that Mark is the mainstay of the team: his strength is legendary.

Doug Ross agrees to carry out an abortion on a 13-year old girl. As he says to her, 'I can help you'. The choices are starkly presented to the child by the doctor: 'You can have the baby and keep it; you can have the baby and give it away, or you can have an abortion. 'The girl says that she cannot have a baby and the choice becomes clear. Doug is sure of how to proceed. His approach is to put the choice to the patient and to fulfill their wishes. Later, however, his lover, Hathaway the nurse, calls the girl's mother who also summons a Catholic priest. Hathaway herself has been refused the opportunity to adopt because of a suicide attempt in a previous series and is clearly sensitive to the role of the mother in such circumstances. Doug becomes angry with Hathaway because the presence of these people, as he says, 'prevents him from helping' the girl. This signifies that the presence of the mother and the priest prevents him from going ahead with the abortion. Eventually, however, he forgives Hathaway who is herself a Catholic. This incident is dialogically related to the previous one: in the case of pregnancy, it is the wishes of the patient which dictate the best course of action, given that the medical options are clear. Doug Ross, however. has to agree that the girl's feelings are not clear and therefore her indecision cannot be ignored. Bringing the priest to her bedside is therefore consistent with respecting her wishes. His forgiveness of Hathaway is ultimately consistent with his professional decision: the girl must be sure of her choice or it would be the wrong one. The doctor is not there to intervene in the decision-making process.

It is the newly-qualified John Carter who has a rather more elevated concept of his role as a doctor: he announces when he manages to resuscitate a young man whose heart has stopped for a considerable time 'I am an instrument'. Whereas previously we have seen more experienced doctors act out of professional obligation or the wishes of the patient, here the more idealistic doctor regards himself as the person who acts to bring about divine intervention. He finds, however, that the man is brain dead and he can only be kept alive artificially. The mother is alone in the world except for her son and pleads to be allowed to 'wait for a miracle', but she is told that this is impossible. The 'miracle-worker' is disappointed, but another family bring in their daughter who is dying and needs a liver transplant. The young man who is being kept alive artificially is of the same blood group and this inspires Dr Carter to consider transplanting the boy's liver into the young girl. Against the mother's wishes, and against the professional code of conduct, he resuscitates the young man again when he is near to death so that the possibility of a transplant remains open. Carter then goes to see the mother who is in the chapel. He explains the circumstances and asks her to believe that this is such a fortuitous coincidence that God must have intended it. The mother, however, is curt and states that she cannot think of other people's children while her son is dying. She wants him to be buried whole. The mother departs and leaves her neck chain with what appears to be a religious symbol such as a cross, behind on the bench. Carter picks it up absent-mindedly.

Dr Carter's dismay, however, is inappropriate. His use of the term 'instrument' is ambiguous. He seems to regard himself not as the conduit for fortuitous events but the instigator: the person who makes them happen. He sees himself as an agent of the divine helper, rather than a passive 'instrument' which obeys a higher law. There may even be a touch of naïve vanity here. Janine Pourroy writes that Carter 'bridges the gap' between the medical profession and lay people because he is new to the job (Pourroy, 1996 : 82). The term 'instrument' implies that he carries out the will of the agency who use him, not that his own individual decisions interpret the divine will. Later it transpires that Susan Lewis has introduced the mother to the family of the dying girl in the corridor and that she has agreed to the transplant after all. She has expedited the miracle rather than trying to make it happen herself. She is describable as the 'instrument', by the way she expedites the process rather than trying to direct it. This touching incident is consolidated in the final stages of the episode when Carter meets the mother in the corridor after she has agreed to the transplant and drops the crucifix necklace in her hand. She accepts it and her rejoinder is a barely perceptible nod. The action signifies that she has accepted the explanation of a divine coincidence and is possibly prepared to acknowledge faith once more. The emotion-evaluation of the nod is half-hearted, however, because Dr Carter is not the bearer of the divine truth.

Within the same episode Dr Corday is treating a middle-aged man who is about to undergo an operation for the removal of his prostate gland and will most probably lose his sexual function. Mr Gardner is a concert musician with a leading symphony orchestra and Dr Corday is clearly attracted to him. Her behaviour is clearly unprofessional when she feigns embarrassment as she confesses to going through a 'disco phase'. As she does this she moves very close so that she can only confess this shameful fact to him. Although she counsels him to donate sperm in order to be able to have children at a later date should be be incapable of sex, Dr Corday continues to show a personal interest in her patient. Mr Gardner has an anxiety fit and is suspected of heart problems because he is so nervous of the operation. He clearly needs counselling, but the attentions of the doctor are comforting. The fact that he is still attractive to a woman obviously boosts his morale and Dr Corday invites him to a restaurant. Here the relationship between doctor and patient is personal and although it may be beneficial to the patient, it transgresses professional ethics. Dr Corday has made a mistake by attempting to influence the patient's medical condition by her own actions. Decisions about the best way of treating a patient are meant to be made by balancing the professional consensus, the personal interests of the patient and the feelings of the family. A professional decision is never a personal one, rather it must be made in such a way that another professional would come to the same conclusion.

There are many examples of debates about the ethics of medical treatment in the media, but one highly significant case, which this episode is dialogically related to, is that of Dr Jack Kevorkian who is famous in America for publicising his actions in assisting various terminally-ill patients to die. In several high-profile cases in the media, the doctor announced his intention to assist euthanasia and was acquitted by five juries. On these occasions, however, the doctor had set up the medical equipment so that the patients could administer the fatal dose of drugs themselves. In this way, he was the 'instrument' for the suicide and not the instigator. More recently still, and after the *ER* episode under consideration, Dr Kevorkian actually televised his administering of a fatal dose himself and was arrested and successfully prosecuted. The moral distinction is made between killing and assisting suicide. Although Kevorkian's crime is not directly referred to in this series, it forms part of the social atmosphere within which the series is experienced. When a doctor actively intervenes in the fate of a patient, she or he is guilty of misconduct. The precise definition of this act, however, is something which dramas such as *ER* bring to popular attention.

In contrast with this issue, Peter Benton has a patient who is obese and who collapses suddenly as one of his stomach staples bursts. On the operating table, Peter suddenly discovers that his patient is going into toxic shock and will shortly die unless something is done. He decides to operate and to remove the food from the abdomen which is causing the problem. This is against the professional consensus which says that he may not operate without another doctor present. When Dr Romano the surgeon arrives, he is drunk and orders Peter to stop, reminding him of the fact that he should be operating. A scuffle follows and Dr Romano is knocked to the ground. Here Peter Benton shows how to act in a case where there is a conflict between the professional consensus and the needs of the patient: the patient's well-being is the ultimate good and this superseded the interests of an egotistical surgeon. Egotism is inappropriate when the job is to direct the course of nature and not to act oneself. No individual is in ultimate control where the interests of a patient are concerned and the doctor is enmeshed in a social situation where he must act in harmony with others to arrive at the best possible decision. This is another kind of inflated self-belief which suggests that Dr Romano regards himself as an indispensable 'instrument'. This factor also explains one of the best-remembered aspects of *ER* which is the use of the steadicam to add dramatic realism to the sudden arrival of a seriously ill patient. In the operating theatre the camera which circles the entire trauma team gives us a non-hierarchical view as well as disorientating us in keeping with the emergency. The camera does not settle on one major character, but insists on showing us the entire team. If the camera framed the surgeon as the hero, this would signify that she or he was the person who saved lives by their actions alone, and this is not borne out by the drama. Doctors control an entire patient environment rather than acting as their sole saviour.

The theme of the episode, therefore is, in a sense, the drama's unconscious. The theme outlined above remains latent throughout: it is never mentioned in detail. There is no one character who personifies all the wisdom that the series attempt to display. This can become the viewer's unconscious in that they may absorb the same ideological message of metaphysical optimism on an emotionally-charged Christmas Eve. The problem for psychoanalytic theory, as Sandy Flitterman-Lewis observes, is that the varied positions which are taken up in showing the action tend to create a fagmented perspective for the viewer and prevent the identification with an authorial voice or a gaze as in the cinema (Flitterman-Lewis in Allen ed. 1992 : 220). The use of the steadicam in the series, enables the director to cut across the line of movement and switch from following one character to another as they come into view, heading in a different direction. The effect is to present multiple points of view which eventually mean that we have seen the activities of the entire cast each series.

The effect of this technique gives rise to what Dudley Andrew refers to as 'psychological montage': 'an event is broken down into those fragments which replicate the changes of attention we would naturally experience were we physically present at the event' (Andrew, 1976 : 157). The viewer can identify with the camera's curiosity and the micro-narratives which occur at frequent intervals, but this is rather like Lacan's 'mirror stage': the drama seems to reflect recognisable human emotions, which we can appreciate and identify with, but they do not enter into the 'symbolic stage' where we can clearly articulate the overall significance of the individual scenes. The 'dream-wish', or the unconscious desire which motivates the drama and the viewer is obscured. The full statement of the theme is always suspended until the concluding moments of the drama, allowing any identification by the viewer to be suspended as well. Given that the television set is always a material reminder of the act of enunciation, we cannot readily identify with the drama and experience it as though we were sharing the same perspective as the characters. Any identification can only take place with the utterance, the entire act of broadcasting seen in full. The act of identification with drama such as this is one in which we come to regard the utterance as an expression of our own thoughts and beliefs.

In cinema, the apparatus of the filming process is hidden from our view in the darkness, and we can imagine ourselves to be one of the characters, but in television we are always conscious of a material source of the images we watch. Cinematic psychoanalytic theory tends to propose that the spectator becomes one with the gaze which is in reality part of the *énoncé*, or the content of the enunciation. The very fragmentation of the series is what makes us wait until we have seen the whole drama because only then can we appreciate the coherent theme. Flitterman-Lewis, therefore assumes that the fragmentation of the televisual glance, which is the nearest equivalent to the cinematic gaze, must mean that there is no thematic coherence.

> If the enunciative source is conceived of as a source of unconscious desire that we are meant to share, where is this "site" in *Knots Landing* for example? Is the authorial subject-position held by David Jacobs (the series co-creator), by Lawrence Kasha (co-executive producer) by Bernard Lechowick, Mary-Catherine Harrold, or Lynne-Marie Latham (producers), by writers such as Parke Perrine, or Mimi Kennedy? ...And – especially with television – couldn't the sponsor be considered the author as well? (Allen, ed. 1992: 221)

By not offering the viewer one subject position to identify with, the series gives the impression that it is transparent and simply shows us the complexities of dilemmas which a genuine hospital would encounter. The source of our desire to believe that doctors can act as the conduit for divine intervention, is not one particular doctor.

The list of possibilities, which Flitterman-Lewis puts forward, displays the fact that she is concerned primarily with the origin of the *text*, not the utterance. The act of broadcasting the show at Christmas, for example, would be an utterance, which endows the text with a special significance as a means of expressing the unconscious desires of the viewers for them. The source of the desires is the broadcasters themselves, assisted no doubt by their sponsors Volvo. Whereas actors and writers and producers may come and go, the ultimate power lies in the hands of the programmers who authorise the broadcasting at a certain time. The image, which displays the name of the famous carmakers, shows a pulsating organic mass, which resembles internal organs and the caption 'Volvo is for life'. This deliberate ambiguity associates the security of Volvo's long-lasting technological stability and its support for the series, which concerns saving lives. There may be a collective group who is deemed responsible, consisting of MGM, Volvo and the network owners. As an utterance it purports to celebrate the importance of life over all other priorities. The position on medical ethics which is adopted may be described in the old adage, 'let nature take its course'. The doctors who attempt to ingratiate themselves with patients or to aggrandize themselves are not trying to hasten natural processes. When a doctor intervenes in a natural process such as pregnancy, this is not acceptable in this episode because it is not endorsing the value of 'life'. Underlying the whole drama is a metaphysical belief in the course of nature, which can be assisted, but not diverted.

John Caughie, in a chapter entitled, 'Playing at Being American: Games and Tactics' (1994), points out, however, that it is possible to watch television with 'an ironic sensibility already formed outside the space of television'. This sensibility may withhold assent from any 'unconscious' theme. The audience may recognise the games being employed and choose to suspend their suspension of disbelief. Rather than absorbing the position offered to the viewer the ironic sensibility may watch knowing that such covert tactics are being employed, yet not dismiss the message completely. Television may offer a position of aesthetic distance, which are not an ultimate rejection, but a healthy scepticism. The idea of a 'semiotic unconscious' is of a set of signifiers, which cannot readily be connected with their signifieds, so that underlying, currents of signification are not immediately identified. It is not to be identified with the classical Freudian unconscious. There may be a sense that the whole drama is a ploy to serve commercial interests, for example. We may derive pleasure nonetheless. It is television especially, however, that reminds us of the complexity of semiosis because a drama may be both a narrative about the world and a decisive intervention in our affairs at the same time.

NYPD Blue: The semiosphere

*N*YPD *Blue* is another television drama which uses the techniques described in the case of *ER*. In an episode broadcast in England on 29 April 1999, the episode begins as usual, *in media res*, with the announcement of two cases which the detectives have to solve: the brutal robbery and assault on an elderly couple who ran a shop by two black men, and the murder of a man in a strip club. Andy Sipowicz and his young partner Danny Sorenson are assigned to the robbery and the two women detectives are asked to deal with the strip club called 'The Gentleman's Hour'. A gay man has arrived at the fifteenth precinct to take the place of the secretary, Dolores who has reported ill. When he is introducd to Sipowicz's new colleague, Danny Sorensen, he balances on one leg a little like a dancer and the camera momentarily shows us Sipowicz's disparaging glance at this. A close-up of Sipowicz's disgusted face then reveals his attitude towards what appears to be a gay man, and he looks askance before leaving abruptly. This is a sign of Sipowicz's now legendary intolerance, which sets the scene for later acts of hot-headedness. The viewer in *NYPD Blue* is often presented with the glances that an actual participant observer would make as they search the faces of those present to see what reaction certain utterances have provoked.

Sipowicz, who is later described perhaps ironically as the 'Buddha' of the department – a spiritual leader – is by far the most famous character in the show, and his facial signs tend to cast a meta-comment on the events we witness. When he and Sorensen visit the scene where the elderly couple have been robbed and badly beaten, the sight is particularly harrowing. The husband asks only that his seriously-ill wife be tended and his desperate clutching of her hand in the ambulance, create a moving, emotionally-charged scene. Close-ups of Sorensen reveal that he is deeply affected by this and he promises the elderly man that they will catch the people responsible. Again, Sipowicz looks sideways at him as if to see how serious this promise is. As a professional he seems to be concerned at such a promise which there can be no guarantee of keeping. This introduces the theme of this episode which is the police worker's struggle to accommodate his or her natural emotions within their professional role.

The remedy for this problem of dealing with the emotions evoked by police work is alluded to by the police informant who reveals the names of the culprits to Sorensen. The informant congratulates Sorensen on his promotion to detective and says that 'all the people on the corner is making the adjustment'. 'Adjusting' is a word which Sipowicz later adopts when he is explaining to Sorensen how he keeps his fish tank in the police station clean and healthy. The care of the fish tank becomes an ecological metaphor which develops into a philosophy of life in Sipowicz's speech. This is an example of displacement as the banal analogy with fish begins to take on a new dimension of meaning. It is also an example of condensation as the metaphor can also be used to explain many of the other aspects of the latent theme.

He tells Sorensen how the welfare of the fish is affected by the presence of algae on which they feed. The maintenance of the fish tank therefore depends on both preserving the ph balance to stimulate algae growth and also maintaining the levels of oxygen available to the fish. In other words, an eco-system is one where various factors have to be held in balance. An excess of one can impact on the others. If there is too much of one element, however, this can be remedied by 'adjusting': adding more of others until the balance is restored. Sipowicz refers to his own shortcomings as a professional policeman, but he asserts that he is capable of dealing effectively with a fish-tank. If you can maintain the fish-tank you can call yourself 'a man who knows fish', he concludes. The statement is significant because it implies that each environment is different and the general principle does not translate into an effective programme of action in all contexts. His rueful smile as performed, signifies that he frequently does not apply the metaphor to his own life. Sipowicz exploits this metaphor to explain to Sorensen that in interviewing one of the robbery suspects he was wrong to throw him off his chair and lose his temper. This is not a moral failing, but a badly-timed gesture. Sorensen showed, however, that he could adjust. Danny signifies that he has taken the homily to heart when he declares (with no discernible irony) that he will catch the violent suspect 'in his net'.

The episode as a whole utterance can be regarded as a rejoinder to the ecological metaphor which has become such a prominent feature of contemporary social thought. The pioneer work, *Socio-biology:the New Synthesis* by E.O.Wilson was published in 1975 by Harvard University Press. In that book it is defined as 'the systematic study of the biological basis of human behaviour' (Wilson,1975 : 595). Since then, socio-biology has grown into a recognised discipline with a vast literature. The theory implies that the same evolutionary laws which govern the animal world can be applied to predict human behaviour. It therefore offers an approach to the work of the police, which could be highly effective. What the drama does is to offer a view of how such a principle might be put into practice. It is an example of praxis.

Danny has begun to take the crime personally and this means that its solution is becoming a matter of self-interest. The loud percussion music which punctuates the series is played over the apprehending of two suspects on a basketball court. The music is closely related to the pace of the action and sometimes signifies the level of tension as the detectives converge on the two possible murderers. Two black men are taken into custody for the crime. Danny has also thoughtlessly revealed to the suspect who seems to have carried out the violent attack on the elderly woman which proves fatal, that his silence will mean that he cannot bargain with the District Attorney to reduce his sentence. He will be seen as the guilty party. The information, however, is an open invitation to confess and reduce his sentence through plea bargaining. As Sorensen tells Del Ray, the suspect who shows no remorse, he is always able to go home early when there is more than one perpetrator of a crime since someone always 'cuts a deal', or offers to give information on the others.

In making this statement the drama is establishing a dialogical link with the discipline of socio-biology. The fundamental problem of socio-biology however, is how altruism has survived when it appears to work against the interests of the individual. The answer is expressed in the 'Prisoner's Dilemma'. This is a hypothetical situation in which two prisoners, each guilty of belonging to an outlawed party, and interrogated separately, face the dilemma of whether to confess. Socio-biologists explain the dilemma as follows. If they both confess, they will each receive five years in jail each. If one confesses, he will go free and the other will serve eight years. If neither confesses, they will be kept for a maximum of three months. The dilemma is whether to confess. The conclusion which socio-biologists have reached is that, as Peter Singer puts it, 'a pair of altruistic prisoners will come out of this better than a pair of self-interested prisoners , 'even from the point of view of self-interest' (Singer, 1983 : 47). The self-interested, tend to confess whereas the altruistic tend to remain silent.

The repentant offender makes a full confession when he hears that the woman is dead. As he reveals the terrible story of how his accomplice attacked the woman, he is deeply affected and shows abundant remorse. Sorenson too is seen with a tear falling from his eyes as he has to listen to the story of the old couple pleading for their lives. It is not clear whether his tears signify that he appreciates the pathos of the whole affair and also sympathises with the robber who is horrified at the consequences of the crime. For his confession to cut a deal with the district attorney however, there must be corroboration. Sorensen then begins to work on Del Ray, who does not know of the previous confession. Sorensen has guessed that he has a self-interested offender and the self-interested tend to confess in the hope of making a plea bargain with the District Attorney. On this occasion, however, because his accomplice has already confessed, it is he who will benefit. When Del Ray confesses, all this does is ensure that his partner will serve a shorter sentence. The interrogation, therefore, reflects the socio-biologist's views very closely. Sorensen's change of direction is a professional success motivated by an emotional reaction. As the women detectives say of him later on, 'he seems to take it all personally – he should do well'.

This remark is also interesting from the point of view of socio-biology. Sorensen has shown that his own altruism is the basis of catching the guilty and ensuring their punishment. He has acted on behalf of Terry when he could have simply accepted one confession. Thus he has shown that altruism is compatible with being a tough policeman. E.O.Wilson commented that the evolutionary function of altruism is 'the central theoretical problem of socio-biology', and here there is a rejoinder which answers the problem. Sorensen has made a mistake because his emotions overcame him, but he adjusts and later tricks the violent offender into making a confession. Justice is, therefore done. What is more the American justice system is shown to be an entirely 'natural' process of social regulation which can be fully justified. In this respect we see Sorensen succeed by adapting his approach to the suspect, but Sipowicz is not so fortunate.

Mrs Sipowicz, a lawyer, has for some time asked him to seek out a fellow officer to determine whether a man called Suarez has been wrongly imprisoned. Andy and the other officer have had a disagreement. When Andy does speak with him somewhat aggressively, the other officer reveals that there are reasons to doubt that Suarez was the guilty man. On returning home, however, Andy offers this information to his wife only to find that Suarez has been killed in prison. His adjustment was too late and the friction in his marriage is a direct result of this. The important lesson to learn about making the ecological adjustments is that no-one should expect thanks. Gratitude only comes when the results of the changes made have become clear. Dolores, the civilian office-worker is found in the strip-club hiding in a toilet cubicle to conceal the fact that she has been moonlighting as a stripper. She knew the dead man and used to pose nude for him while he masturbated. In the montage of brief scenes which introduce the episode, Dolores is found in the women's toilet stretching her legs upwards. She explains that she is thinking of resuming her ballet career. In fact the 45 per cent angle of her outstretched leg echoes the sign outside 'the Gentleman's Hour', which shows a woman with her legs at the same angle. Dolores gives her reasons for moonlighting in this way. Dolores signifies someone who has not learnt to adjust. She is a performer and signifies an alternative to the ecological metaphor.

The notion of performance suggests that it is possible to change one's life if you change the way you behave towards others. Changing one's own performance is a different strategy from trying to adjust the ecology of the environment in which you work. Performances bring immediate praise. One vital difference is that the performer herself takes direct responsibility for success or failure. Dolores reveals that what she hated about the police station was that everyone thanked her politely. This amuses the women detectives who interpret it as self-doubt. Because she has so little self-respect she cannot accept praise from people without doubting it. The direct exchange of a 'performance' for money is at least, for her, an occasion where she can believe in the value of the service she is providing, even if it is degrading. Manipulating the eco-system does not produce instant results in terms of praise or gratitude or money – it takes time.

By contrast, Tina, another stripper at the club who was involved with the dead man, displays a purely mercenary character. When questioned, she can recite exactly how much her late lover spent on her to the nearest hundred dollars. The officers describe her as a 'human cash-register'. Tina has exploited her attractiveness in return for material goods and is played as a shallow, unattractive personality. The detectives comment that she is possibly seeking sympathy but express little for such an exploitative person. As she gets up, Tina display a considerable amount of thigh in the extremely brief garment she is wearing and the camera 'glances' at this as a rejoinder to the claims she is making that she has led an unfortunate life. Such glances help to establish the evaluative orientation of the utterance as a whole, which is critical of the people who exploit others and may ask for sympathy. At one point Diane threatens to punch her in the mouth but she adjusts and eventually adopts a reasoned approach to the interrogation.

The ecological metaphor also means that it is better to endure isolated aggravation if one interviewee can tip the balance of the whole situation in the favour of rightness. The police team are not fundamentally mercenary. Their motivation is essentially altruistic, yet their public reception can be brutally unkind. The officers do not work for praise like Dolores, or for money like Tina. It transpires that Tina's other lover, Tod, who is a heavy drugs-user, was extremely jealous of her relationship with the dead man and Tina is persuaded to lure him to the club. When the psychopathic Tod arrives he has a gun to rescue her and is quickly arrested. The two women officers can appreciate the man's nature and they complain that they will not be allowed to claim his arrest as their own since he will probably only confess when the forensic evidence proves conclusive. Tod is so outraged that the two women will not be credited with the arrest that he confesses on the spot. The two experienced women detectives appreciate that getting a confession from Tod is a matter of changing the environment, of subtly altering the factors which affect his behaviour. Tod likes to cut people down to size if they 'act bigger than other people'. This was his reason for killing Tina's other lover and this is why he dislikes the idea of other people claiming credit for his arrest. He does not confess because he likes the women detectives. The detective's satisfaction comes from successfully manipulating the environment to obtain the correct result, not from the admiration they receive.

The final test of Sipowiz's philosophy arrives when Sorensen visits his lover, Nadine after a hard day's work and they are seen naked in bed together. Nadine informs him that she still does not want a serious relationship, and Sorensen comments that he recalls how much this appealed to him when he first met her. His wry smile gives the statement an ironic accentuation. Their relationship is clearly not entirely casual. Nadine then adds that if they do 'go to the next level', this would be OK with her and she wants to know whether Danny wants their relationship to develop. Sorensen is upset that their pleasant evening making love has been disrupted by things being 'stirred up' and does not give an answer. This situation is analogous to the prisoner's dilemma in some ways.

Nadine is trying to trap Sorensen into becoming the first to declare a serious passion. If Sorensen is the first to do this, however, his selfless gesture could backfire: Nadine has contradicted herself and she might now reject him if he is too passionate. The issue is who is to be the first to declare love for the other and what are the consequences.

When he is reluctant to answer, Nadine is offended and asks 'What's wrong with someone saying they like you?' This question is dialogically related to Dolores' problem. Dolores is mocked by the women detectives for her statement because they do not feel so appreciated, but they also understand: 'You're so down on yourself you can't stand anyone liking you'. Sorensen's self-respect has suffered because he has had to extract a confession by devious means and be close to acts of unspeakable violence, but this is a chance for his ecological *modus vivendi* to come to his aid. It is time to adjust, and to change the situation. Sorensen's answer to her accusation that he has come to her just for sex, is that he simply wanted to be 'next to someone good' after a day in his job. The actual human consequences of the ecological metaphor for the people who work in social services is that they simply adjust the environment and are not recognised as the people who are responsible for social order. The contemptible things they encounter and sometimes do, have to be endured while they wait for the higher good to result from their actions. As Sipowicz implies, the person who maintains the fish tank can only claim that he is 'a man who knows fish': the talent is not transferable into other areas of life.

In their personal lives, they may as seems to happen here, forget to adjust and expect admiration as Sipowicz expects praise from his wife for uncovering Suarez's innocence, but this is not to be. Sorensen recovers from this setback enough to offer to see Nadine on Friday when he says that 'if you don't want to talk, I will understand'. Nadine replies, 'Good try; I'm busy on Friday' in a fit of pique. In the private domestic world of these characters, others can also play the game of adjusting the environment. Nadine is also 'fishing' for compliments and reassurance by introducing uncertainty into their relationship. Her comment, 'Good try' signifies that she is aware of Sorensen's ploy. Sorensen, however, does not respond to this retort and instead suggests that they see each other on Saturday. He thereby avoids asking questions about what she might be doing on Friday and being drawn into her game of fostering jealousy. By negating her ploy, Sorensen gets a positive response and Nadine agrees to a Saturday meeting. An uneasy truce has been declared. The principle of the fish tank is that you do not tackle problems head-on but you look at their underlying cause and alter the environment which has caused them. By insisting that he wants to see Nadine, he has reassured her of his feelings without having to name them.

In our dream-wish, we want the metaphor of the fish-tank to work because it means that there is an answer to life's difficulties and we can indulge our feelings knowing that there is always a solution close at hand. Danny Sorenson is also young and handsome and his youthful optimism is a feature which it would be depressing to see destroyed. Sorensen has overcome a personal difficulty by adopting the socio-biological metaphor which supports his morale at work. It remains to be seen whether this philosophy will guarantee his success. The socio-biology thesis is ultimately a rather pessimistic view of human nature and can imply that we cannot lead our lives by rational decision-making. Nature takes over, and as Hume put it, 'reason is the slave of the passions'. Sorensen has got what he wants, but his ability to manipulate the situation has ruled out sincerity and seems to leave him dissatisfied with himself.

The theme of many American television dramas is the role of the professional: the doctor, the police officer and the psychologist are the examples referred to here. In their daily working lives they encounter moral problems continually. Mark Greene in *ER* sometimes has to decide whether to operate on a patient in the accident and emergency area despite the fact that this is against procedure. On occasions he does this successfully and saves a life when no other surgeon is available. Breaking rules about the administering of medication, however, is something he frowns upon. He would not give a patient drugs to prevent pain simply to earn his gratitude. Andy Sipowicz and his colleagues are also confronted with a choice about whether to break the rules. When they know that they have the perpetrators in custody but cannot obtain a confession, they often resort to bullying tactics to ensure that witnesses and conspirators confess. Fitz also chooses to both uncover the guilty party by subterfuge and eventually to act with a clear conscience. In all three cases, the professionals show a higher-level morality. Whereas Kantian ethics would stress the motive on which the professionals act and Utilitarian ethics would place emphasis on the results, these men achieve the best results with the highest motives. Their behaviour shows a concern for the moral law as Kant wanted. They act out of the spirit of saving life or convicting those who take lives. The important thing is not to follow the rules slavishly but to exercise judgement about how to unite motives and consequences in each case. The ideal professional is a pragmatist and follows rules until they conflict with the public's interests whereupon he must make a decision in the particular case. Morality seems to require a cadre of professionals who are capable of such judgement.

The comforting mythology which seems to be prevalent in many series of this kind, is that there is a natural law by which the professional motives and the right consequences can be reconciled. In *ER*, it is recognising that the putting-together of the two sets of parents will result in the agreement to a transplant. The best role for the doctors is to expedite what nature will bring about by itself. In *Fitz* the confession of David Roberge is hastened by appealing to his nature and his psychology: all it takes is to confront him with his own motives which involve recognising the crime as an extension of his nature. *NYPD Blue* also espouses the view that the ideal detective simply sets up the circumstances in which suspects will confess. In this way any infringement of individual civil rights is seen as irrelevant because nature takes its course. Cracking the code of the professional series, therefore means observing its recurrent ideologies and assessing these in the cold light of day.

An example of signifiance which interrupts this dominant mythology, however, occurs when Danny is inteviewing a suspect and begins to cry as he hears the story of how the confessor's accomplice battered the elderly woman to death. It is difficult to see where compassion can intrude if the professionals subscribe to the biological metaphor which is outlined above. Professional behaviour is a matter of judgement and not of feeling. The professional's actions are not motivated by compassion. When Danny Sorensen cries, therefore, is he feeling sorry for himself, for the deceased woman, for the confessor, or for the situation as a whole? Compassion is irrelevant in doing this job which always requires a measures response to the controlling of the determining factors. It is a science, not an art, yet human agents feel emotions which they have to express. Sorensen's emotion is an example of what Barthes calls, 'an emotion-value', the evaluation of a situation which the third meaning can yield. As such it makes a distinctly odd accompaniment to the clinical exercise of professional judgement by suggesting that the whole thing is a tragedy. It is on occasions where the professionals are characterised that the realisation of their personalities can conflict with the demands of the job. Sipowicz's well-known outbursts humanize his character but detract from his status as 'Buddha'. The dilemma for these professional characters is whether they are expediting the course of nature and so improving the world, or whether they are, in fact, using their reasoning to justify their own passions and prejudices. This is an unresolved issue in socio-biology and it remains a perennial counter-narrative in these otherwise complacent dramas.

The X-Files: Thinking above the flow

In one episode of *The X-Files*, a Navajo Indian tribe enables Fox Mulder to keep a computer disk out of the reach of the conspirators who are pursuing it by memorising its contents and passing them on to other Navajo through their oral tradition. The Navajo have long been recognised as a tribe with a spiritual tradition which offers an alternative to America's consumer society. It is easy to conclude that the drama series simply presents a set of fashionably attractive ideas which gullible viewers will prefer to the harsh realities of daily life. Whether Navajo Indians can actually perform such a feat is open to debate. This is an example of the kind of New Age nostalgia for primitive mysticism that the drama has celebrated. What is open to question by exploring the semiotics of the drama is whether the appeal can be reduced to the celebration of alternatives to technology and modernity. Chris Carter, the originator of the series has denounced the attempts to read meanings into the show which he regards as straightforward entertainment. In one sense, this is obviously true, and it is undoubtedly true that the show is not deliberately designed to attract these readings. The semiotic approach which has been developed so far, however, may explain how it is possible to regard the show as a thriller with a more profound social meaning for many people.

Robin Nelson maintains that *The X-Files* 'is grounded in a TV drama referential realism' (Nelson, 1997 : 152) by virtue of its style of situating each scene with a textual display that gives real locations. The word 'grounded' is important here: the drama's narratives originate in real locations but go beyond this to a hypothesis with only a brief recognition. The text which tells us the precise locations situates the events in reality, but the hypothetical worlds which the drama presents are not framed within the conventions of a recognisable naturalism. This drama claims the freedom to insert any kind of non-natural event in its pursuit of closure. The text on screen is actually more akin to a Brechtian panel on stage which announces information to the audience. The font used and the manner in which the text seems to be 'typed' across the screen signify the process of filing reports. We are presented with documentary evidence to be assessed. The initial semiotics of each scene distances us briefly from the facts which are presented.

As Brecht said, of his own work, 'complex seeing must be practised...Thinking *above* the flow of the play is more important than thinking from *within* the flow of the play' (quoted in Williams, 1952 : 381-2). In other words, there are many opportunities to attend to signs which make us reflect on what *The X-Files* is presenting and not to be overwhelmed by its apparent truth claims as if it were simple naturalism. It is semiotics which enables us to perceive moments of reflexivity which take us 'above the flow'. If there is realism in this drama series it is psychological realism. This drama is not so much critical naturalism as *hypothetical* critical naturalism. It offers the prospect of an intolerable society under future conditions where current psychological tendencies of the powerful continue. There is, therefore a link with naturalism, since it does show how people's actions are determined by social pressures, but its style is not that of recognisable reality. The series, therefore, needs to be understood firstly for its cultural significance and not by the content of the dramas alone.

Robin Nelson also correctly observes that the drama is a rejoinder to the Roswell incident where what appeared to be a UFO crashed in the desert near Roswell in the USA in 1947 and the government was reluctant to allow people near. Photographs of corpses which looked like aliens have been widely circulated, although the government has denied that these are genuine. The claims and counter-claims have been numerous since the 1950s, and it is now very difficult to establish exactly what did happen. It is possible to discover files on the internet which claim to be secret government papers relating to cover-ups of the Roswell incident.

Whatever did happen, it is clear that the authorities gave conflicting accounts of the incident. The drama is a rejoinder which demonstrates the kind of logic which would lead a government to conceal such an event from its people. Watergate and the recent Presidential sex scandals have compounded this event. Since government deception is hidden from us, the series speculates on the kinds of incidents which *might* take place and the possible motives for concealing them. If there is any subversive intent on the part of the writers it is not to reflect what people know but what they find credible about their rulers. We may not know all that they do, but as in the case of the American president, we have reason to be sceptical when they speak about themselves. As the mysterious black man says, they (the conspirators) have only one policy: 'deny everything'. The real basis of the series is the highly suspect psychology of the American leaders of state. It is not, therefore, necessary to believe all that we see in the drama as if it were naïve realism.

In many shows the series as a rejoinder demonstrates the rational basis for scepticism about American democracy rather than claims about its actual machinations. If Lyotard's view of contemporary postmodern politics is that the State is concerned only to legitimate its own actions, then the discovery of facts which are suppressed is a sign that the kind of society envisaged by Habermas: the consensual world brought about by the free communication of information, is clearly not the aim of the authorities. Lyotard's description of

State 'terror' is when there is 'a threat to eliminate a player from the game one shares with him', or to de-legitimise a player altogether. The implicit imperative as Lyotard describes it is 'Adapt your aspirations to our end – or else' (Lyotard, 1979 : 63-4). Viewers of *The X-Files* will recognise this threat which hangs over Mulder and Scully constantly. Their actions need to be seen as responses to the generic forms of oppression which occur in America today. They show how it might be possible to survive such treatment. As the 'smoking man' says to Mulder, 'I have respect for you Mulder; you're becoming a player'.

In reading *The X-Files*, however, the most crucial element of a semiotic approach is to decide just what kind of social practice the drama is engaged in. This strategy is liable to be construed as making a cult television drama into an intellectual experience by superimposing ideas and theories which were never intended. The semiotic approach which begins with the nature of the social practice that a drama participates in, however, makes a distinction between the meaning of a drama's content and its social function. The dramatic text on television is not a separate, isolated phenomenon which mirrors or distorts the culture which surrounds it. Instead, the text's signs must be seen in a cultural context as a part of a practice rather than a commentary upon one.

The anthropologist Clifford Geertz refers to the Navajo Indian ceremony of 'sings' in his chapter entitled 'Religion as a Cultural Practice' (Geertz, 1973). By taking this analogy, it is possible to begin to debate whether the semiotics of *The X-Files* demonstrates how to resist hegemony and produce oppositional readings of social life or whether the drama is also a means of coming to terms with psychological discomfort and of easing anxiety in the way that *Fitz* can be argued to do. If the latter is the case then *The X-Files* could be argued to create just as conservative an audience as any other drama. Scully's eventual recovery after abduction, for example, might be seen as a straightforward testament to religious faith. In the three episodes which will be discussed, Dana Scully may be seen as a symbol of old-fashioned Christian values which are abstract and independent of particular regimes. Perhaps the viewers enjoy the picture of a reassuring integrity and take the message that this will enable the virtuous to survive anything. It is also possible that there is a continual ambiguity on this issue which is maintained deliberately throughout the series. This may explain part of its appeal. The constant tension in the series between the feeling that the discovery of the truth, when communicated by virtuous people, might make a difference, and the feeling that even revelations are manipulated by invisible agents of the State, represents a vital contemporary debate. The dark surroundings from the Film Noir genre signify the ambiguity which is never resolved between the completely repressive State as envisaged by Lyotard, and one in which the discovery of truth will liberate the people. The signs are that a sinister plot might always lurk in waiting for Mulder and Scully even at their moments of triumph. Viewers are provided with the understanding to engage in this dialogue.

When the American government concealed facts about the Roswell incident they compounded two crimes in the minds of many people: they both practised political deception and also denied the beliefs which were many people's replacement for religion. Seeing a UFO, for example, tends to be an individual experience and to suppress this testimony relegates the individuals concerned to the status of the insane. This is fundamentally unacceptable in a country which is built on individualism. Geertz's argument is that religion is a means of making the incomprehensible world comprehensible, of explaining how to differentiate between good and evil and of offering a coherent explanation of suffering which makes it tolerable for the individual who suffers. Thus the Christian story of suffering as bringing redemption to those who endure it, can be seen as a means of restoring a sense of purpose to a life where suffering cannot be avoided and evil appears to triumph.

The anthropologist of religion suggests that there is a way of understanding this situation. As Geertz says, the maxim of all religious experience is 'he who would know must first believe' (Geertz, 1974 : 110). If a religious perspective is accepted, then everywhere empirical evidence seems to confirm it. Subjective and objective can be united. Proof follows from belief, not belief from proof. In demonstrating that certain beliefs may give coherence to a set of diverse facts, some of which are taken from actual media reports, the drama tackles the problem of meaninglessness. The postmodern condition is not actually reversed, but certain over-arching narratives can be made much more convincing. This makes us more sceptical as an audience because it demonstrates that the coherence of an explanation is no guarantee of validity. When an alternative world-picture can also give coherence to a set of facts which have hitherto been explained satisfactorily, then our accepted beliefs must be questioned.

In the ceremony which the Navajo call 'sings' a sick person is treated by a symbolic act of purification which identifies them with a divine force. The ritual is in three stages: the purification of the patient and the audience; a statement in chants of the wish to restore well-being; and an identification of the patient with the Holy People. As Geertz remarks, however, the chief purpose of the ritual is not to inculcate belief in the deities invoked, but to 'give the stricken person a vocabulary in terms of which to grasp the nature of his distress and relate it to a wider world' (Geertz, 1974 : 105). The problem of evil is not the problem of how to avoid the apparently arbitrary misfortune visited upon the just and the good, but that it threatens 'our ability to make sound moral judgements' (Geertz, 1974:106). The religious ritual demonstrates the necessity for values in a world where there are no rational expectations of salvation.

The X-Files, therefore, acts to provide a dialogue with evil events which enable the viewer to feel that their fundamental concerns have a voice and can be articulated. The drama shows that a postmodern incoherence only increases the necessity to believe, if only to achieve a resolute voice in the face of deception. An analogy might be made with keeping a memento of a dead family member. Keeping such an item may not be a means of maintaining that person's presence, but a psychological mechanism which links our thoughts to the values and beliefs which that person represented for us. The function is not to overcome nature, by overcoming death, but to live with a recognition of that natural phenomenon transformed into a symbol of hope. The drama can therefore be seen as either showing how to find an oppositional voice, or how to select a comforting mythology which elevates the mystic to the status of hero. The show establishes a fantastic, non-naturalistic hypothesis and then dramatises the means of finding a form of expression which can effectively communicate this and the various cultural and political barriers which will be placed in anyone's way. According to Geertz the aesthetic attitude is divorced from factuality. The hypothetical nature of the worlds created which begin with a requirement that we accept a fantastic belief, mean that we are automatically in a non-natural world where the usual rules need no longer apply. There can be no doubt, however, that some audience members have failed to distinguish the religious from the aesthetic perspectives and have seen in the drama a description of real conspiracies.

In the three-episode video entitled '*Abduction*' from the second series, a man called Dwayne has escaped from a state penitentiary institution and taken a doctor hostage. His motive is to escape being abducted again by aliens. The doctor is kidnapped in order that he may also be abducted with him and believe Dwayne's story. At the outset we see Dwayne from above, screaming and bathed in brilliant white light as a number of alien figures gather behind a translucent window to observe him. The shot then widens to take in the house in which he is alone. It is full of a brilliant white light which streams from each window. Next we see a column of light descending onto the roof of the house. The style is a sign that we are not automatically supposed to believe Dwayne's account. This is a non-naturalistic sign. The actual performance of the scream staring upwards at the ceiling, borrows from images of nightmares and suggests that he may be dreaming. The scene is abruptly abandoned and an on-screen graphic tells us that the scene has shifted to a correctional institution where Dwayne is a prisoner. This sudden transition condenses the intervening narrative. In a conversation with the institution's doctor, a reference is made to the fact that he 'hurt someone' which explains how he came to be there. It is characteristic of the series that the action should be discontinuous in a manner which accelerates the narrative. The actual plot is composed of episodes which detail the reactions to Dwayne's accounts of his abduction. These are the crucial elements in the editing process and these are closely focussed. The *plot* is not what happens to Dwayne, in which case, his attacks on others would be shown; it is the history of the reception of his account of abduction. This, therefore, is not in a logical, cause-and-effect sequence of continuity editing. For this reason, the plot selects highlights from the story.

Dwayne refers to himself in the third person as 'Dwayne Barry' to signify his alienation from the self he once possessed. He later takes further hostages inside a travel agents and Mulder is summoned to help negotiate with him. The pattern which the conversation is supposed to take in such negotiations is 'honesty/containment/conciliation'. When Dwayne reveals that he knows that Mulder will adopt this strategy, Mulder knows that he must also have been a member of the FBI who had received the same training. He asks to have further details of the man's case in order to understand what happened to him, but the agents in control of the situation do not regard the man's history as relevant to his capture. This immediately creates a dialogic relation between the scene commander's disregard for the perpetrator's history and the audience's knowledge. Our privileged knowledge has revealed to us that Dwayne's personal account would be extremely helpful in calming the hostage crisis. Before Mulder goes inside the building to assist a wounded hostage, he is told by the other agents that he must not 'jump into his (Dwayne's) delusion'. Mulder repeats this as a catechism: it represents the conventional FBI wisdom in hostage-taking negotiations. The accentuation which Mulder gives the words as he recites them, however, constitute a sign: this utterance signifies a weariness and scepticism on his part with the Bureau's approach. The reason for this approach is that as Mulder recites it, 'I can't negotiate with him if he thinks I believe him'. When the women police officer leading the operation to free the hostages shows herself to be sceptical, Mulder asks whether she knows what aliens do to women's ovaries. The rhetorical question signifies his compassion towards the abductees. It also looks forward proleptically to the moment when we see a tube making contact with Scully's distended belly when she is operated on by the aliens who abduct her. This moment is 'pregnant' in that it signifies the choice which Mulder makes when he is confronted with the imperative expressed by Lyotard as ' Adapt your purposes to our ends or else'. Mulder chooses to ignore the threat and this has consigned him a to play a specific role in the events which is not of his choosing.

Once inside the hostage scene, Mulder begins to behave differently. The reason why identification with the hostage-taker's delusion is discouraged is that this means that it becomes increasingly difficult to make the perpetrator face reality. The theory is that he must be discouraged from persisting in his delusional world. Mulder, however, goes further than identifying with him: he actually begins to give him information. He tells Dwayne things which only someone who knows about the abduction experience could know. 'They don't speak', he tells Dwayne. He also gives him the vocabulary to express his knowledge. Mulder tells Dwayne that the aliens' ability to see into their victims' mind is called 'mind-scanning'. It is at this point that Dwayne relates more of the events which happened when he was abducted. His flashbacks show glimpses of the aliens and also dark-suited men who he claims to be agents of the state present at the abduction. His flashback takes us to the alien ship where he is spreadeagled on a table to be subjected to the aliens' scientific experiments. We see from his point of view the terrifying high-tech machinery used to drill tiny holes in his teeth which are then filled with a strange metallic substance. As we see this high-tech drill slowly lowering to deliver a powerful and painful beam which drills Dwayne's teeth, the scene abruptly changes to the room next to the hostage scene. In the room next door a more primitive drill is being used to make a hole in the wall for surveillance purposes. One drill is immediately replaced with another. The abrupt montage editing signifies a visual analogy with thematic significance: the Federal agents are thereby explicitly compared with the aliens as they regard Dwayne as a mere scientific curiosity to be observed. This analogy-sign also relates dialogically to the claim that there is a conspiracy between the State and the aliens: it becomes a counter-narrative. When Mulder fails in his attempts to persuade Dwayne to give up the hostages, he lures him to the front door do that the police marksmen can get a clear shot at him. A small red dot, of the same brilliant red as the tooth-drilling beam locates Dwayne to signify that he is in a laser sight before he is shot. A further sign which does not contribute to the narrative but complicates it, is the next shot which shows the hostage-negotiation team from above. This proposes a perspective which has not been offered to the viewer so far. The possibility of another presence which is observing the whole scene is a hint of the conspiracies which might be taking place. The observers too may be in the process of being observed.

Dana Scully meanwhile has been investigating Dwayne's past in the FBI at Mulder's request. She discovers that he is suffering from a psychosis and tends to act out his fantasies. He was shot in the line of duty and his 'moral sense has been destroyed'. When Dwayne acts out his fantasies, according to his records, he becomes violent. Scully warns Mulder via the microscopic receiver he is wearing inside the travel agents. Mulder, however, continues to tell Dwayne that he understands. The FBI record is, in fact, a useful way of explaining the spiritual crisis which has sent Dwayne Barry almost insane.

At this point, we can see how the series engages in a dialogue with many of the newsworthy incidents of a similar nature which have happened in America. As Geertz has pointed out, the religious perspective actually creates an alternative belief system which establishes a moral order. In situations such as the storming of David Koresh's compound at Waco, a similar situation was encountered where the inmates had a radically different perspective on the world. The authorities, however, had the task of removing what they saw as an obstruction to law and order. Witnesses have commented that the authorities believed that loving parents would release the children when the building came under attack. In fact, those who believed that this was the Apocalypse they had prepared for, felt that the best way was to ensure their children were taken with them to salvation. In the apocalyptic movements in particular, it may be necessary to consider what the perpetrators actually believe rather than regarding them as a logistical problem with a military solution. As Mulder states in relation to Dwayne, honesty and respect are needed. The diagnosis which Scully gives is one which is perfectly compatible with Dwayne's abduction experience. Both may be true, and yet the existence of one cancels out the other in Scully's scientific mind. The political problem which such a situation poses has genuinely important, far-reaching consequences.

In semiotic terms such a dilemma is signified in the poses struck by Mulder and Scully in what Genette call the 'paratext' (in Stam *et al* 1992): the various images which are allied to the drama such as pre-publicity stills and advertisements, all of which help to establish the drama's atmosphere and govern its social significance. One memorable image shows the two main characters conservatively dressed, often back to back, staring in an almost accusing manner at the image's viewer. Often they are also looking downward with their arms folded as if their task has been fulfilled and they now claim the authority of exclusive, superior knowledge. This is an example of the third meaning, where this pose signifies something which can only be described rather than clearly named. The somewhat staid dress styles of the characters signify their social positions: they are not natural radicals with an alternative society in mind. Their strait-laced contemporary Puritanism makes their espousal of the paranormal all the more exceptional and worthy of note. The opposing approaches of Mulder and Scully: the believer in the paranormal and the scientific rationalist, are constantly in tension. The internet fans make up stories about the consummation of their very close relationship, but symbolically, science and the paranormal remain separate. The acknowledgement of the viewer suggests that they present us with the final choice as to how their discoveries should be evaluated. The unsmiling directness of their deadpan gaze is a further sign that this is almost a moral imperative for the viewer: they are expecting a judgement. If the truth is 'out there', the series' slogan can be seen as an imperative exhorting the audience to seek it out. Bakhtin's 'responsive understanding' is suggested by their look.

The Navajo 'sing' consists of three parts: the purification of the patient and audience by repetitive chants; purification rites which may involve an ordeal and physical symptoms such as sweating; and the identification of the patient with the divine. The three-episode video 'Abduction' can be correlated with these three dramatic elements. In the first episode Dwayne Barry is vindicated despite his anti-social behaviour and the audience is assimilated with the knowing people who comprehend his pain and make the correct judgements about efforts to contain him. In the second episode, Scully is substituted for Dwayne as the victim. Since she is a much more attractive and well-loved character than Dwayne, once she is abducted, the audience experiences a natural concern for her well-being and hints of the dark practices of the aliens only serve to heighten the tension. The third section of the 'sing' is usually accomplished by drawing a symbolic divine figure in sand and laying the patient upon it. The act enables the holy man to touch the sand figure and the patient and to establish a symbolic identification between them. In the case of Dwayne Barry, the editing of the drama forces the viewer to contemplate and empathise with the drilling of Dwayne's teeth. The insidious beam of light is shown being lowered into position and the agonising drilling taking place. The perspective then shifts to that of the victim and the audience then see the drill from below as if they are experiencing it. This makes the suffering of the patient both an objective and subjective phenomenon. We have to watch it taking place which can also be painful. The audience are also ennobled by having to endure this agonising image. This process is analogous to the use of the sand figure in that it establishes an identification between the audience and the victim. The identification of the divine and the human makes the patient's pain comparable to the divine sacrifices which guarantee the survival of the race. This both establishes a meaningful context for suffering which dispels the notion that it is without purpose and also provides a vocabulary to express this.

If, in a postmodern society, the proliferation of beliefs only increase, then there will be many people whose alternative moral opinions become incompatible with society's objectives. An ominous political warning-note is sounded by the series. The proliferation of moral beliefs in a pluralist society might be impossible to contain and repression might be the only answer. Oliver Stone, in an article in defence of his own version of American conspiracy theories wrote.

> The lessons of history repeatedly point out the virtue of independent thinking. The need to question. Disbelieve. Defy. Allow us in our million-dollar a TV minute culture, a little space and time for the contrarian and allow that paranoia in moderation. (*The Sunday Times* 8 November 1998)

The drama series *Dark Skies* which sought to imitate and extend the style of *The X-Files* attempted to establish a mythology which would link facts as remote as the assassination of President Kennedy and contemporary accounts of alien abduction.

The naïve response of the alternative believer might be that we only need to demonstrate the truth of our position and the authorities would have to accede to us. *The X-Files*, however, has already considered this possibility. The truth is not enough: the truth is 'out there' but the utilitarian logic of the State would not allow the powerful to listen even if it were found. For this reason, Mulder is sometimes portrayed as the dupe of the authorities and not the agent who will subvert them. The worthwhile point of the drama is not that the fantasies could be real but that if they were, contemporary governments would be liable to consider conspiracies. Like most science fiction, the drama has a great deal to tell us about the present. Chris Carter has acknowledged that he is swayed in his writing and editing of the series by the feedback he finds on the internet. In this sense there is a continual dialogue between the series producers and the fans.

As Geertz points out, however, the 'Problem of Meaning' involves, 'recognizing the inescapability of ignorance, pain, and injustice on the human plane while simultaneously denying that these irrationalities are characteristic of the world as a whole' (Geertz, 1974 : 108). The motto, 'The truth is out there' has a further echo in that it maintains that despite the variety of interpretations which are possible, it is ultimately likely that one perspective will unite the diverse facts that the agents of truth discover. The pain and injustice, in other words, can be seen as man-made rather than a metaphysical inevitability. Empirical facts alone will not change the world-view of the powerful, but a complete picture is ultimately possible which will re-cast all the facts into a coherent perspective. The series is fundamentally optimistic, but its ultimate 'truth' is a tantalising, unrealised prospect which helps to maintain interest throughout the episodes.

The return of Scully after her abduction by the aliens heralds the final section of this dramatic trilogy where Scully has to undergo a psychic struggle for survival. The aliens have tested what the Lone Cowboys, a band of hackers, call 'branched DNA' on her. This is an attempt to merge two diverse beings through joining their molecular structures. The experiment, however, has been abandoned and the residual DNA is now poisoning Scully's system. Mulder is told that there is nothing he can do. Dana's sister, Melissa jons her mother at her bedside and claims to make contact with her soul. Unusually, this is dismissed by Mulder as insufficient to rescue her.

Scully is faced with the fundamental philosophical question which was once posed for existentialists by Camus: why not commit suicide if the world has no meaning? Why should she not allow herself drift away and not regain consciousness? Mulder too is undergoing a crisis. He is furious that Scully has been taken and he decides to track down the apparent conspirators. When a man tries to steal a sample of Scully's blood from the hospital, Mulder captures him, but Mulder's secret ally shoots the man before he can be interrogated. Mulder is prey to feelings of revenge and he is tempted to revenge himself on the 'Cancer Man', a senior FBI agent who has engineered Scully's disappearance.

Mulder is given information that his appartment will be searched that evening and he is told by his black ally that he can kill the men who come to do this. As he waits, however, he is visited by Melissa, Dana's sister who tells him that he is living in 'a dark place' both literally and metaphorically. When Scully is seen, she is often pictures bathed in a dazzling white light. She asks why Mulder does not tell Scully how he feels, and he abandons his wait for the searchers and goes to visit the weakening Scully. Melissa wears a black band around her neck, a kind of choker with a small white crystal attached to it. This somewhat dated fashion helps to signify that she is pagan. Mulder is not attracted to a simple pagan alternative and when Melissa practices what appears to be Reiki healing by holding her hands at a distance from Dana's body, Mulder is not impressed. Mulder is actually seeking not merely a physical cure but a completely new moral order to substitute for the lawlessness he has discovered. What sociologists call 'anomie', the breakdown of all recognised values, has taken place in his life.

Scully, meanwhile has also been tempted to give up the struggle, but the vocabulary which she needs to strengthen her resolve is made clear to her. She is seen in a small rowing boat without oars which is tethered to the side of a lake. She sits in the boat resting on a cushion facing the figures of Mulder, a small boy and 'Nurse Owens' on the bank. The image is redolent of various female figures in mythology of an elevated status. Scully becomes a goddess.

Despite the pleading of Nurse Owens, we see the rope which hold the boat dripping with water and finally snapping to release Scully. Mulder visits her and tells her that he believes she has the strength to continue and that her faith will help her. When Melissa suggests that Mulder switches his approach, she is therefore recommending a gender shift. Scully's late father visits her in a dream and in his sparkling white naval uniform reveals his regret at a life lived according to masculine values. Mulder's visit signifies that he has been converted to the values which Dana holds dear. Belief in a fundamental dichotomy between the darkness and the light is essential to sustain the search for the truth. Mulder gives Scully a small gold cross on a chain. She put this around her neck and fondles it. The cross moves in the light and gleams with a bright light to signify that Mulder and she are both now determined to pursue the source of illumination.

This could be seen as a comforting mythology of the most conservative Christian kind, in keeping with the ideology of 'middle America', but it must also be seen as a sign. In narrative terms, this is a gesture which shows the bonding of Mulder and Scully. In symbolic terms they both espouse an abstract ideal: goodness of light as against darkness, Abstract ideals are, of course, something which the pragmatics of postmodernism cannot accommodate. The postmodern approach which defends the State's actions on the basis that to maintain the existence of the State is the highest goal, cannot accept that some values override its own existence. Scully also signifies scientific rationalism, which, perhaps surprisingly, is not linked with the possibility of State 'terror' by Lyotard. In *The Postmodern Condition*, Lyotard argues that science is an 'open system': one which does not result in a closed loop, which which continually entertains and assimilates new knowledge. Science does not reject that which appears to confound its very premises, but has to explain it. In symbolic terms, therefore, the rapprochement between Mulder and Scully and her return to the task of uncovering the truth, signify that science and belief in the paranormal can be consistent. Science is, in one sense, an avenue through which the truth may subvert that State's grip on power. Skinner, Mulder's boss at the agency refuses to accept his resignation and gives his reason as an out-of-the-body experience he underwent whilst wounded in Vietnam. This is dialogically related to Scully's experiences whilst in a coma which are similar. Both signify that the one experience which will change an individual's attitudes and beliefs is that of confronting the paranormal.

The preceding remarks, in other words, demonstrate the existence of Barthes' second meaning: the symbolic, codified message. The third meaning is more elusive, but it disrupts the view that the ending is a settled and complacent closure. When he has been admonished by Melissa for retreating into darkness, Mulder return to Scully's bedside and while she is in the coma, tells her that he believes that she feels that it is not time to go and that she has always lived by her beliefs. This is a dialogic reference to her father's intervention in her dream. When Scully does eventually wake up and Mulder visits her, Scully tells him that it was his beliefs which sustained her. At one level this looks like simple mutual support, but it is actually more complicated. The editing of the drama inserts a number of signs which make the ending ambiguous. Scully says that she attributes her revival to Mulder's beliefs, but she dreamt that her late father visited her and gave the same advice. He too said that he believed her work was not over. In addition to her father a 'Nurse Owens' also encourages her to refuse to give up the fight for survival. Mulder and Scully do not share a religious faith. When Mulder returns to his appartment after seeing Scully in a coma, he squats on his haunches and holds his outstretched hands about six inches apart. This unusual posture is, perhaps, half-way to prayer. It seems like a gesture of despair, but it does not quite become a position of supplication. This is an example of a signifier without a codified signified. Mulder needs Scully to continue the keeping of the X-files. This, as they say, is what the authorities fear most. This is the best form of retribution. Oddly, perhaps, Mulder, the member of the duo who usually does believe in the paranormal, cannot find a faith to sustain him. Scully's loss would probably mean the end of his struggle. His posture partly signifies the recognition of existential emptiness. In the end what he actually says to Scully represents a belief not in a faith, but in the struggle to find the truth itself. Until the truth is discovered, he awaits revelation.

Scully, therefore has a number of possible sources for her recovery of spirit: her father, Melissa, Mulder and the enigmatic 'Nurse Owens' who turns out not to exist. The drama leaves open the whole range of possibilities: spiritualism, New Age therapy, the romantic relationship with Mulder, and divine intervention. Any of these agents could have been responsible for Scully's miraculous recovery. The gesture of returning to Scully the golden crucifix necklace which Mulder says he has been 'holding for her', might seem to signify a romantic bond. At this point, however, we cut to a glimpse of Scully's mother who is searching Mulder's face for a sign of romantic involvement. The glance here is a psychoanalytic moment where the audience's unconscious thoughts are reflected in the screen action. The gesture is not followed up by a close-up of Mulder and any romantic significance evaporates. The meaning of life for Mulder and Scully inheres in the pursuit of truth itself, and not in any specific doctrines.

As an ending, therefore, a careful consideration of the various signs which problematise it, makes the conclusion more than a comforting return to the ideology of middle America. The ambiguity makes the place of faith in the search for truth clear. Belief may sustain individuals but the facts which will confirm it, the 'truth' to be discovered, is still sought after. The concluding, signs have, therefore, shown how what might be read as a comforting assertion of traditional Christianity, is, in fact, not the whole meaning of the final episode. The drama does, therefore offer some comfort in ennobling the figures of Scully and Mulder through a process analogous to the Navajo 'sing'. They have therefore become the nearest we have to gods. Their continued search is reassuring. On the other hand, we have also seen how the drama encourages the viewer not to be complacent and to rest easy with this comfort. It also usurps the dominant ideology by showing how easy it is to concoct a comprehensive explanation. The paradox of the series is that it seems to be premised on some postmodernist principles, yet it offers a totalising explanation: the conspiracy also explains everything coherently.

New Technology and TV Drama: *Wilderness*

In 1996, at an international writer's workshop in Madrid, Roger Gregory wrote:

> A delicious irony is that as social realism has established its dominance over television drama, the technology of the system has become increasingly less dependent on real images. Television is 'soft'; the image can be manipulated. Though its output is, for the most part, naturalistic, television itself is becoming progressively less so. At some stage, this new grammar of computer-generated images of immense detail and flexibility will be absorbed by drama producers. But there is not much sign of it yet. (Friedmann, ed 1996: 71)

Janet H. Murray speculates on the advent of the 'hyperserial' in which a digital archive such as a website is integrated with television drama. Murray suggests that the characters in *ER* could have their naturalistic background enhanced by making the area interactive so that further data on each of the characters can be found (Murray, 1998). The existing *ER* website, already contains the biographies of characters and the actors who play them. Lynda La Plante's experimental approach to television dram in which the screen is split into four, looks forward to television drama being issued on DVD so that different perspectives on the action can be selected by choosing one of the camera angles available.

Robin Nelson also states that he does not find any great change in television drama as a result of new technology, although the interconnectedness of all the new technologies promises to draw television drama into a more intimate relationship with other forms of communication such as the internet. The feedback from viewers on *The X-Files* which can be found in internet discussions may well have influenced the content and style of the series (Nelson, 1997 : 28). The prospect of a series which is dictated by public opinion in much the same way as Dickens' serialised novels were in the nineteenth century, is becoming much more likely. There is an argument that some audiences are already governing the form and content of media products through their viewing and purchasing habits which can now be scrupulously monitored. There have been audience-dictated soaps on the internet itself but these have been seen as experimental forms which have not had any great impact on mainstream offerings on television.

There is clearly a relationship between the technological forms of television, their funding and the style of actual broadcasts. The celebrated drama, *Boys from the Blackstuff* was notable for the fact that it was shot using the latest hand-held video technology. This enabled a low-budget programme to be shot on location whereas normally, it could only have used such locations if expensive film technology was used. The drama was therefore able to present the action against the backdrop of actual locations in Liverpool where many of the social problems it dealt with really existed. This was a spur to the drama's naturalistic 'authenticity'. When *Boys from the Blackstuff* was made, the technology for digital manipulation did not exist so plentifully that it could be used to edit the video scenes. Analog technology tends to restrict the fundamental signifying unit to the shot, whereas digital technology enables the analytical process to separate the elements of shots into, for example, naturalistic and non-naturalistic simultaneously. This will also raise the possibility that in some scenes a dialogical relationship between various signs can be established. The emphasis on the shot also tends to foreground the director's role over that of the writer or editor, for example. Post-production technology will increasingly become the point at which artistry is explored, however, and the editor will have many more opportunities to augment the work. Julia Kristeva was perhaps the first major theorist to draw attention to a distinction in technology which will make a considerable difference to semiotics. 'An analog computer is defined as any device that computes by means of real, physical, *continuous* qualities and some other set of variables, whereas the digital computer presupposes *discrete* elements and discontinuous scales' (Moi, ed, 1986 : 116). Kristeva goes on to say that the semiotic is made up of both. Television drama is increasingly in a position to employ digital technology which enables each element of a shot to become a signifier in its own right.

Wilderness is an example of a television drama which shows how new technology is likely to accelerate the gradual transition from pure naturalism to a mixture of naturalism and expressionism. The drama is based on a novel by Dennis Danvers and concerns a young woman called Alice White who is a university librarian. This is a kind of television drama which does not allude explicitly to a particular event in society, but does depend on a knowledge of contemporary dialogues about women to appreciate its rhetorical stance. She is a predatory woman who seeks out men for sex and does not wish to see them again. She tells her psychiatrist about this behaviour. She also tells him that she turns into a wolf once every month when the moon is full. This is something which it is tempting to interpret, but Alice also informs her psychiatrist quite categorically that 'it is not a metaphor'. This is a good example of a dialogue which is essentially 'echoic': it is a pregnant moment and a kind of counter-narrative. It is a dialogue between characters, between writer and the audience and between the text and history. The dialogic relation between Alice and her psychiatrist is more than a mere rebuttal. It is an acknowledgement of his patronising strategy and it establishes the fact that Alice knows exactly how his mind is working. As a semiotic gesture it is intended to cut short his analysis of her condition, to signify that she has anticipated it. Alice can see the dialogism in his language but he cannot perceive the same quality in hers. Simultaneously, the dialogue speaks to us as the audience and also disrupts our attempts to understand this drama. At a more refined level, the dramatic text is offering a statement on women in general and their role in society. This aspect of the dialogue refers beyond the immediate situation of Alice and women who feel like her and makes a statement about women throughout history. Perhaps there could be a sense in which they do find a nature which is inimical to contemporary society.

Just like the psychiatrist, we too need to ground our understanding. We see Alice lying down in the basement when the moon is full with a bowl of raw meat, but we do not see what happens. In her conversations with her psychiatrist, she recalls childhood experiences where she ran naked in the woods at the age of thirteen. We see a flashback of the young Alice running and images of a wolf taking a rabbit. The flashback convention allows for an expressionist scene with fantastic elements, since it is not presented as a literal scene.

This is a classic case of what Freud called 'the uncanny'. The uncanny, according to Freud, expresses drives which have to be repressed for the sake of society. Furthermore, the uncanny is a phenomenon which although not supernatural or beyond explanation, cannot be fully understood. The drama underlines this with a continually dark and gloomy set. As Rosemary Jackson writes, the uncanny 'empties the "real" of its "meaning", it leaves signs without significance' (Jackson, 1981:68). Alice is a signifier, but we have been deliberately thwarted in our attempts to understand what she signifies. The uncanny takes a sign which looks as as if it *ought* to have a meaning and makes the attribution of a meaning complicated.

There is clearly an intertextual dialogue between her name and the story of Red Riding Hood. Angela Carter has written a short story called 'Wolf-Alice'. Carter has also written short stories, filmed as *The Company of Wolves* which challenge the prevailing mythology of the folk-tale where men are predatory, sexually rapacious and women are desperate to preserve their virtue. The wolf is generally taken to be a sign of predatory male sexuality, invading the domestic security of the chaste female in the folk-tale. Angela Carter's women are able to divert and contain the energy of the wolves: they show how to control 'the beast in man'. In one story the beast is contained by accepting his sexual advances and gratifying him. This gesture deflates the triumphal aspect of male aggression. The imagery of a monthly transformation is, of course closely allied with menstruation, but this by no means exhausts the meaningful potential of the various signs. Alice's wolf has killed a boy who tried to rape her. The uncanny sign is not necessarily a part of the genre known as the fantastic because it can clearly be explained by natural means but we are unaware of exactly how. The main emphasis of the drama is on the understanding of this woman's mentality and an attempt to find a signified for her as a sign.

The dialogues with which this engages and which it extends through the Brechtian device of the 'theatre of consequences', is the social discussions on the nature of femininity and the implications of femininity for adult socialisation. Alice wants to settle down and have a family, but she feels unable to do so unless she can gain control of the wolf. This relates to social debates about the way in which the female gender has been seen as an inescapable burden to be carried. It is a social contradiction that she must escape: her sexually predatory nature is not conducive to a traditional nuclear family. What this drama represents is a hypothetical situation where the burden of nature is completely unacceptable to society and also inexplicable to men. It raises the possibility that there is no ultimate compatibility which is a satisfactory compromise for both parties. In this sense, the drama enters into a current debate and draws the audience into consideration of an unresolved issue of great importance.

Freud attributes the uncanny to a repression of taboos, and here the taboo against intercourse with animals is shown. We are shown the consequences for a woman. The denial of the attempt by Alice's psychiatrist to explain her condition, is an example of an echoic dialogue which spans both text and history, responding to various dialogues. It short-circuits intellectual explanation of the sign within the text and it also simultaneously addresses the male tendency to try to understand women's position in society. Alice begins to realise that her psychiatrist has no understanding of what she is. The utterance which denies that we can analyse the wolf as a metaphor and asserts its literal status, addresses the psychiatrist, the viewer and the historical society which as always sought to pigeon-hole women who are unusual.

Alice meets a man called Dan, the university Reader in Animal Behaviour, when they both stop to rescue an injured dog, and they begin a relationship. In the novel, the name of Alice's lover is Erik. Both Alice and Dan love the wilderness, which gives the drama its title, although in his case it is the Antarctic. Alice is initially troubled by a dream in which he dissects her on an operating table and shows revulsion when the wolf's skin appears through the slit in her stomach. It is significant that Dan's specialism is penguins which are monogamous animals which mate and return to the same place each year. His nature is dynamically opposed to that of Alice. When his ex-wife calls with a bottle of wine, he is again drawn to her as his behaviour echoes the penguins' need for security.

Alice and Dan begin a passionate affair by making love in the university library. This in itself has become a sign, since Alice states that she loves the sense of order which the library gives her. It is the antithesis of the wilderness, and it is here where she is able to enjoy a relationship with him. Dan argues that the wilderness as he knows it is full of order. Alice's psychiatrist is also a man who 'would not even sleep with his ex-patients', according to a colleague. Masculinity here is a more passive element. As Alice and Dan sleep together, however, the camera cuts to a shot of the full moon and Alice wakes up. The full moon signifies and connotes many things – it is a code for the female gender for example – but here in this text, it has acquired a specific meaning. It is the night of her transformation and she becomes very disturbed. Her skin glistens with sweat and her eyes glow green like those of a wolf. This is the first use of new technology to enable a sudden transformation in the primary narrative of this drama. Previously, as Alice related the story of her attempted rape, she claimed that she transformed into a wolf and killed the boy responsible. Here in the reminiscence scene, we see the morphing of her face into that of the wolf at the moment of the rape. At this stage, however, the convention of the televisual recollection is that it can break the rules of nature in showing us supernatural events because memory plays such tricks.

Following Alice's awakening from her sex with Dan and the green glow in her eyes, we then see the library from a low perspective as if we were looking through the eyes of a wolf loping along the bookstacks. A wolf is seen padding through the bookshelves and wandering along the road, scavenging. At this point, the conventions of television drama are not clear. Are we witnessing an expressionist sequence designed to illustrate Alice's feelings, or are we actually viewing what is happening? We do not see any sign which would settle this ambiguity. Alice eventually makes her way home, naked and dirty, a feral creature surviving amongst the town. Whether she has dreamt this or whether she has actually lived through it is not clear. The transformation comes to an end as another shot of the moon shows it disappearing behind clouds. The ambiguity is partly related to a story such as Henry James's *The Turn of the Screw*, where the narrator sees many manifestations of characters who have died and is unsure of whether she is actually witnessing a supernatural event. The reader, is also unsure whether we are meant to find the narrator or the tale to be the main focus of our interest.

In the first of the three episodes, we experience the uncanny. The second element begins to answer some nagging questions and turns to the fantastic. In this mode, we are unsure of whether the explanation for the events we witness is supernatural or natural. The end of the previous episode has implanted this problem. 'The fantastic', as Rosemary Jackson puts it, 'pushes towards an area of non-signification'. The gap between signifier and signified dramatises the impossibility of ever arriving at a definitive meaning or absolute reality (Jackson, 1981 :41).

The second episode begins with a series of abbreviated clips to summarise episode one. This sequence continues the process of disrupting the analysis of the plot which we might be tempted to make. The various 'candidates' for the signified of Alice's wolf-sign are gradually eliminated to add to the sense that we have moved from the uncanny to the fantastic mode. In one short clip we see the psychiatrist explaining to a colleague that Alice experiences her sexuality as such a powerful force that she cannot reconcile herself to it. The next clip shows Alice enjoying a passionate sexual encounter with Dan in the library, which shows that the psychiatrist, Luther, is wrong. The composite sign created by editing, of statement and contradictory action, is further evidence that we are moving toward the 'fantastic'.

Shortly after she leaves Dan in the library, Alice hears that a student has been attacked by a large dog and is now dead. It is clear that she suspects herself of this act. The relationship with Dan deteriorates and we are gradually presented with more and more signs of the reality of the transformation to a wolf. At one point, Dan's ex-wife with whom he has been sleeping, is surprised by Alice calling at Dan's house. In a fit of rage, Alice transforms into a wolf. The conventions of editing do not make it clear whether this is an expressionist statement to signify the extent to which Alice is enraged, or a transformation which is flouting the laws of nature. As Todorov would call it, this representation of a supernatural act is called in genre theory, 'the marvellous'. Shortly after Alice has threatened Dan's ex-wife we see the wolf emerge from the house and disappear. The audience is left puzzled as the drama moves towards the hybrid genre of the fantastic-marvellous, a combination of the ambiguous sign which may or may not be supernatural and the clearly supernatural.

Alice decides to return to the wild as a wolf. The decision is one which signifies her belief that she can never live happily in conventional society, or that this woman's essential nature is incompatible with what society expects. Despite a last-ditch attempt by Dan to dissuade her, Alice returns to the wolf sanctuary run by the wolf expert who has befriended her, and prepares to integrate with the resident wolf-pack. The final scene is one where Alice is seen actually morphing from a woman on all fours to a wolf for the first time. This use of new technology to make the transformation seem both credible and even in some sense, 'natural', finally confirms the fact that we are watching a 'marvellous' drama in which the impossible happens. The morphing seems to bring out a characteristic of the original image, so that the woman on all fours almost looks like the wolf she eventually becomes. The morphing develops a natural resemblance.

In the history of intellectual movements, naturalism in the theatre gave way to expressionism as a reaction against it. In contemporary television drama, naturalism and expressionism are mixed to create a dialogue between them. As Alice transforms before our eyes, the scenery is still that of the Scottish highlands where the wolf-sanctuary is based. Naturalism plus new technology means that signs can be altered to make it constantly necessary to evaluate every element of a scene. *Découpage*, the implanting of ready-made images in a scene, is an increasing aspect of television practice which digital technology has made increasingly easy. Naturalism today is a choice and not a form which the medium imposes on the drama-makers.

Conclusion: The Emergence of Expressionism?

The textual studies which have been presented here do not justify conclusions about all television drama or the development of the genre, but they do allow us to reflect on the range of signs which can be used in the form and the aesthetic effects these may produce. Naturalism continues to be the dominant variety of television drama, and it is, therefore, important to consider whether this does restrict the semiotic function of signs. As Bakhtin remarks, conventional Naturalism aims to establish a '*causal* (my italics) explanation of man's acts and thoughts' (Bakhtin, 1986 :112) and once this is demonstrated, the individual character becomes representative of a process of social determination. 'The voices are simply transformed into 'signs of things (or symptoms of social processes)', in Bakhtin's words. A poor man, in other words, comes to signify 'the poor', rather than an individual who is suffering from poverty. Naturalism tends to reduce semiotic functions to allegory. Codes help to explain this situation where a visual signifier can be linked to a particular concept. The drama therefore rapidly seems to become a conceptual scheme to represent a particular social situation.

In the preceding examples, however, some characters are not so easy to assimilate into this process. The wife in *The Politician's Wife*, for example, does not easily fit into any of the categories which codes might refer us to. She is neither progressive nor reactionary: she is not a feminist nor is she a traditional Tory wife by the end. The signs are that she might have adopted some of the characteristics of her husband, although she is also admirable in many respects. By creating an artificial mythology, to use Barthes' term, we resist the temptation to resort to conventional concepts which might describe the ideological status of women. The naturalism here is not 'conventional'. The code which translates characters into straightforward ideological functions is redundant in this example.

This is not to say, however, that Naturalism is no longer fashionable or relevant in television drama. Raymond Williams describes Ibsen and Chekov's underlying naturalistic theme as 'the dramatic tension between what men feel themselves capable of becoming, and a thwarting, directly present environment' (Williams, 1952:386). This might apply equally well to *The Politician's Wife*, the police officers of *NYPD Blue*. and to Dana and Scully in *The X-Files*. Three very different styles of drama all serve to illustrate the struggle of individuals with the *status quo*. Williams argues that naturalism does not change from one era to another in its aim, merely in the means it uses to achieve it. Hence he argues that expressionism is 'the action that succeeds to, rather than contradicts, the great tensions of the major naturalist play in the nineteenth century' (Williams, 1952 : 391). The reason why expressionism begins to infiltrate naturalism is perhaps explained by Brecht. He argued that literature needed the cinema because it provided the complementary external perspective to literature's internal treatment. A recent example of this was the dramatisation for television of Ian McEwan's *The Crow Road*, which combined inner monologue with conventional narrative. The combination of introspection and externality provides a complete account of the individual's behaviour, but it does not suggest a determinist relationship. It allows for individual differences in the responses to external determinants and finds signs to convey these. The obtuse meaning, as Barthes puts it, 'carries a certain *emotion*'. The transformation of the leading woman into a wolf in *Wilderness* is a poignant moment where the sadness of having to relinquish the human world to find happiness is felt. In the absence of a particular signified, however, the precise value and meaning of the emotional rejoinder can be debatable. This is the point at which the audience are able to interpret signs in accordance with the dramatic context in which they occur.

In a talk at the National Film Theatre in 1997, Steve Bochco maintained that *NYPD Blue* was not designed to present solutions to the dilemmas facing American policeworkers. His task, as he saw it, was simply to present the problems, not the solutions. Fay Weldon has also asserted that she simply described what she knew to have happened in her experience of the Women's Movement when she was criticised for *Big Women*. This attitude may seem like the obvious outcome of a naturalistic drama which exposes all the determinants and reactions which affect the characters' behaviour. If every aspect is authentic then viewers can simply draw their own conclusions. One approach, therefore, is to simply lay the facts before the audience. Didacticism is felt by many writers to be out of place in television drama.

This approach highlights the importance of semiotics in this genre of drama. The naturalistic authenticity invites a comparison with viewers' own experience. Rather than aiming to transmit an author's insights, which might result in an idealist theory of drama, the television genre aims to focus on and draw attention to those aspects of the world we know. Jimmie L. Reeves (1994), in his discussion of television authorship as dialogism, refers to the 'open orientation' of the dialogic rewriting of culture. Since the television text takes a number of other texts and rewrites them so that they constitute something new yet their diverse origins are recognisable, the text is both 'conventional and innovative'. As Bakhtin puts it, the author is 'outside the world depicted', but 'occupies a position precisely in this real dialogue and is defined by the real situation of the day' (Bakhtin, 1986 : 116). Authorship is a matter of bringing together various signs which exist in society to create a unique focus which highlights what Reeves calls 'latent correspondences in the cultural order'. The act of combining these signs is deliberate, and therefore a matter of artistry, but the correspondences are not simply ideas in the minds of the artists: they can be seen to exist elsewhere. Furthermore the correspondences can be open to negotiation by audiences, and are not beyond dispute. The original inspiration for semiotics, therefore, was to address communication in a more scientific manner and not refer to idealist notions such as the author's conceptions. The audience must judge whether their knowledge and experience corroborate the patterns which emerge, and not search for the author's key to the meaning. Recognisable signs must, therefore, be used to communicate. The drama makers orchestrate sets of signs to invite interpretation. Hence when Fay Weldon's drama was debated, the criticism focused on Virago and whether actual feminist publishers did behave as she implied. Although the orchestration is intentional, the intention is not what is judged.

It is true that naturalistic television drama does attempt to signify on the basis of publicly-acknowledged signs, but it does not follow from this that the drama is detached and objective. *NYPD Blue* addresses the issues which face real policeworkers in America, but it does imply that certain approaches can overcome these dilemmas. In fact, as we have seen, the American professional drama series seems to be dialogic on the surface, but can be understood as monologic at an unconscious level. A consistent message emerges in what appears to be a faithful reflection of the diversity of police problems. As Bakhtin/Volosinov state, the sign is always ideological, though it is based on public materialist procedures. Entering into the dialogue means entering into the ideological struggle and following the many ideological implications of signs to the social conditions which gave rise to them. *Cracker* illustrates how the sign need not be ideologically determined as in the case of Eisenstein. In the case of *Cracker* the main character signifies a set of contradictions: the conflicting impulses of a postmodern man. As Edward Said would describe it, the speech by Fitz in the restaurant where he tries to convince his friends that they are unable to escape ideological contradictions, is an act of the will. It does not have a meaning, in the sense that it can be related to a code of actions, but it does signify an attempt to *do* something: to penetrate an emotional defence, to exonerate himself and so on. The context of this action is needed to understand what is at stake here and it is threefold: it is the dramatic context; the broadcasting context; and the historical context. The 'pregnant moment' has distant repercussions.

'Morse code', or the coded semiotic systems which enable us to read meaning clearly, however, will not enable us to arrive at the ideological perspectives on the social issues which signs can offer to the audience. In general, the conventional signs simply assist us to piece together the narrative. The ideological aspects of television drama often exist in opposition to the narrative, or as what Barthes calls a 'counter-narrative' in elements of the shot and its juxtaposed signs which do not feature in the story-telling. The three bottles of whisky which Morse buys as the body is exhumed in 'The Wench is Dead' are not essential to the plot, but they do help to signify the possibility that Morse's endeavours are ultimately on behalf of men and not in the interests of an abstract notion of justice as the story suggests. Ironically, the techniques which Morse uses are more intuitive than logical in a traditionally masculine style. The coded signs also do not tell us how the drama as a whole might be related to its social and historical context. *The Politician's Wife* does not need to refer directly to its context in the drama itself in order to be understood as a rejoinder to Tory sleaze. A relationship between a sign and its context is always unique and there is no explicit connection between text and context here. That relationship is an example of what Baudrillard calls 'silent signification' when the relationship is understood without a code to make the connection. The connection between *The Politician's Wife* and a certain phase in British history is via a family resemblance which gives the drama its essential signifying function. The family resemblance is perceived immediately rather than decoded.

Naturalism may, therefore present an opportunity to indulge in a version of social semiotics on the contemporary, but the preceding studies admittedly do not deal extensively with the past and the future. Costume drama may seem to be outside the scope of the approach adopted here, since it often adapts a historical novel, for example. Even though this may seem to have no dialogic relationship, it does often challenge preconceptions and raise questions. An athletic Mr Darcy in *Pride and Prejudice*, for example, challenges our assumptions about the novel and its realism and can nonetheless be related to our preceding debates about Jane Austen. The studies offered here hopefully pave the way for a more detailed examination of adaptation in its social context.

Fantasy drama and the genre category of the marvellous, also seem to lie outside the realm of dialogue with the present at first glance, but the example of Beckett's work shows how audience expectations are always at the forefront and a context can always be found to situate the most extreme examples of interior characterisation. *The X-Files* may also help to dispel this view. Although the drama starts with the genuine trappings of the FBI and authentic locations, it rapidly moves into speculative fantasies and imagination. This is another example of what Raymond Williams called 'a hypothesis within a recognition'. The naturalistic beginnings help to ground the drama in recognisable situations, from which speculative dialogues may emerge which bear on the contemporary political situation. Drama such as this present an imitation of the current dialogues followed by a rejoinder to ensure coherence of the dramatic discourse.

This drama above all, perhaps, also shows how there is no definitive interpretation of signs despite the fact that they have some definitive social effects at a particular moment in history. Once Mulder and Scully have uncovered a conspiracy or a mystery, they do not find that the knowledge leads to a spectacular revelation. As Lyotard puts it, 'The State... must abandon the humanist and idealist narratives of legitimation in order to justify the new goal... the only credible goal is power' (Lyotard, 1986:46). The media show, however, that the State can never fully determine the interpretations of current affairs and that bad publicity can be generated. The Foucauldian view that State power is absolute is not borne out. Spin-doctoring, however, is perhaps another example of refunctioning or reaccentuation in the transformation of unacceptable news into 'good' publicity. Every confession of misconduct is hailed as an example of how the government is adept at rooting out its miscreants. In this way the continual refashioning of the sign does not allow any interpretation to remain permanently valid and State conspiracies can, for example, survive media revelations.

The recognition that the signs used in television can feature in a number of social practices and serve different purposes, is perhaps the closest we can come to a television aesthetic. An ironic suspensiveness, for example, may be due to the feeling that the fantastic elements of *The X-Files* are meant to offer a veiled criticism of another aspect of State policy. As Bakhtin puts it, the dialogue, is always 'double-voiced'. The fact that the sign is enmeshed in a network of related dialogues and can be 'deconstructed' by following these ramifications does not mean that it has no immediate social impact. In the same way, for example, money can be said to have no absolute value yet this does not prevent financial transactions from taking place. The televisual sign always offers a range of interpretations: as *studium* or *punctum*, signifier or *signifiance*, representation or social intervention, and the skilled makers can exploit these varied roles to enable viewers to enter into the social dialogues of the day. The alert viewer may be able to entertain these varied functions simultaneously. Television drama is above all a vigorous, dynamic practice in which audiences are encouraged to respond. It can sometimes be seen to fulfil John McGrath's maxim that it should 'use words, images and ideas with a historical awareness as well as an awareness of the audience' (McGrath, 1984:114). McGrath's assertion in the early 1980s that such radical television drama was not possible in any other country except Scandinavia and Holland, however, may neglect the ability of audiences to read the signs and to 'crack' the codes which conceal the awareness of history and its discontents.

References

Allen, Robert C. ed. 2nd edition (1992), *Channels of Discourse: Television and Contemporary Criticism*, Chapel Hill, University of North Carolina Press.

Althusser, Louis (1971, repr. 1976), *Essays on Ideology*, London, Verso.

Alvarado, Manuel (1982), *Authorship, Origination and Production*, University of London Institute of Education Media Analysis Paper, no.4.

Alvarado, Manuel and John O. Thompson eds. (1990), *The Media Reader* London, BFI.

Andrew, Dudley (1976), *The Major Film Theories*, Oxford, Oxford University Press.

Bakhtin, Mikhail Mikhailovich and P. N. Medvedev (1978), *The Formal Method in Literary Scholarship: An Introduction to Sociological Poetics*, Baltimore, John Hopkins University Press.

Bakhtin, Mikhail Mikhailovich (1986), *Speech Genres and Other Late Essays*, Austin, University of Texas Press.

Barthes, Roland (1977), *Image-Music-Text*, Glasgow, Fontana.

Barthes, Roland (1972), *Mythologies*, London, Jonathan Cape.

Barthes, Roland (1980, repr. 1993), *Camera Lucida*, London, Vintage.

Baudrillard, Jean ed. Mike Gane (1993), *Baudrillard Live: Selected Interviews*, London, Routledge.

Baudrillard, Jean trans. Sheila Faria Glaser (1994), *Simulacra and Simulation*, Michigan, University of Michigan Press.

Baudrillard, Jean (1988, repr. 1996), *Selected Writings*, Oxford, Blackwell.

Bazin, André (1967), *What is Cinema? vol.1* California, University of California.

Beckett, Samuel (1985), *Collected Shorter Plays*, London, Faber.

Bell, Ian A. and Graham Daldry eds. (1990), *Watching the Detectives*, London, Macmillan.

Bennett, Tony (1979), *Formalism and Marxism*, London, Methuen.

Bennett, Tony *et al* eds. (1981), *Popular Television and Film*, London, BFI.

Bentley, Eric (1968), *The Theory of the Modern Stage*, Harmondsworth, Penguin.

BFI, ed. (1994), *TV Holdings of the National Film and TV Archive 1936-1979*, BFI.

Bleasdale, Alan (ed. David Self) (1984), *Boys from the Blackstuff*, London, Hutchinson.

Bondanella, Peter (1997), *Umberto Eco and the Open Text*, Cambridge, Cambridge University Press.

Bradbury, Malcolm (1982), *The After Dinner Game: Three Plays for Television*, London, Arrow Books.

Brater, Enoch, (1987), *Beyond Minimalism: The work of Samuel Beckett*, Milton Keynes, Open University Press.

Brand, Neil (1998), *Dramatic Notes: Foregrounding Music in the Dramatic Experience*, Luton, University of Luton Press.

Brandt, George ed. (1981), *British Television Drama*, Cambridge, Cambridge University Press.

Brandt, George ed. (1990), *British Television Drama in the 1980's*, Cambridge, Cambridge University Press.

Brecht, Bertolt, trans. John Willett (1963), *Brecht on Theatre*, London, Methuen.

Brecht, Bertolt, trans. John Willett (1965), *The Messingkauf Dialogues*, London, Methuen.

Bronfen, Elizabeth (1992), *Over Her Dead Body: Death, Feminity and the Aesthetic*, Manchester, Manchester University Press.

Brunsden, Charlotte (1998), 'What is the "Television" of Television Studies?' in Geraghty and Lusted, eds., 1998.

Burnett, Ron (1991) *Explorations in Film Theory*, Indiana: Indiana University Press.

Caughie, John (1994), 'Playing at Being American: Games and Tactics', in Newcomb ed., 1994.

Corner, John (1986), 'Codes and Cultural Analysis' in Richard Collins *et al* eds. *Media, Culture and Society*, London, Sage.

Crace, John (1994), '*Cracker*': *The Truth Behind the Fiction*, London, Boxtree.

Currie, Gregory (1990), *The Theory of Fiction*, Cambridge, Cambridge University Press.

Davis, Desmond (1960), *The Grammar of Television Production*, London, Barrie and Jenkins.

Day-Lewis, Sean (1998), *Talk of Drama: Views of the Television Dramatist Now and Then*, Luton, University of Luton Press.

de Lauretis, Teresa (1991) 'Semiotics, Theory and Social Practice: a Critical History of Italian Semiotics', in Ron Burnett ed., *Explorations in Film Theory*, Bloomington, University of Indiana Press.

Deleuze, Gilles (1986), *Cinema 1: The Movement-Image*, London, Athlone.

Deleuze, Gilles (1989), *Cinema 2: The Time-Image*, London, Athlone.

Eco, Umberto (1986a), *Semiotics and the Philosophy of Language*, London, Macmillan.

Eco, Umberto (1986b), *Travels in Hyperreality* , London, Picador.

Elsaesser, Thomas *et al* eds (1994), *Writing for the Medium: TV in Transition*, Amsterdam, Amsterdam University Press.

Erdinast-Vulcan, Daphna (1995), 'Bakhtin's Homesickness: a Late Reply to Julia Kristeva', in *Textual Practice* 9 (2), pp. 223-242.

Esslin, Martin (1968), *The Theatre of the Absurd* , Harmondsworth, Penguin.

Esslin, Martin (1983), *Mediations: Essays on Brecht, Beckett and the Media*, London, Abacus.

Esslin, Martin (1987), *The Field of Drama: How the Signs of Drama Create Meaning on Stage and Screen*, London, Methuen.

Fiske, J. and Hartley, J. (1978), *Reading Television*, London, Methuen.

Fiske, John (1988), 'Meaningful Moments', *Critical Studies in Mass Communication*, Sept., 246-50.

Fiske, John (1990), *Introduction to Communication Studies*, London, Routledge.

Fiske, John (1994), 2nd edition *Introduction to Communication Studies*, London, Routledge.

Fletcher, B. *et al* (1978), *A Student's Guide to the Plays of Samuel Beckett*, London, Faber.

Geertz, Clifford (1973), *The Interpretation of Cultures*, Princeton, London, HarperCollins.

Genosko, Gary (1994), *Baudrillard and Signs: Signification Ablaze*, London, Routledge.

Geraghty, Christine and Lusted, David, eds (1998) *The Television Studies Book*, London, Arnold.

Greenblatt, Stephen (1990), *Learning to Curse: Essays in Early Modern Culture*, London, Routledge.

Hallam, Julia and Margaret Marshment (1995), 'Framing Experience: Case Studies in the Reception of *Oranges are not the Only Fruit*, *Screen* 36:1 pp 1-15.

Hall, Stuart (1973), 'Encoding and Decoding in the Television Discourse', Ocasional Paper no. 7, Birmingham CCCS.

Harris, David (1996), *A Society of Signs?*, London, Routledge.

Harris, Roy (1996), *Signs, Language and Communication*, London, Routledge.

Hawkes, Terence (1977), *Structuralism and Semiotics*, London, Methuen.

Hebdige, Dick (1978), *Subculture: The Meaning of Style*, London, Routledge.

Hodge, Bob and Gunther Kress (1986), *Children and Television: A Semiotic Approach*, Oxford, Polity.

Hodge, Brian and Gunther Kress (1988), *Social Semiotics*, Ithaca NY, Cornell University Press.

Husson, William (1994), 'A Wittgensteinian Critique of the Encoding-Decoding Model of Communication', in *Semiotica* 98-1/2 , pp 49-72.

Hutcheon, Linda (1989), *The Politics of Postmodernism*, London, Routledge.

Ishikawa, Sakae ed. (1996), *Quality Assessment of Television*, Luton, John Libbey.

Jackson, Rosemary (1981), *Fantasy: The Literature of Subversion*, London, Methuen.

James, Henry (1977) *The Turn of the Screw and Other Stories*, Harmondsworth, Penguin.

Jameson, Fredric (1981), *The Political Unconscious: Narrative as a Socially Symbolic Act*, London, Methuen.

Jameson, Fredric, (1990), *Postmodernism or the Cultural Logic of Late Capitalism*, Durham NC, Duke University Press.

Jenkins, Ray (1995), 'Facts Fashioned from Fiction', in *20:20 the National Magazine for Photography and Media Education*, (ed. Jim Hornsby) Issue 2, pp 34-37.

Jensen, Klaus Bruhn and Nicholas W. Jankowski (1991), *A Qualitative Handbook for Mass Communication Research*, London, Routledge.

Jensen, Klaus Bruhn (1995), *The Social Semiotics of Mass Communication*, London, Sage.

Katzman, David ed. (1998), *American Studies: Special Edition: TV and US Culture* vol. 39, no. 2.

Leavis, F. R. (1962), *The Common Pursuit*, London, Chatto and Windus.

Liszka, James Jakób (1996), *A General Introduction to the Semiotic of Charles Sanders Peirce*, Bloomington, Indiana University Press.

Lindgren, J. Ralph and Jay Knaak, eds. (1997), *Ritual and Semiotics*, New York, Peter Lang.

Locke, John (1690), *An Essay Concerning Human Understanding*.

Lotman, Yuri (1990) *Universe of the Mind*, London, IB Taurus.

Lovell,Terry (1980), *Pictures of Reality: Aesthetics, Politics and Pleasure*, London, BFI.

Lukács, Georg (1963), *The Meaning of Contemporary Realism*, London, Merlin.

Lyotard, Jean-Francois (1979), *The Postmodern Condition: A Report on Knowledge*, Manchester, Manchester University Press.

Macherey, Pierre: (1978), *A Theory of Literary Production*, London, RKP.

Mandelker, Amy (1995), 'Logosphere and Semiosphere: Bakhtin, Russian Organicism and the Semiotics of Culture', in Amy Mandelker ed. *Bakhtin in Contexts*, Chicago: Northwestern University Press.

Marx, Karl (1977), *The German Ideology*, London, Lawrence and Wishart.

MacCabe, Colin (1981), 'Realism and the Cinema: Notes on Some Brechtian Theses', in *Popular Television and Film*, ed. Tony Bennett *et al*, London, BFI.

— 'The Revenge of the Author', *Critical Quarterly*, vol.31, no. 2, 1989.

McArthur, Colin, (1980), 'Points of Review: Television Criticism in the Press', in *Screen Education*, Summer 1980, no. 35, pp 59-61.

McGrath, John (1977), 'TV Drama: The Case Against Naturalism', in *Sight and Sound* 46, pp 100-105.

McGrath, John (1977), *The Cheviot, the Stag and the Black, Black Oil*, London, Eyre Methuen.

McGrath, John (1981), *A Good Night Out: Popular Theatre: Audience, Class and Form*, London, Eyre Methuen.

McHoul, Alec (1996), *Semiotic Investigations: Towards an Effective Semiotics*, Lincoln and London, University of Nebraska Press.

Melrose, Susan (1994), *A Semiotics of the Dramatic Text*, London, Macmillan.

Merrell, Floyd (1997), *Peirce, Signs and Meaning*, Toronto, University of Toronto Press.

Metz, Christian (1974), *Film Language: A Semiotics of the Cinema*, New York, Oxford University Press.

Millington, Bob and Robin Nelson (1986), *Boys from the Blackstuff: The Making of TV Drama* , London, Commedia.

Moi, Toril ed. (1986), *The Kristeva Reader*, Oxford, Blackwell.

Morley, David (1980), *The 'Nationwide' Audience*, London, BFI.

Morson, Gary Saul (1982), *Bakhtin: Essays and Dialogues on his Work*, Chicago, University of Chicago Press.

Murray, J. (1998), *Hamlet on the Holodeck: The Future of Narrative in Cyberspace*, Massachussets, MIT Press.

Nelson, Robin (1997), *Television Drama in Transition: Forms Values and Cultural Change*, London, Macmillan.

Newcomb, Horace ed. (1994), *Television: The Critical View*, New York, Oxford University Press.

Nöth, Winifred (1995), *A Handbook of Semiotics*, Bloomington, Indiana University Press.

Oliver, Kelly (1997), *The Portable Kristeva*, New York, Columbia University Press.

Pavis, Patrice (1992), *Theatre at the Crossroads of Culture*, London, Routledge.

Pechey, Graham (1989), 'On the Borders of Bakhtin: Dialogisation, Decolonization', in Ken Hirschkop and David Shepherd eds *Bakhtin and Cultural Theory*, Manchester, Manchester University Press.

Petrilli, Susan (1993), 'Dialogism and Interpretation in the Study of Signs', in *Semiotica* 97 - 1/2, pp 103-118.

Poliakoff, Stephen (1998), *Shooting the Past*, London, Methuen.

Potter, Dennis (1984), *Waiting for the Boat: On Television*, London: Faber and Faber.

Pourroy, Janine (1996), *Behind the Scenes at ER*, Ebury Press, London.

Poutney, Rosemary (1988), *Theatre of Shadows: Samuel Beckett's Drama 1956-76* Gerards Cross, Colin Smythe.

Ralph, Sue, Jo Langham Brown and Tim Lees (1998), *What Price Creativity?*, Luton, University of Luton Press.

Reeves, Jimmie L. (1994), 'Rewriting Culture: A Dialogic View of Television Authorship', in Newcomb, ed. (1994) pp.188-201.

Said, Edward (1978), 'The Problem of Textuality: Two Exemplary Positions', in *Critical Enquiry*, 4 , pp. 673-714.

Samuels. Robert (1995), *Mahler's Sixth Symphony: A Study in Musical Semiotics*, Cambridge, CUP.

Saussure, Ferdinand de (1974), *Course in General Linguistics*, Harper Collins.

Selby, Keith and Ron Cowdery (1995), *How to Study Television*, London, Macmillan.

Shaw, Marion and Sabine Vanacker (1991), *Reflecting on 'Miss Marple'*, London, Routledge.

Silverman, Kaja (1983), *The Subject of Semiotics*, New York, Oxford University Press.

Simons, John, '*Real* Detectives and *Fictional* Criminals', in Bell ed, (1990), pp 88-96.

Singer, Peter (1983), *The Expanding Circle: Ethics and Sociobiology*, Oxford, Oxford University Press.

Stam, Robert (1989), *Subversive Pleasures: Bakhtin, Cultural Criticism and Film*, Baltimore, John Hopkins University Press.

Stam, Robert, Robert Burgoyne and Sandy Flitterman-Lewis (1992), *New Vocabularies in Film Semiotics: Structuralism, Poststructuralism and Beyond*, London, Routledge.

Staniland, Hilary (1972), *Universals*, London, Doubleday Books.

Storey, John, ed. (1996), *What is Cultural Studies? A Reader*, Arnold, London.

Strindberg, August (1888). *Plays One: The Father, Miss Julie, The Ghost Sonata*, London, Methuen.

Thibault, Paul, J. (1997), *Re-Reading Saussure: The Dynamics of Signs in Social Life*, London, Routledge.

Thomas, Lyn (1995), 'In Love with *Inspector Morse*: Feminist Subcultures and Quality Television', in *Feminist Review* No 51, Autumn, pp 1-25 .

Thomson, Clive (1983), 'The Semiotics of M.M. Bakhtin'. *The University of Ottowa Quarterly*, 53, 1 pp 11-21.

Thompson, John O. (1978) 'Screen Acting and the Commutation Test', in *Screen* vol. 19, no. 2, p. 55-71.

Thompson, John O. (1980), 'Tragic Flow: Raymond Williams on Drama', in *Screen Education*, Number 35, pp 45-58.

Todorov, Tsvetan (1980), *The Fantastic*, Ithaca NY, Cornell University Press.

Tomaselli, Keyan, G. (1996), *Appropriating Images: the Semiotics of Visual Representation*, Aarhus, Intervention Press.

Tulloch, John (1990), *Television Drama: Agency, Audience and Myth*, London, Routledge.

Volosinov, V. N. (1973), *Marxism and the Philosophy of Language*, London, Harvard University Press.

Weldon, Fay (1984), *The Lifes and Loves of a She-Devil*, London, Coronet.

Weldon, Fay (1997), *Big Women: Big Girls Don't Cry*, London, Penguin.

Weldon, Fay 'Pity Poor Men' *The Guardian*, Tuesday 9 December 1997.

Williams, R. (1973), *Drama from Ibsen to Brecht*, Harmondsworth, Penguin.

Williams, R. (1974), *Television, Technology and Cultural Form*, London, Fontana.

Wittgenstein, Ludwig, (1951), *Philosophical Investigations*, Oxford, Blackwell.

Wolff, Janet (1993), 'Death and the Maiden: Does Semiotics Justify Murder?', in *Critical Quarterly* 35, ii, pp 38-43.

Wood, Charles (1987), *Tumbledown*, Harmondsworth, Penguin.

Yeats, W.B. (1971), *Collected Poems of W.B. Yeats*, London, Macmillan.